how to start a home-based

Catering Business

seventh edition

Denise Vivaldo

Globe
Pequot

Guilfor

This book is dedicated to my mother and father.

Interior spot art licensed by Shutterstock.com.

"How to Write a Press Release for Pickup" on page 124 reprinted with permission of Martha Hopkins, martha@terracepartners.com.

"Ways to Write Clear Recipes" on page 142 reprinted with permission of Dianne Jacob, diannej.com.

Distributed by NATIONAL BOOK NETWORK

ISBN 978-0-7627-9641-0

Printed in United States of America

Contents

Acknowledgments

There were days when I was writing this book that I felt I would never get to the end. I discovered that putting my knowledge on paper required a lot of discipline, dedication, and personal motivation. During the moments that I possessed none of these traits, I was lucky enough to have a support system of people to pull, drag, and push me forward to the last page.

I need to thank Kit Snedaker, not only for her skill and her suggestions on this book, but more importantly for all the years she has listened as I read my work aloud and, no matter how awful the pages were, encouraged me to keep on writing.

I'd like to thank everyone who works behind the scenes at Globe Pequot. I'm amazed at the amount of talent, energy, and people it takes to publish one book.

Last but not least, thank you to my husband, Ken Meyer, and my sister, Joan Vivaldo, two firstborns who enrich my life with their love and support. The two of them have taught me to keep my eye on the ball, always eat dessert first, and not be afraid to ask for what I want.

Introduction

As I sat down and reread my own book to work on this seventh edition, what I read was practical, achievable business advice that was as true in 1993 as it is today in 2013. In fact, with the competitive nature of catering and the cost of doing business, the information I shared then and the timeless worksheets included are more useful than ever. (I would type the worksheets into your computer program and have them at your fingertips. Keep a party folder for every event. Use them.)

What I deducted from my twenty years of upgrading this book is this: As much as our culture changes, successful business habits do not.

The additions in this new edition vary from chapter to chapter. Included are several new diagrams, new menus, tips for photographing your food or parties, and tips spurred by the explosion of social media. And I'm warning you: If you don't use Twitter, Facebook, LinkedIn, or Tumblr, start today. No excuses.

I do get reader mail from people that have bought my book and want to thank me or ask a question. I am still thrilled and humbled. The questions they ask are usually already answered in the book, so I suggest they reread a chapter or send them directly to the page they need.

I am proud that this little book has helped many and will continue to do so. If you have questions or success stories, please contact me at denise@denise vivaldogroup.com. I'm happy for both of us!

01

So You Think You
Want to Be a Caterer?

One night as dinner guests were leaving after another spectacular party, I thought, *I should get paid for doing this!* The next day I made some phone calls from the real estate office where I worked to see how I could realize my dream of becoming a caterer. A year later I was cooking foods I loved to fix and learning how to make catering my full-time job. Now more than thirty years and thousands of parties later, I'm a home-based caterer. On average I direct five or six events each month, parties ranging from a fund-raiser for several thousand guests on a Hollywood soundstage to a wedding reception for one hundred guests in someone's backyard.

I also work with people who want to start their own catering business, and I train other caterers who want to expand. My services include recipe and menu development, public relations and promotional events, marketing pieces and website portfolio design, as well as custom-tailored programs designed to solve my clients' problems.

For more than twenty years, I've taught catering courses across the country to men and women who want to entertain—people just like you. Like you, my students read cookbooks and food magazines the way other people read newspapers. I'll bet you buy every new kitchen gadget on the market. Chances are you're already throwing parties for friends, colleagues, and family without getting paid for it. You may even have gone so far as to investigate cooking schools. Bravo! You're well on your way to becoming a caterer.

Of course, becoming a caterer doesn't happen overnight. As we'll discuss, if you want firsthand experience, the best thing to do is apprentice with another caterer or go to a cooking school. You will also need to learn the nuts and bolts of running a catering business. That's where this book comes in. Follow the suggestions outlined here and learn how to:

- set up your home office
- be "the boss"
- write a business plan
- charge for your talent
- bid for and close deals
- write a proposal
- ask for deposit money up front
- package your own press kit
- set up a successful website
- put together a winning team of employees
- hire entertainers and musicians
- design the menu for a perfect party
- cook recipes in quantity
- find new clients by referrals
- deal with elements beyond your control
- profit from every opportunity
- make money at something you love to do

Do You Have What It Takes?

As much fun as it is to cook and to give wonderful parties, catering is not for every-one. To evaluate your experience, motivation, and interest in this business, look at the following questions. If you can answer "yes" to most of them, you too can be a caterer.

- ❑ Do you have basic cooking skills?
- ❑ Do you have a working knowledge of food preparation and menu planning?
- ❑ Do you enjoy serving people, making them feel comfortable and at ease?
- ❑ Do you like to solve problems?
- ❑ Are you creative and resourceful?
- ❑ When you read a recipe, can you "taste" the finished dish before you even begin?
- ❑ Are you comfortable enough in the kitchen to cook without recipes?
- ❑ Do you dine out often and like different kinds of food?
- ❑ Are you gracious and polite in stressful situations?

- ❒ Are you good with a budget?
- ❒ Do you have money set aside to start a new business?
- ❒ Have you ever worked in sales?
- ❒ Will you be comfortable promoting yourself?
- ❒ Are you willing to leave your current career behind and start all over again as a caterer?

Opportunities in Catering

Hotels, country clubs, restaurants, charter yachts, even airplanes—all present catering opportunities, or you can create your own catering opportunities by "chefing" in private homes or executive dining rooms, directing catering for department stores, or supervising take-out counters in supermarkets. One way to jump-start your new career is to contact an existing food purveyor and offer a specific item you'd like to sell—mocha-chip chocolate cookies, for instance.

Hotels

Most hotels have a separate catering division to handle banquet rooms. Entry-level positions, which are frequently available, may give you a chance to meet local clientele and thus build a client base of your own. You can also get a close look at how in-house catering works, and you might discover some service you alone can provide.

When hotels rent out banquet rooms to outside caterers for a party, they usually let the caterer use the hotel kitchen. I got to know one hotel chef this way and saw what culinary needs he had that I could fill after the party was over. It turned out that he needed appetizers, so I began making them on a weekly basis, and we cut a profitable deal.

Airplanes

Everyone complains about airplane food. Here's your chance to do something about it. Approach international or charter carriers with ideas for providing first-class dinners every other day. They might welcome the notion of fresh meals from a local caterer. Don't forget private charters and private planes, for that matter. All pilots and passengers eat. Think of box lunches and creative picnic baskets you could provide.

Private Parties

Personal catering in private homes is always in demand and is a good source of income. Often big catering companies don't like to take on parties for fewer than thirty people. That's where you come in. A home-based, one-person caterer can handle a party of five to fifty (buffet) with just an assistant. And because you're small, you can be ready with only two days' notice.

At the start of my career, I kept private party costs down by using my clients' kitchens. I could turn out elegant and money-making dinner parties for six this way. For more than six, I learned to hire a waiter. I calculated my prices with an eye on the competition and charged between $60 and $80 per person. Sometimes this gave me a profit margin of as much as 60 percent!

Local Markets and Stores

If you have a signature item—a dynamite cheesecake, dazzling cookies—think about manufacturing it. Make a few samples and take them around to local cafes and bistros. If possible, use their facility to produce at least the first few batches. That way you will be cooking in a commercial kitchen (which will help you get used to industry standards and health department regulations) while test-marketing your product. If the cafe owner needs persuasion, point out that he or she will reap the fruits of your labor without having to put you on the payroll.

Special Events

I started my home-based catering business by selling food to special-event planners, many in the motion-picture industry. My partner and I split the work. She did most of the food preparation while I did most of the marketing and sales.

I made up a promotional package that showed event planners the services we could provide and our wholesale catering prices. I described beautiful presentations, good working staff, superb food. Then I sent this package to public relations companies that hire caterers for press and publicity parties and anyone else connected with special events. It worked. In short order I had a potential client list of people who called me first before looking in the Yellow Pages under "caterers."

In order to be legal (California law requires all caterers to manufacture their food in kitchens licensed and inspected by the California State Health Department), we prepared the food in a commercially retrofitted kitchen that we shared with a brownie manufacturer. That way two companies split one overhead. By organizing carefully, my partner and I made the food for three or four big events a month. Although this sounds like a lot, we managed to do it in fifteen days, cutting expenses in half and showing a 40 percent profit.

In order to set up your business, you'll need to check the city, county, and state requirements for manufacturing food in your area. Start by calling your health department. Your local restaurant association may also have useful information. In order to protect the public's safety, most localities do not permit caterers to sell food that has been prepared in a home kitchen. Make sure you find out the laws that pertain to your area. You'll find tips in chapter 2 on sharing and renting kitchens.

Does It Pay to Go to Cooking School?

In my experience, giving parties for friends and family was easy. Nothing was too much work. No mess was too great to clean up. Even asparagus out of season wasn't too expensive for my taste. I loved it all. When it came to turning professional, however, I realized how much I didn't know about the business of entertaining. I was scared. My solution was to enroll in a professional chef's program at the California Culinary Academy in San Francisco.

Even though I had studied cooking on my own, the sixteen-month program at CCA taught me how to run a commercial kitchen and gave me good practice preparing meals for the school's 300 students. Between and after class I worked off-premises parties catered by the school and gained experience being a party manager. In class we studied with expert Chinese, Italian, and French chefs, learning techniques and presentations of classic ethnic dishes.

Best of all, the school gave me a degree—recognized credentials to support me when I entered the catering field. (A list of respected culinary schools follows at the end of this book.)

Everything I did in school helped me in my career, but that doesn't mean it's the only way to go. Many of my colleagues trained by apprenticing with experienced caterers, as I did after I graduated from CCA. Catering is learning by doing, and apprenticing gives you plenty of opportunities to do.

Starting as a Personal Chef

Whether you are a culinary school graduate, an experienced restaurant or hotel chef, or a self-taught home cook, starting and operating a business as a personal chef can be a deeply satisfying career. Begin with a client or two and add more clients as you gain experience and become faster and more efficient in the kitchen. The United States Personal Chef Association (7680 Universal Blvd., Ste. 550, Orlando, FL 32819; 800-995-2138; uspca.com), founded in 1992, is the largest professional organization representing personal and private chefs that specialize in virtually every culinary discipline, supporting busy professionals and parents, families on the go, seniors, senior caregivers, people with special dietary needs and restrictions, and more. Members have the opportunity to start or grow their personal chef businesses through the use of seminars and training materials, and to share techniques with other successful personal chefs.

What is the difference between a personal chef and a private chef?

A private chef is employed by one individual or family full-time and prepares up to three meals per day. A personal chef serves several clients, usually one per day, and provides multiple meals that are custom designed for the clients' particular preferences. These meals are packaged and stored so that the client may enjoy them at their leisure throughout the week.

Where do I cook the food?

For legal reasons, meals are prepared in the client's kitchen, although some personal chefs make enough to cook out of licensed kitchens and use a delivery service. On the agreed-upon cooking date, the personal chef will bring the fresh ingredients for meals along with their own pots, pans, and utensils and prepare entrees on-site. At the end of the day, you leave the kitchen clean and the refrigerator/freezer stocked with meals for the rest of the week (or however many days is agreed upon).

How long will it take me to cook the meals?

You will likely be cooking several different entrees and side dishes from scratch, so it will take several hours. The more experience you have, the faster you will become. Be willing to work with your client's schedule or situation, and make arrangements in advance so that the cooking date and time is compatible to both of you.

How do I leave the finished food?

Store food in the refrigerator or freezer, depending upon when it is going to be eaten. Always leave easy-to-follow heating instructions for each entree. Frozen food should be defrosted overnight in the refrigerator and heated according to your directions, so as to be enjoyed at the peak of its flavor. Uniform-size containers take less storage space. You should bring the appropriate containers for the food you prepare. Ask clients to return used containers to you so that you can use them again, saving on their cost.

How do I justify what I charge?

Although your fees are expressed per entree or per serving, they actually represent all of the components that make up your service. Part of your service is a thorough assessment of your clients' likes, needs, and special dietary requirements so that you can customize their menu. Your recipes are modified for each client. You submit meal selections for their approval. The cost of groceries are included. Their meals are prepared in the safety of their own kitchen. Packaging, labeling, and storing their meals are all features included in your price. If you were to compare a personal chef service to restaurant service, you could think of it this way: For a restaurant, they must drive to get there, possibly wait for a table, and take a chance that their server is having a good day. If they have allergies or a special request, they have no guarantee that it will be honored, since most entrees are premade up to a certain point. After eating their meal they must pay for it, tip the server, and get back in their vehicle and drive home. If they had a personal chef service, they could heat up a beautiful meal prepared specifically for them and eat it in the comfort of their own home.

Do I request payment ahead of each cooking date?

It is customary to get paid for your service in advance of your cooking date. After you have established that they are a good client, you can get your check upon arrival at their kitchen each week.

How often will clients need my service?

You will determine with your clients how often to schedule your services to best serve their needs and support their lifestyle and your schedule.

What if a client wants half of my regular service?

For this to be a profitable business for you, you cannot take the same amount of cooking time and produce half the amount of food. It takes the same amount of planning, shopping, and preparation time to cook ten portions of food as it does for twenty portions of food. Instead of losing a client, suggest more portions of the same food and cooking less often.

Chefs say figuring out how to price and what to charge is always a challenge. Your pricing in this field depends on what level of service you offer and where you do business. Big-city jobs usually pay more than rural locations, while wholesome, everyday meals earn you less than fine-dining meals. Play up your unique talents to tantalize clients in your market. Again, join one of the personal chef organizations listed below. Learn from experienced pros to help you build your business.

Apprenticeships: Learning by Doing

I worked with many different caterers after graduating from cooking school. Some were good and some were not so good, but I learned new menus and dishes from all of them. I made a practice of taking my camera along to parties in order to shoot pictures of the way the food was presented and of the decor. Afterward I had two prints made of each shot.

Personal Chef Associations and Information on the Web

American Culinary Federation
www.acfchefs.org

American Personal & Private Chef Association
www.personalchef.com

The Chef Alliance
www.thechefalliance.com

International Association of Culinary Professionals
www.iacp.com

United States Personal Chef Association
www.uspca.com

Women Chefs and Restaurateurs
www.womenchefs.org

Further Reading

Cooking for a Crowd, Susan Wyler (Rodale Books, 2005)

Cooking for Company, Nicole Aloni (HP Trade, 2003)

Food Safety Fundamentals: Essentials of Food Safety and Sanitation, David McSwane, Nancy R. Rue, Richard Linton, and Anna Graf Williams (Prentice Hall, 2003)

How to Start a Home-based Personal Chef Business, Denise Vivaldo (Globe Pequot Press, 2006)

Perfect Party Food, Dianne Phillips (Harvard Common Press, 2005)

Prevention's Low-Fat, Low-Cost Freezer Cookbook: Quick Dishes for and from the Freezer, Sharon Sanders (Rodale Press, 1998)

Quick Simple Food, Susie Quick (Clarkson Potter, 2003)

Seriously Simple: Easy Recipes for Creative Cooks, Diane Worthington (Chronicle Books, 2002)

Seriously Simple Parties, Diane Worthington (Chronicle Books, 2012)

One I gave to my employer, who was so happy that she generally reimbursed me for the film. The other picture I kept to build my own portfolio. Images are even easier to take today using your smartphone. You can easily snap pictures for your clients, yourself, or an employer.

Apprenticing also allowed me to make valuable contacts. As a caterer's apprentice, I met and networked with servers, florists, designers, and musicians whom I was able to call on when I went into business for myself.

Catering is more than cooking, I quickly learned. Catering can mean furnishing table linens, flatware, glasses, plates, even chairs for some parties. Few clients have the makings of a party for even fifteen, let alone fifty. It's up to the caterer to pull the party off, from colored tablecloths with matching napkins to comfortable chairs. Fortunately all these things are rentable, as you'll learn in chapters 9 and 10.

To find a good caterer to apprentice with, call your local rental companies and ask them about the different caterers in your area. They know which caterers are busy, organized, and successful. This information will help you decide with whom you want to work.

Learning from the Mistakes of Others

The best advice I can give you is to approach every apprenticing opportunity with an open mind. Even the worst caterer can teach you something, if only not to make his or her mistakes.

For example, early in my new career I got to a job on time and found myself alone with the staff. There we sat, eating up time and money waiting for the caterer, the rentals, and the food. I couldn't help but see that being late was not only unprofitable but also stressful.

Another caterer I worked with tried to befriend all her clients. She treated them like family, thinking they would forgive her slipshod style. Imagine how the father of the bride felt arriving an hour before the reception to find tables bare and the waitstaff in shorts sitting around with soft drinks in their hands. I discovered on the spot how important it is to create and maintain a professional atmosphere.

At other affairs I found out what happens when a caterer runs out of food, fails to set a time for a party to end, is short a waiter, or neglects to set budget limits and stick to them. One caterer I worked for, called "Promise Them Anything" by his staff, always said yes to whatever his clients requested. When these special requests turned out to be impossible to fulfill, his staff paid the penalty. I watched an angry and disappointed client who expected one wine but received another take out his frustration with the caterer, in front of everyone, on an innocent bartender. I made a silent vow never to put my staff in that position. (I wasn't surprised two years later to hear that Promise Them Anything had filed for bankruptcy.)

Learning from Your Own Mistakes

Of course, you can also learn a great deal from your own mistakes. Working yacht parties right after graduating from cooking school, I learned no fewer than ten lessons my first day at sea. The chef had said that he wanted a "pair of hands" to help for a party on board over the Fourth of July weekend. What he didn't tell me was that the yacht was 107 feet long, with the galley situated within the last 7 feet—that's all the kitchen there was. From that tiny space I was to feed eighty strangers a "make-your-own omelet" breakfast, a lunch of grilled swordfish and barbecued chicken, and two complete dinner buffets that began with appetizers.

Against all odds I succeeded, even though I forgot to

- crack and strain twenty-dozen eggs ahead of time
- slice bagels in half for easy eating
- make a backup tray of cooked bacon and sausages
- make backup bowls of butter balls and dressing
- parboil chicken pieces before the barbecue to cut down on the cooking time
- time the appetizers and main course properly
- bring cold drinks and food for the crew
- turn the leftover swordfish into an antipasto tray
- check my equipment when I came on board
- bring a second, clean chef's jacket for dinner

Catering my first party on my own gave me a new respect for money. Cooking, I learned, was the least of my worries. The party was a financial disaster. I spent more than I collected, my waitress left with the best-looking male guest before the party was over, and I had to do the dishes alone.

Nevertheless, I survived that first party, and what I've learned since then forms the basis of this book. I'd like to spare you some of my disasters and share tips for success. I wish I had a dollar for every student who has called me after taking my catering course to tell me that all the forms I provided really worked. You'll find the same forms sprinkled throughout this book, together with information on catering courses you can take, some of my favorite foolproof quantity recipes, suggested reading lists, and even tips for "culinary" computer software. Please write when this book pays off for you!

Getting Organized

Before you quit your day job and leap into catering, you need to know how much it will take to keep you afloat, which means considering some things you may never have thought about before. Sit down with pencil and paper and think about specifics. Do you have a spare room or a spare corner of a room where you can set up a home office? Do you already have voice mail, a stand mixer, and a food processor? If not, you'll need to buy them. You will also need between $3,000 and $4,000 for a business license, insurance, a lawyer, and the services of an accountant. On top of all that, remember that you will need stamps, stationery, notepads, and a calculator. You will also need to pay for your own transportation, medical insurance, and business calls.

Figure how much you need to keep going and to put money away for later. Add in something extra for emergencies and other unforeseen expenses. Ask other caterers how much of a nest egg they suggest you start with. Then make a budget by the week and the month and stick to it.

Leaving the Security of a Job

Leaving the security of a paying job is the hardest part of getting started. My solution was to begin to set up my business while I was still employed. My calendar read like this:

March 1: Purchase a desk and a file cabinet.
March 15: Think up a name for company.
April 2: Arrange for design of company logo.
April 17: Print business cards.
May 1: Clean out spare bedroom.
May 15: Secure a business phone number (with call forwarding and voice mail).
June 1: Establish an Internet and social media presence (website, blog, Facebook, Twitter, LinkedIn, Tumblr, Pinterest).
June 15: Quit job.

With this system and setting aside half of each paycheck, I acquired a nest egg over several months to meet anticipated as well as unanticipated costs. I also had booked several parties by the time I left my job.

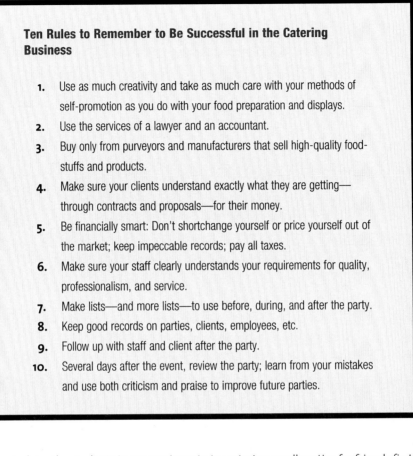

Ten Rules to Remember to Be Successful in the Catering Business

1. Use as much creativity and take as much care with your methods of self-promotion as you do with your food preparation and displays.
2. Use the services of a lawyer and an accountant.
3. Buy only from purveyors and manufacturers that sell high-quality foodstuffs and products.
4. Make sure your clients understand exactly what they are getting—through contracts and proposals—for their money.
5. Be financially smart: Don't shortchange yourself or price yourself out of the market; keep impeccable records; pay all taxes.
6. Make sure your staff clearly understands your requirements for quality, professionalism, and service.
7. Make lists—and more lists—to use before, during, and after the party.
8. Keep good records on parties, clients, employees, etc.
9. Follow up with staff and client after the party.
10. Several days after the event, review the party; learn from your mistakes and use both criticism and praise to improve future parties.

I advise the students in my seminars to try catering small parties for friends first, before they quit their day job. Turning a hobby or a passion for cooking beautiful foods into a successful career isn't going to work for everyone. You need to start small.

Of course, it's no mean feat to cater a party on the weekend and still work forty hours a week, but it can be done; I know people who do it year-round. The trick is to bite off exactly what you can chew and no more. Avoid weddings for 250. Instead stick to parties of manageable size. Do a whole series of small jobs well, and before long you'll have the confidence, the contacts, and the income stream you need to tackle more ambitious projects. At that point it will be much easier for you to figure out whether it makes sense to leave your day job.

How This Book Is Organized

Undoubtedly, you will make mistakes in your business—everyone does—but if you read this book chapter by chapter, you'll get an excellent idea of what it takes to succeed as a home-based caterer. You'll begin by learning what you need to set up your own business, how to research the health regulations that affect caterers in your area, and how to structure your business and create a business plan. Then you'll learn how to line up work, charge for your services, find good help, and get your name around. Two full chapters discuss what it takes to stage a successful party, from planning all the way through execution. Of course, keeping your books isn't nearly as fun as throwing a good party, but you'll learn that, too, along with information on the legal aspects of your catering business.

You're about to embark on an extraordinary adventure. Good luck!

02 Working Out of Your Home

During the first few days working out of your home, you may feel as though you're on vacation. No boss. No deadlines. No dress code. If it's a warm day, you may even put on shorts and take your cell phone outside in the sunshine to make sales calls. If you are to succeed, however, you'll have to become your own boss, setting working hours and daily goals. To do this effectively, it pays to take a look at your energy cycles and living patterns.

Are you a lark, bright-eyed in the morning? Or are you an owl, with energy in the afternoon? When do you feel most effective? Make sure you work hard for several hours at that time.

Don't be surprised if the demands of your new career require you to work more hours, or at least different hours, than you put in on your former job. After all, much of a caterer's work needs to be done in the evenings. Many clients can't talk about parties until after they get home from work, and if you're out delivering promotional packages and menus to prospective clients during the day, evenings may be the best time for writing proposals, going over menus, or fine-tuning events.

To give you an idea of how your day might look, consider the following blow-by-blow description of a recent day I spent working from home:

9:00 a.m.   Returned phone calls from existing clients. Made notes about changes on the party information form I had in front of me.

9:30 a.m.   Called rental company to check on items needed for anniversary party on Saturday. Made sure to ask them what time they would deliver and what the total amount would be so that I could get a check from my client to give them.

10:00 a.m.	Added two waiters to staff for Saturday party because guest count grew.
10:15 a.m.	Started two employee folders for new waiters. Included I-9 forms and W-4s for income tax purposes. I planned to have them fill these out as soon as they arrived.
10:30 a.m.	Called catering director at the hotel where I would be exhibiting bridal shower food and props on Sunday. Verified where I should park to unload.
11:00 a.m.	Called fish purveyor at the specialty grocery store and got the lowest price for imported caviar for the anniversary party. Called client back with dollar quote per person. To keep costs down, suggested serving caviar on blini instead of letting guests serve themselves. (Note: Client decided against caviar after hearing the price and stuck with the smoked salmon she chose originally.)
11:30 a.m.	Called bakery to tell them that the order they filled for me last weekend had been a dozen rolls short. Deducted the price from the invoice.
11:45 a.m.	Called client of last weekend's party to say what a joy it had been working there and to ask for names of three friends who might need a caterer in the future.
Noon	Lunched on lasagna left over from the weekend. Yum!
12:20 p.m.	Tossed waiters' black aprons in the washing machine, checking pockets first. Soaked kitchen towels and chef's jacket in bleach before washing, drying, and pressing. Loaded clean jackets and towels into the van.
12:30 p.m.	Called fifteen corporate event planners from convention center referral list. Set up dates to show them my portfolio, DVDs with footage of my parties, and suggested menu packages. Sent each one a brochure and a handwritten note telling him or her how much I was looking forward to our appointment.
3:30 p.m.	Printed pictures from my phone from last weekend's party and to put photographs in album for tomorrow's appointments.

4:30 p.m.   Wrote out checks to suppliers for products received last weekend.

5:00 p.m.   Read society page in newspaper to find upcoming events that I might attend or get involved with for business networking. Relaxed until 7:00 p.m.

7:00 p.m.   Spent an hour on the phone calming a nervous bride.

And that was an easy day!

Setting Up an Office

Working out of your home allows you to keep overhead low, but you have to create a workable environment. Although space might be at a premium in your home, it's still important to set up an area you can call your own. A quiet corner of a family room, a small room with a door, even the basement or a corner of the garage will do for a start.

To make my first work space, I divided a walk-in closet in half, placed my desk in that space, and built two shelves above my desk. From this tiny place my business grew to the point where I was booking six parties a month.

The Ten Most Common Mistakes That Home-Based Caterers Make

1. Not taking one day off every week
2. Setting appointments for early Monday morning after a weekend of parties
3. Answering the business phone during family time
4. Answering the family line during working hours
5. Expecting family to know and sympathize when you're worried or rushed
6. Letting friends or neighbors stay and visit when they drop in unannounced
7. Turning on the TV
8. Accepting errands from people who say, "You don't mind, do you? You're home all day!"
9. Having clients come to your home instead of meeting them at their home or office
10. Not getting up and dressed at the same time every day

Once you've set aside office space, you'll want to outfit it with a desk, a business number, and voice mail. A computer, printer/scanner, and Internet connection are all you really need.

Start-Up Costs

Basic food preparation equipment	$_____
Initial food costs and staples	$_____
Location for cooking	$_____
Business license	$_____
Lawyer and accountant fees	$_____
Insurance	$_____
Transportation	$_____
Advertising	$_____
Office supplies	$_____
Telephone and Internet provider	$_____
Stationery and business cards	$_____
Website and blog	$_____
Medical insurance	$_____
Taxes	$_____
Money to live on	$_____
Nest egg (unexpected expenses)	$_____
Total projected start-up costs	$_____

For right now, make sure you have the basics covered. The first law of catering is Make Do. Don't buy anything until you can't function without it.

Doing without a computer, however, is not an option. It stores vast amounts of information and retrieves it instantly. It saves you space and time. You'll have access to the Internet and e-mail.

Still, I know a caterer who grosses $1 million a year tapping out proposals on a typewriter. Information on every party she's produced is stored in old-fashioned paper files. Her best resource is her great memory for names.

On your computer, file parties under the date and cross-reference with the client's name. Then create an index of your party files. An up-to-date list of completed parties with the clients' names and phone numbers will be handy if quick information or referrals are necessary.

As a caterer, you'll find that working within each client's budget is your biggest challenge. (There are only two kinds of clients, as the sparrow said: cheap and cheaper.) It helps if you have first learned to work within your own budget. See how little you can spend setting up an office. Use this as an opportunity and a challenge, not as a bore and an obstacle.

For example, when I started my catering business, I decided not to buy stationery with printed letterhead. Instead I had business cards, envelopes, thank-you notes, and return-address stickers printed with my company logo. I never missed the letterhead. Instead I printed proposals or correspondence on a variety of different colored paper, often using clip art or photographs to jazz them up. I used cartoons, stickers, anything I could think of that was different. I wanted my proposals to stand out from the high stack of competing proposals on a client's desk.

I'm glad to say my strategy worked. Not ordering letterhead saved me $500 in the beginning. Now I don't have letterhead by choice. My proposals are lively and creative. My presentations work for me, and every day I'm getting interest on that $500 in the bank.

The moral of the story is this: In the beginning of a new career, don't get hung up on what you don't have. Concentrate instead on the ideas, talent, and energy you possess. Setting up an office is not that different from cooking. When a recipe calls for a spice you don't have in your cupboard, you make do. Substitution and imagination are essential in running a business, too. Don't sweat the small stuff, as the saying goes. Look at the big picture.

ESSENTIALS

- ❏ Pens and pencils
- ❏ Ruled legal pads for taking notes
- ❏ File folders
- ❏ Filing cabinet or box for vendor information or past party files
- ❏ Laptop computer with catering software installed and a printer/copier/ scanner
- ❏ Large envelopes in several sizes
- ❏ Stamps
- ❏ Return-address labels
- ❏ Business cards
- ❏ Business line with voice-mail system
- ❏ Internet provider
- ❏ Paper clips and stapler
- ❏ Basic accounting software or accounting ledger from a stationery store
- ❏ Calendar for marking party dates
- ❏ Rolodex for important names, addresses, and phone numbers
- ❏ Small digital camera to document your work
- ❏ An easy-to-read clock only a glance away
- ❏ An easy-to-read handheld calculator
- ❏ Smartphone, which can be used as a calendar, Rolodex, camera, clock, and calculator all in one

WHAT YOU WILL WANT LATER

- ❏ iPad or tablet to show portfolio of work
- ❏ A monthly payroll service
- ❏ Printed stationery or an alternative branding strategy, including postcards, to make dropping notes to clients and purveyors easier
- ❏ An office fridge with cold drinks and an automatic coffee/tea machine

Working Green as a Caterer

Here are five simple things you can do to reduce waste and save money in the process.

- Cut down any wastepaper that is blank on one side to use as notepaper.

- Buy recycled copier and printer paper, envelopes, etc.

- Use e-mail as often as possible to cut down on postage.

- Collect tote bags to use as grocery bags. Washable bags are especially useful.

- If you must use disposables, look into using biodegradables, which are available at online restaurant supply stores.

Training Family and Friends to Take You Seriously

When you make the career transition from everyone's favorite party host to professional caterer, family and friends will need to see you in a new light. Here are some tips on training them to view you as a professional.

At first your family will think that working at home instead of going to the office means you have tons of time to run errands and tie up loose ends. Establish clear boundaries right away. Now is a good time to write down the first draft of your business plan (see chapter 3) and read it to family members. Not only will this help clarify your thoughts and get you organized, but it will put your family on notice that you mean business. You will also want to explain how success in your new career will benefit everyone.

To keep family members from disturbing you while you work, make a time schedule, tack it on your office door, and stick to it. Explain to them the amount of time involved in finding clients and planning a party. Also explain why you may need to work some evenings.

Enlist your family's aid in marketing your new catering business. Perhaps your husband's corporation is planning its annual Christmas party or your daughter's basketball team is planning an awards banquet. Both events could use a caterer. There's no better representative for you than a proud relative.

Friends can also be helpful in getting your new business off the ground. Look for every chance possible to work with people you know. If a friend has a daughter getting married or a neighbor is throwing a baby shower, offer to cater the event for a nominal fee that will cover your costs. You'll get experience, and guests at the party may become future clients.

When you are first setting up shop, it is important to get your name around. Look for every opportunity to flaunt your new business. Say your son plays Little League baseball. Why not suggest a barbecue for the whole league at the local baseball field? Suddenly sixty or seventy parents know you're in business. You might even consider sponsoring a team. Not only will you have raised your profile, but by making your children part of your business, you'll have given them a sense of pride and satisfaction in what you do.

Think of how many tweets and followers will come from a party like that: #mysistertheworldsbestcaterer #myfamilygivesperfectparties!

Employing Family Members

Many caterers are tempted to hire family members as employees, but before you hire them, they need to know your policies, guidelines, and rules. What do you expect from them? What can they expect from you?

For this and future hiring, you need to learn successful interviewing and hiring techniques (see chapter 4). The best way to get the results you want from an employee (family member or not) is to tell the employee, preferably in writing, exactly what he or she is expected to do.

I learned this the hard way. Once I hired my sister to help me with a small party. She understood her role to mean she would go with me to the location, carry in the food, sit on a stool, critique the food, and watch me sweat as I ran around doing everything. I had pictured her passing appetizers, pouring wine, and helping with the cleanup, but I had neglected to tell her that. Later, when I exploded in the car, she simply said, "You should have told me what you wanted."

Employees who want to work for you again will often tell you what you want to hear. Family members, on the other hand, are usually more than willing to tell you when the cake is dry or the meat is overdone. Hear them out and use their feedback to improve your performance the next time.

Twelve Commonsense Measures for Safe Food Handling

1. Maintain good personal hygiene and health.
2. Date and label incoming stock items and be sure everything is packaged correctly.
3. Check in and refrigerate or freeze all products the moment they arrive.
4. Rotate stock constantly.
5. Keep work areas clean, especially when you're busy.
6. Don't reuse bowls, knives, or pans without washing them first.
7. Keep pantry food on shelves and racks away from rodents and pests.
8. When in doubt, throw the food out.
9. Contract for a professional extermination service.
10. Buy products from respected and approved purveyors.
11. Cook all foods thoroughly; use a thermometer and learn the proper temperatures.
12. Instruct your staff about the temperature "danger zone" in foods, and have them attend a Certified Food Handler seminar.

Complying with City Ordinances

Most caterers begin working out of their homes without a business license, a caterer's permit, or product liability insurance. Because such a casual approach to running a business can get you in trouble with local and state authorities, the most important advice I can give you is to find out—before you set up shop—about government regulations in your state that pertain to catering.

Most businesses are required to register and publish a DBA "doing business as" statement, also known as a fictitious business name (FBN). DBA registration is necessary when a business operates under a name other than its owner's personal name. In such cases, conducting business and opening a business bank account are only possible after you have filed and published your DBA. There are a variety of online services that will file your DBA and put the required notices in newspapers for you for a fee. State and county laws differ, so check out a service that is familiar with your area.

Your first step should be to check with the city or county clerk's office to see whether it is legal for you to have an office in your home. Remember that regulations vary from one locality to another. In West Los Angeles it is legal for me to have my office in my home for phone and mail purposes, so long as I create no extra foot traffic.

The city business tax license issued to my home address the first year cost about $100. I got it at the city clerk's office. From there I went to the State Board of Equalization to apply for a seller's permit and resale number, which allows me to

Cottage Food Laws

Having your name on delicious food products is a great way to get your catering business recognized and could be an additional income source.

Since 2013 cottage food producers in California have been allowed to sell certain foods made at home, joining thirty other states that already allow selling homemade food products. Some states require attending a food safety course, some require ingredient labels, and some only allow very specific foods. There may be a permit fee or a requirement that you register with your county health department. Certain states and counties may require that you obtain a separate permit from the health department if your products are being indirectly sold through restaurants, grocers, or food trucks. As there can be strict limits to the number of employees and a limit to the amount of money you can make, you may need to separate your catering business from your cottage food business.

Check your state's laws before selling anything made from your home.

Below is the list of foods that are allowed under the California law:

- Baked goods (without fillings) such as breads, biscuits, churros, cookies, pastries, and tortillas

- Candy, such as brittle and toffee

- Chocolate-covered nonperishable foods, such as nuts and dried fruits

- Dried fruit

- Dried pasta

- Dry baking mixes

buy goods without paying taxes on them, so long as I charge sales tax to my clients. Understand that as a business, you are expected to collect the city and state tax from your clients and to turn it over quarterly to the city and state. (Check in your state; you may be lucky and not have sales tax.)

In Los Angeles I charge clients 9.25 percent of the total amount spent on food, staff, rentals, and entertainment. For more information call your own State Board of Equalization or Department of Revenue for a free tax guide.

- Fruit pies, fruit empanadas, and fruit tamales

- Granola, cereals, and trail mixes

- Herb blends and dried mole paste

- Honey and sweet sorghum syrup

- Jams, jellies, preserves, and fruit butter*

- Nut mixes and nut butters

- Popcorn

- Vinegar and mustard

- Roasted coffee and dried tea

- Waffle cones and pizelles

*A very important note on jams, jellies, preserves, and fruit butter: Inclusion of additional ingredients changes the chemistry of food, which can allow growth of bacteria and toxins under the right conditions. For example, adding jalapeño peppers to jelly to make pepper jelly can cause the formation of botulism. Any business that produces such potentially hazardous products needs to come under stricter health department rules for professional kitchens than those spelled out in the cottage food laws.

If you give food as gifts, you don't need any type of permit. The same usually goes for bake sales where the money goes to a school or charity. But do take into account the list of foods above: There's a reason these foods are considered safe.

Working as a caterer from home is trickier than working as a home-based writer or accountant because in addition to an office, you need access to a kitchen. Most state or local health protection agencies do not allow food prepared in a private home or kitchen to be sold to the public. True, in many parts of the country many caterers begin cooking out of their homes, but you are risking a hefty fine if this is against the law in your area. Once you are fined, you may not be able to get a business license in the future.

Until you have established a commissary or commercial kitchen for your company (see pages 28), one solution is to cook in your client's home. Your client can buy the food, you can charge for your services, and you aren't breaking any laws.

Working with Your Local Health Department

As a new caterer, one of the first calls you make should be to your county health department to ask: Do I have to cook in an approved city-licensed kitchen? If so, which safety and sanitation features are required for a kitchen to qualify? Generally you will find that the health department mandates such features as ventilation for the stove, stainless-steel worktables, special nonskid flooring, and thermometers in all refrigeration units.

The aim of the health department is not only to protect the public from unsafe food but also to educate people in the food-service industry. Check with your local health department to find out what laws apply in your area. The health department staff inspects and approves kitchens on an ongoing basis. Each year, they issue me a caterer's permit, the cost of which is based on the square footage of my processing area.

Working in an approved kitchen and using your local health department as a safety resource will help ensure your success by protecting your reputation as a professional. Be sure to ask for the guidelines for bringing a kitchen up to code or building one from the ground up. Working out of an uninspected kitchen is a mistake. Not only are you breaking the law, but you run the risk of being shut down entirely.

Your local health department may also have helpful tips about ways to prevent the growth of bacteria in cooked food; transport food safely; cook and handle foods on party sites; and avoid spoilage, accidents, and illness. All this information is extremely valuable to a new caterer.

Steps to Making Your Business Legal

- Find out about state and local zoning regulations in your area pertaining to having an office in your home (page 24).

- Set up your office space (page 17).

- Establish your business address (consider renting a post office box).

- Establish your business telephone number (a separate line just for your business).

- Apply for a DBA if you need one (page 23).

- Apply for a city business tax license, usually issued by the city clerk's office (page 24).

- Apply for a seller's permit and resale number from the State Board of Equalization (page 24).

- Get business cards, letterhead, and envelopes printed (page 20).

- Comply with city ordinances regulating where to cook (page 23).

- Work with your local health department (page 26).

- Find a kitchen (page 28).

- Permit your kitchen (page 29).

- Find an attorney (page 58).

- Get the insurance you need (page 59).

- Establish agreements and contracts (page 61).

- Learn about subcontractors and suppliers (page 62).

- Establish your needs for employees—permanent, part-time, or independent contractors (page 63).

- Understand labor practices (page 71).

Sharing a Kitchen

Your best bet when you're first starting out is to find an approved commercial kitchen and share it with another caterer. Your goal should be to avoid the overhead of a full-time facility. To do so you will need to be resourceful and flexible, but it's worth it. Your savings in rent your first year alone can amount to $10,000 or more.

Consider running an ad in a local newspaper specifying what you want. Expect a response from caterers who want to shave their overhead. A typical ad might look like this:

> **Wanted:** Experienced Caterer to Share Commercial Kitchen
> Let me help you cut your overhead. Share 8 to 15 days a month.
> My flexible schedule of clients can accommodate your business.
> Own many props and decor pieces to share. City licensed and
> insured. Extensive knowledge in safety and sanitation.
> Excellent references from industry professionals.

In deciding which kitchen to share, you'll want to consider how near it is to your home and how much parking there is for pickups and deliveries. Also look at the layout, size, equipment, and storage areas. It's not likely you'll want to spend thousands of dollars to outfit a rental kitchen, so finding one that best suits your needs is the goal.

A well-designed kitchen will save you time, money, and product. First, look for stairs and steps. Everything on one level is most desirable. Are there double doors for big floral arrangements or props? Are there screen doors with overhead fly-traps? Is the floor smooth and in good condition? Are there thick, black rubber mats to protect your legs when standing? Are the walls free of holes? Is there enough room for your entire crew to work side by side in the busiest months? Are there adequate bathroom facilities for your employees, if you hire any, with extra hand sinks? Are there tables and chairs for workers to sit and eat at? Is the equipment in reasonably good shape? Have the ovens been calibrated recently and the refrigeration temperatures checked with thermometers? Is the place freshly painted? Are storage areas accessible and dry?

If a kitchen has been recently approved by your local health department, building and safety department, and fire department, you should be issued your own necessary caterer's permit without any problem.

Make sure you're not violating any existing lease and zoning laws. A real estate broker or an attorney will suggest the right questions to ask and help you work out the best agreement with your co-tenant or landlord.

My first catering partner and I shared commercial kitchen space in Santa Monica with a brownie manufacturer who sold other caterers great dessert trays. The only major piece of equipment we had to buy when moving in was a double-door reach-in refrigerator. Stoves, worktables, shelves, and a freezer were there and included in our lease. We didn't need a walk-in refrigerator; instead we rented refrigerator trucks at weekend rates when we needed to transport a lot of food for large parties.

Your goal should be to share space that includes just about everything you need in the way of heavy equipment. If you find yourself in a position where you need to invest in refrigeration equipment, it pays to buy the best you can. Poor refrigeration shortens the life of your product, reduces the quality, and adds to your food cost by increasing spoilage. Commercial refrigerators such as Delfield or Hobart are designed to keep food at lower temperatures than average home refrigerators can maintain.

Dishwashers are sometimes missing from commercial kitchens, but you can lease them from food brokers or restaurant-supply houses. I negotiated a good deal for a brand-new dishwasher with a cleaning supply company by signing a two-year contract for detergent and a rodent-control program.

Renting a Kitchen on a Per-Day Basis

If you need a kitchen only two or three days a month, look into day rentals from private clubs or churches. Often places like these use their kitchens only a couple of days a week, and the rest of the time they stand empty. Without signing a lease, you can negotiate a per-day price and use the kitchen only when you need to. Most of the time these types of kitchens have been commercially retrofitted and approved by the health department, but you'll have to check.

Outfitting Your Kitchen

Let's assume that you've decided on a kitchen. Your next challenge is to figure out what you need in the way of pots, pans, and other equipment to do a good job. Unless you've worked for some time in a professional kitchen, you probably don't know much about commercial-quality equipment. The best way to learn is to visit a restaurant-supply house with the checklist on page 30 in hand.

POTS AND PANS IN ALL DIFFERENT SIZES

- [ ] sauté pans
- [ ] roasting pans
- [ ] stockpots
- [ ] saucepans with covers
- [ ] sheet pans, full- and half-size
- [ ] chafing-dish liners
- [ ] stainless mixing bowls in various sizes

UTENSILS

- [ ] small and large ladles
- [ ] tongs of different lengths
- [ ] kitchen spoons
- [ ] measuring spoons
- [ ] measuring cups for dry and wet ingredients
- [ ] carving board
- [ ] cutting boards
- [ ] spatulas
- [ ] wire whisks
- [ ] potato peelers
- [ ] can opener
- [ ] colanders
- [ ] knives of different sizes
- [ ] wooden spoons

- [ ] portion scale
- [ ] scissors
- [ ] strainers
- [ ] pepper grinder
- [ ] pot holders
- [ ] towels
- [ ] corkscrew

APPLIANCES

- [ ] freestanding mixer with two bowls
- [ ] food processor
- [ ] blender
- [ ] ice-cream maker
- [ ] coffeepot (for crew)
- [ ] portable slicer
- [ ] microwave
- [ ] portable convection oven

HOUSEKEEPING

- [ ] garbage cans
- [ ] broom and dustpan
- [ ] mops
- [ ] buckets
- [ ] first-aid kit
- [ ] carpet sweeper
- [ ] cleaning supplies

You'll notice immediately that pots, pans, food processors, and the rest of the equipment you see is larger and heavier than the equipment you use in your home kitchen. It has to be sturdier in order to hold large quantities of food and to stand up to constant use. Everything costs more than the home kitchen version, too. You can expect to pay anywhere from $3,000 to $5,000 if you're starting from scratch.

If you don't already own them, you will need assorted sizes of sauté pans and saucepans, sheet pans, chafing-dish liners, and roasting pans to prepare, deliver, and serve food. Be sure to get sizes that fit both home and commercial ovens, as you'll be cooking in your clients' home kitchens as well as in your own commercial setup.

Stainless-steel mixing bowls, colanders, and strainers are important and come in all prices. Find the most durable.

Also get a lot of clear plastic storage containers with lids in every size. You'll need a couple of insulated box carriers for transporting food to and from party sites. And don't forget to invest in a few rolls of heavy-duty plastic wrap and aluminum foil.

Get special equipment, as you need it, for offbeat recipes (madelines, for example) or new party menus. A good source of such equipment is industry trade shows such as the Fancy Food Show or the National Restaurant Association Show at the McCormick Center in Chicago. Equipment purveyors haunt those places. You can buy anything from pots and pans to walk-in refrigerators, but you can also find such novelties as chocolate mints to imprint with your company logo or lace wrappers for your halved lemon garnishes. For example, I once found thermal holding bags for bakers' racks at the Western Foodservice and Hospitality Expo (used to be held in San Francisco, then Los Angeles, but is now in San Diego). I still use these nifty bags—which cost me $200—to keep my warm desserts at the right temperature and to protect them at party sites.

Smallwares and Utensils

As a caterer, you'll be dealing with a jumble of small items: metal and wooden spoons, whisks, spatulas, tongs, funnels, vegetable peelers, matches, pastry brushes, and cake-decorating tips and bags.

The first thing you need is a storage place so that you'll be able to find each item when you need it. A metal or plastic toolbox works fine. So does a fishing-tackle box. Look for them at a hardware or building-supply store. Any of these boxes is a natural for organizing kitchen tools.

Finding Used Equipment

I've had great luck buying used kitchen equipment at auction houses. I check under "Kitchen Equipment" in the Sunday paper's classifieds online. Restaurants closing or hotels remodeling often sell their kitchen equipment and smallwares off to an auction house. As a customer, you just need to show up and bring cash. I've paid as little as 10 to 20 cents on the dollar for items. Many pieces are clearly marked and no bidding is necessary.

The best bargain I've bought, to date, is a brand-new food processor—still in the box—for $10, at a church garage sale. What a miracle!

What to Look For in a Good Knife

Since a knife is a chef's most important piece of equipment, you'll want to look for good knives that will last a lifetime and a long, thin steel whetstone to keep the blades sharp. You want a sharp short-bladed knife not only because it makes cutting easier but also because a dull blade is more likely to give you a nasty cut than a sharp one.

When you go shopping for a knife, notice the variety of blades and handles. Heft a few knives before you buy to see which ones feel best in your hand. Most blades today are made from high-carbon stainless steel, which has the strength of stainless steel plus carbon steel's ability to hold an edge. Not only is it stronger than stainless steel, it does not discolor on contact with high-acid foods, such as tomatoes or onions, or rust if not dried immediately. Though some knife handles are still made of wood, these eventually crack and split. Most handles today are plastic, made to look and feel like wood, and they have the same life span as the knife blade.

Wüsthof Trident and Henckels are two brands I can recommend. No matter what knives you buy, use your steel to sharpen them every time you use them and have all knives professionally sharpened once or twice a year.

When I set up shop, I bought a starter set of Henckels from a catalog. It included a chef's knife, a boning knife, a slicer, and a couple of paring knives. That was all I needed for several years. These sets, easily available to home chefs, are a bargain for the new professional.

Setting Up Your Pantry

Every caterer needs to set up a pantry in order to be ready for last-minute parties. As you bring in dry goods, you'll need to calculate what I call your *mise en place* cost. This is French for "everything in its place." That means flour, salt, spices, and other staples stocked and ready to be used before you buy the perishables for your first event.

If you keep careful track of your receipts, you can incorporate these costs into your per-person food charge. I calculate a per-person party mise en place figure by dividing the monthly cost of staples by the number of people I plan to serve that month.

Transportation

After a job or two, you'll find that carrying the food, props, equipment, and staff is an important part of catering. A van, an SUV, or a truck is the best thing for a caterer to work from, although loading and unloading are always a challenge. Think about conserving your energy so that you don't get hurt. Practice careful lifting. A dolly or a hand truck is essential for getting everything on and off easily.

If you don't already own a van, don't rush out and buy one. By doing your homework and charting the number of days you're likely to need a van each month, you will see why it makes better sense for your cash flow to rent for eight days a month than to own for thirty. My strategy is to rent vans and trucks as I need them. I built a good relationship with a van rental company in my community. I asked for and got bargain weekend rates and weekly rates when I needed them. I even managed a monthly rate for December (the biggest party month) by reserving early. You can do the same. Remember to pass the cost of renting a van on to your client when you figure your costs per head (see chapter 9).

Establishing Relationships with Wholesale Purveyors

Until now you've probably purchased all your meats, fish, produce, and other supplies at a grocery store. When you go into business for yourself, however, you can no longer afford to buy food at retail prices. Buying wholesale will save you 10 to 35 percent, and you'll enjoy a better selection to boot. Research wholesale purveyors in your area, and visit their warehouses. Find out how long each company you're considering has been in business, whether the company is licensed and insured like you, and whether the two of you see eye to eye on supplying the finest product to your clients. One of the best ways to find out about quality purveyors is to ask other caterers.

A good working relationship with a purveyor's sales representative can save you time designing your menus, help you control your food cost, and even help you solve food production problems. Sales reps are knowledgeable about how to calculate the right portions, keep food from spoiling, and take advantage of the availability of special seasonal items.

I work primarily with three different wholesale food purveyors. I'm able to buy chicken and fish from one, dry goods and beef from another, and produce, flowers, and fresh pasta from the third. I do almost all my shopping over the phone or e-mail, which saves me a considerable amount of time, gas, and money. I've used the same purveyors for over twenty years. Not only do they sell the finest-quality foods, but they also take the time to negotiate price, suggest alternative products, and provide

Staples Checklist

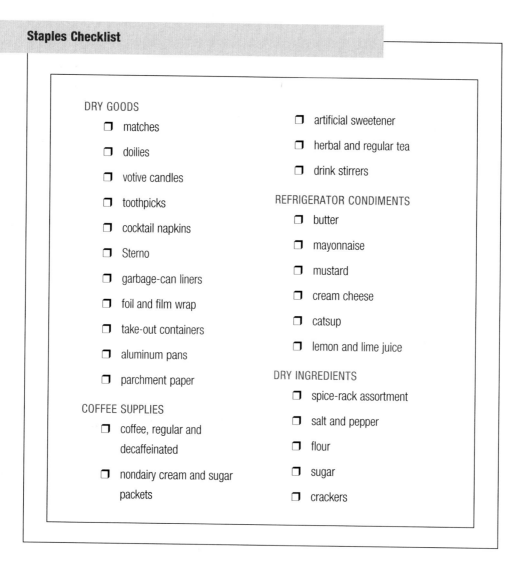

DRY GOODS
- ❏ matches
- ❏ doilies
- ❏ votive candles
- ❏ toothpicks
- ❏ cocktail napkins
- ❏ Sterno
- ❏ garbage-can liners
- ❏ foil and film wrap
- ❏ take-out containers
- ❏ aluminum pans
- ❏ parchment paper

COFFEE SUPPLIES
- ❏ coffee, regular and decaffeinated
- ❏ nondairy cream and sugar packets

- ❏ artificial sweetener
- ❏ herbal and regular tea
- ❏ drink stirrers

REFRIGERATOR CONDIMENTS
- ❏ butter
- ❏ mayonnaise
- ❏ mustard
- ❏ cream cheese
- ❏ catsup
- ❏ lemon and lime juice

DRY INGREDIENTS
- ❏ spice-rack assortment
- ❏ salt and pepper
- ❏ flour
- ❏ sugar
- ❏ crackers

Seven Money-Saving Tips for the New Caterer

1. Always use reusable grocery or tote bags.
2. Store leftovers in reusable food-storage containers.
3. Encourage your clients to use their own plates instead of disposables where appropriate.
4. Make fresh bread crumbs from stale bread.
5. Puree unused fruit and freeze for simple dessert sauces.
6. Grate unused cheese to make cheese blends. Rinds from hard cheeses can be used to flavor soups and stews; remove rinds before storing or serving.
7. Shop locally and at farmers' markets whenever possible, saving transportation costs and fuel.

---

safe packaging and reliable delivery (even to the party site if I've forgotten anything). After years of a successful business relationship, I've also reaped the benefits of building a solid credit history and have thirty days to pay my invoices if I need it.

My network of purveyors has supplied me with tips on finding good staff, with job leads, and even with presentation ideas. As we often say in the trade, you're only as good as your purveyors. Make sure you find the best.

Your Next Step

By the time you've read this chapter carefully, you'll have learned how to set up a home office, how to enlist the help of family and friends, and how much equipment to buy (and where) to get started. You're a lot closer to catering your first party than you were pages ago. But before you jump in, take the time to create a formal business plan, the subject of the next chapter.

Running a successful business is like cooking a meal: The more time and care you put into the preparation, the better the results. In this chapter you will learn how to write a business plan. In the process you will learn how to take yourself and your business seriously.

If you have not run a business before, consider attending seminars on starting and running a business. Check local colleges or business schools for courses taught by financial experts. Such courses are invaluable, and the fees are usually reasonable.

Local business organizations can also be helpful, both in increasing your visibility and in gaining you access to good advice. When I first started out, I joined a local chamber of commerce group that invited consultants and professionals to speak at weekly breakfast meetings. An added bonus of my membership was the chance to network and share information with other businesspeople, including other caterers. To get started yourself, pick up the phone and call a local chapter of Rotary, Kiwanis, or another business group. Ask if you might attend as a guest the first few times.

In your search for free information on running a business, be sure not to overlook your local library. Look for texts or online sites dedicated to business problems and management. Also ask the manager of your favorite bookstore for any outstanding books written by or about new entrepreneurs.

Not far from my house, I discovered that the local chapter of the California Restaurant Association had a library available for members' use. No one was ever there. I had the place and all its books to myself. I read all about marketing a food business and writing profitable menus.

Certain government services may also be worth investigating. For example, I learned from a flyer I found in the city clerk's office that the Small

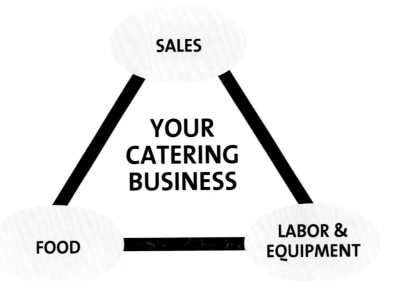

SALES

YOUR
CATERING
BUSINESS

FOOD

LABOR &
EQUIPMENT

This figure illustrates the equal importance of food costs, labor and equipment costs, and sales to your bottom line. Keep this balance in mind as you develop your business plan.

Business Administration makes retired businesspeople available as consultants to budding entrepreneurs. My partner and I spent hours with an accountant who had owned and managed his own firm for thirty-five years. He helped us project and estimate our first-year financial data, pointing out start-up costs, showing us how to keep an accounting ledger, and teaching us about gross profit margin and standard operating percentages. Working as a consultant not only filled his needs (he missed his business) but also helped us as partners to understand the necessity of good accounting practices from day one. Call your local Small Business Administration office and ask about SCORE (Service Corps of Retired Executives). Also check the SBA website at www.sba.gov to see what resources are available, including business forms, podcasts and RSS feeds, and online training.

How to Structure Your Business

Before you can write a business plan, you need to know what sort of business you plan to operate. Will you operate as a sole proprietor? Or do you plan to have one or more partners? Does it make sense for you to incorporate? These are some of the questions we'll explore. Before you make any decision, however, be sure to consult a certified public accountant.

The structure of your business depends on your background, skills, and interests. Often caterers start as sole proprietors and later expand into partnerships. The appeal of operating as a sole proprietor is that it's easy. You're in control, you don't have many start-up costs, and the record keeping required by law is minimal. Any money you make is simply taxed as personal income. The disadvantage is that for the rest of your life, you personally are liable for any business debts you incur.

A partnership is also low in start-up costs. Like the sole proprietorship (and unlike a corporation), it's relatively free from government control. Profit from the partnership to the partners is taxed as personal income, and the partnership is required to file an information return. One real advantage is that with a compatible partner working at your side from the start, your new business has a broader base of knowledge and two people to share the problems.

The trick is to make the terms of your partnership agreement as explicit as possible. My catering partner and I began by dividing our responsibilities according to our interests and talents. We decided that she would take care of the food ordering, purchases, and cooking and I would meet with clients and deal with sales and marketing. We had our attorney draw up an agreement to reflect our understanding of our roles and to minimize problems and surprises later. The agreement listed what personal equipment was brought to the partnership, the hours each of us was expected to work, the days we had off, what time of year we could vacation, how we intended to divide the profit each month, what percentage of profit we would put back into the company each year, and even what to do in the event of one partner's death. (We each purchased our own insurance policy and made the other partner the beneficiary upon death. In this way we created cash—the insurance money—for the remaining partner to purchase the deceased partner's interest based on a preset value.)

We took plenty of time to talk it over so that we both knew what the other person expected. If you are interested in establishing a formal partnership, you might take a look at *The Partnership Book: How to Write a Partnership Agreement,* by Denis Clifford and Ralph E. Warner, published by Nolo Press, June 2008.

The disadvantages of a partnership are similar to the disadvantages of a sole proprietorship, but they're multiplied by the number of partners. The main disadvantage is that each partner has unlimited liability for the partnership's debts. If your partner orders $10,000 in new equipment and then skips town, you're stuck with the bill.

Also, remember that a partnership means divided authority. As a sole proprietor you don't have to compromise; as a partner you can't avoid it. For this reason, getting along with and trusting your partner are absolutely critical. In fact, finding a suitable one might be the hardest thing you ever do, short of finding a suitable mate.

Your third option for structuring your company is to set it up as a corporation. The appeal of a corporation is that it may allow you to limit your personal liability in the event the corporation incurs debts you can't repay. It's also much easier to raise investment capital if you incorporate and to make sure the business will continue if you die.

Each state has different corporate record-keeping requirements. A good accountant should be able to acquaint you with what's involved before you take the plunge. You'll also want your business to be making enough money to benefit from the corporate structure; otherwise you may be stuck paying a hefty minimum tax, whether or not you can afford it.

If you decide to incorporate, you will need the advice of an attorney in setting up. The initial costs and filing fees vary, depending on the attorney's fees and state regulations. Remember that as a corporate entity, you're subject to double taxation—first on the corporation's profits and later on the salary you pay yourself.

Writing a Business Plan

Now that you've decided how you want to structure your business, you're ready to write your business plan. This meaty document is intended to help you express your plans, both immediate and long-term, as concretely as possible. If you're hoping to get a bank loan or to raise money from outside investors, you can't do without a business plan. Even if you plan to work alone and pay as you go, writing a detailed business plan is an informative and challenging exercise.

A business plan isn't something you whip together in a few days. In fact, I usually give my catering students an entire semester to pull it together. None of them wants to do it, of course. I hear all sorts of groans and mumbling about "not having time." My reply is: "You can't afford not to make the time." Starting a business without a plan is like getting in a car to go on a long trip without a map or any gas. You simply won't get where you think you're going.

Writing a business plan is the best way I know to create a vision of your company. It's a tool you can use to measure and then improve your performance. It offers a basis for making decisions, defines your partnership if you have one, and ultimately lets you share your vision with employees. Of course, some sections described below—particularly company management and projections for the future—may be tough to write when you're just starting out. My advice is to put these sections aside until you have enough information and experience to go on.

Step One: Writing the Summary Statement

Starting with your business name and location, write an overview of your business. Tell who you are, your credentials for starting your business, the market you plan to reach, and your plans for dealing with the competition. Then give a good, clear idea of your goals and objectives, including your plans for the future.

Some business consultants suggest writing the summary statement last; once you've got the entire plan on paper, it's a cinch to summarize. I prefer writing the summary statement first because I need to focus my energy and inspiration on the project. Either way works.

The first few paragraphs of a summary statement for a new home-based catering company might look like this:

> Food Fanatics caters parties for private individuals and businesses
> in Los Angeles County. Started by Denise Vivaldo, the company

specializes in parties where the decor is just as spectacular as the food. Many of the company's clients come from the city's entertainment industry. Clients call not only when they want value for their money but especially when they want to create a memorable and complete environment for their guests.

Food Fanatics' mission statement is printed on its business cards: The company strives to produce first-class menus for any occasion and to complement the vision of its clients. Everyone with whom Food Fanatics works—from waiters, bartenders, and hostesses to rental companies, florists, and entertainers—must meet its high standards.

What distinguishes Food Fanatics from other caterers in the area is Ms. Vivaldo's extensive background in food and wine. Having cooked in Shanghai, Cairo, San Francisco, Tokyo, New Orleans, Rome, and Honolulu, she is an expert in an unusually broad range of food styles.

Step Two: Defining Your Niche

This section gives you the opportunity to understand your market, size up the competition, and define your specialty.

Begin by developing a list of competitors. Consult the Yellow Pages under "caterers." Be sure to check restaurant listings, too. Highlight ads that mention take-out food, banquets, or special events. Then pick up the phone and talk to the owners and managers of these places. Ask them what dollar volume they did last year and how many years they've been in business. Most owners or operators are happy to share information because they're either winning or losing the game. While you're on the phone, you should also try to find out the biggest problem they face from year to year and how they solve it. Obviously, once you have talked to everybody in town, you'll have a much better idea of the sort of competition you're up against.

Another option is to hire professionals for a demographic study. Often restaurant management firms have up-to-date information on hotel chains or restaurants currently in "plan check" (that is, waiting for approval from the city building and safety department). Most likely their information is not free, but you can negotiate—maybe you can provide them with a fabulous Christmas party.

If you're planning to market a product or service to restaurants or other caterers, it's even easier for you to do market research. One caterer I worked with wanted to introduce a premium chocolate-covered fortune cookie. She didn't know whether or not people would like it. I told her to call every caterer in town to see who was interested in buying it. Armed with their positive responses, she went ahead.

When you're ready to write up this section of your business plan, focus on the opportunities and challenges that lie ahead for your new business. What are you offering that other caterers don't offer? What audience are you targeting? What are the demographics for your area? How's the local economy? Can you define the niche you'd like to fill? How do you know your service is a valuable addition to the community?

A typical market analysis might look like this:

Orange Blossom Catering
Redondo Beach, California

Redondo Beach is a very desirable place to live and offers a wonderful climate on a year-round basis to its 65,000 residents. In addition, within a 3-mile radius there are 175,000 residents and within a 5-mile radius 366,000 people.

The most prominent age-group is from twenty to forty-four, prime ages for first and second marriages and other special events. The average income within a 3-mile radius is $69,000 per household.

In 2011 almost 2.1 million couples were married. The Association of Bridal Consultants estimates that couples and their families spent an average of $28,082 on weddings in 2012, and of that amount nearly 50 percent went to receptions.

Southern California leads the nation in the bridal market; $2.7 billion is spent annually in bridal-related products and services. Unlike other regional areas, California's bridal market is year-round.

Given the lack of upscale, full-service catering companies in this area, Orange Blossom Catering expects the community to give its full support as clients. With the current strength of the bridal market, it is an excellent time for Orange Blossom Catering to enter this special-event market.

Step Three: Drawing Your Organizational Chart

A typical organizational chart for a catering business run from your home might look like this:

The number of employees you have at any given moment will vary depending on the size of the parties you cater. (For much more about employees, see chapter 4.)

It makes good sense to include in this section a copy of a staff sheet from a recent event, showing how many chefs and waiters it took to do the job. Indicate what each employee did and how much each got paid, as shown on page 47.

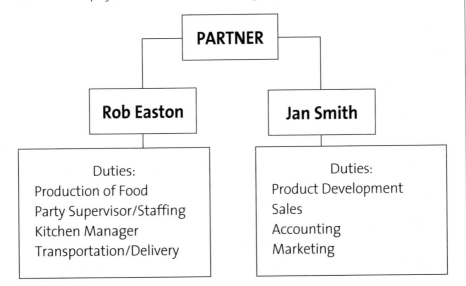

PARTNER

Rob Easton

Duties:
Production of Food
Party Supervisor/Staffing
Kitchen Manager
Transportation/Delivery

Jan Smith

Duties:
Product Development
Sales
Accounting
Marketing

If you're writing your business plan for the purposes of getting a loan or raising money, you'll want to write a paragraph on where you get your staff, the techniques you use to train them, and your experience in handling employees.

Such a paragraph might look like this:

> I plan to use culinary students, local college students, and/or servers who have impressed me with their skill and training. I will provide each server with a job description and list of policies. Everyone will also receive a party flow sheet to round out the details of the event. Finally, before the event we will meet to discuss the overall game plan and answer any questions. My experience working in restaurants and with other caterers has made me a firm believer in hiring polite and considerate people who can think on their feet.

Step Four: Describing Company Management and Operation

This section has four parts:

1. **Key personnel:** Bios of your company's key players go first. Be sure to emphasize special talents and attach up-to-date résumés. How you "sell" your management skills to an interested investor, partner, or loan officer may mean the difference between success and failure.

2. **Office and kitchen plans:** Next include a description of your office setup and your plan for either sharing, renting, building, or buying an approved kitchen. The results of your research into permits, licenses, and health regulations belong here. Indicate that you intend to conform to any legal requirements that affect you. You want any loan officer reading your business plan to know that you intend to be a full-time, legal caterer, not just a weekend warrior.

3. **Capital investments:** If you have made capital investments in office furniture or kitchen equipment, list them here. Note the priority and importance of your purchases. If items have already paid for themselves, say so.

4. **First year's operating agenda:** This is where you lay out a specific operating plan. A three-month schedule of events for a small home-based caterer might look like this:

January

- Place ad in a local paper online, inviting "This Year's Spring Brides" to call my wedding-consultant hotline. Answer one question, get their name and number, and send them a letter of introduction explaining the complimentary services I provide as their caterer.
- Attend local bridal fair and leave each vendor with a wrapped "Mexican wedding cake cookie," together with a price list by the dozen. "This is something I'm selling as the first edible party favor for every bride to order."

February

- Contact American Heart Association regarding its annual bake sale.
- Send valentine cookies to PTA board.
- Call local food editor to pitch article on the "Spring Bounty of Vegetables."

March

- Deliver six "American-Made Lunch Boxes" to the local convention center meeting planners. Follow up from my "cold calls" of last December about supplying lunch boxes and brownie baskets. Leave a typed price list with each lunch box.
- Give complete written proposal to the convention center's director of operations about the convention center purchasing one hundred boxes and baskets for its annual employee party and gift giveaways.
- Check with local ad agencies for campaigns featuring "real businesspeople" as the models. Find out to whom to address a promo pack with pictures. Stress that I would be happy to appear in the ad and feed the crew.

Food Fanatics
SPECIAL EVENTS

www.DeniseVivaldo.com

Biography of Denise Vivaldo

Denise Vivaldo is a professional chef de cuisine with more than thirty years' experience teaching and consulting in all areas of the hospitality industry. Recognized as a respected food professional, her expertise ranges from food styling for print and television to event planning, buffet design, innovative menu conception, recipe development, and restaurant consulting.

Beginning her culinary training at The Ritz Escoffier and La Varenne in Paris, she graduated chef de cuisine from the California Culinary Academy in 1984. Following graduation she was hired as kitchen manager for Charter Concepts International, a worldwide yacht chartering company. Soon afterwards Ms. Vivaldo transferred to CCI's sister company California Celebrations, where she was made executive chef during her first year. She orchestrated special events at exotic locations with both international menus and celebrity guests.

In 1988 Ms. Vivaldo founded Food Fanatics, a full-service catering company, where she received commissions for such prestigious events as the Academy Awards Governor's Ball; Macy's/American Express's PASSPORT, starring Elizabeth Taylor; Sunset Magazine's "Tastes of Sunset" and Los Angeles Magazine's "Taste of LA." In addition, Chef Vivaldo has catered and coordinated post-premiere and wrap parties for many Hollywood films.

An accomplished author, Ms. Vivaldo has written How to Start a Home-based Catering Business, currently in its seventh edition; How to Start a Home-based Personal Chef Business; Do It For Less! Parties, an entertaining guide and cookbook with quantity recipes; and Do It For Less! Weddings, which won an IACP cookbook award. She has also served as a creative consultant, developing original recipes for cookbooks authored by nationally recognized diet and fitness gurus.

Ms. Vivaldo has worked as a food stylist on such shows as Inside Dish with Rachael Ray on Food Network, The Ellen DeGeneres Show on NBC, The Tonight Show with Jay Leno on NBC, Donny and Marie on ABC, and Method and Red on Fox Television. She was also the culinary producer of Fine Living's NapaStyle with Michael Chiarello.

Party Date _____   Party Coordinator _____

Party File Number _____   Party Name _____

DATE	EMPLOYEE NAME	JOB DESCRIPTION	TIME IN/OUT	RATE PER HOUR
9/21	Alan Dune	Party Manager	4:00 P.M./11:00 P.M.	$22/hour

Responsibilities: Buffet decor, dinner timing and serving with kitchen, staff check-in, waiter job assignments, staff breaks, feeding musicians, locking up gifts, party breakdown, separating linens, washing, storing, and securing all rentals until pickup.

9/21	Cheryl Flower	Chef	2:00 P.M./9:00 P.M.	$20/hour

Responsibilities: Leave kitchen with food and loaded van; drive to location; set up temporary work kitchen; heat, finish, and serve appetizers, dinner buffet; and help bakery set up wedding cake. Direct job assignments to kitchen assistant. Refill buffet as needed, oversee breakdown of kitchen, leave kitchen clean, remove all garbage, recycle cans and bottles, repack van, and off-load at commissary. Put any extra food in the commissary refrigerator.

9/21	Fred Stone	Server	5:00 P.M./10:00 P.M.	$15/hour

Responsibilities: Buffet monitor—count plates, roll silverware, polish glasses, fill and light chafers, check tables for ashtrays, salt and pepper, and water pitchers. Pass appetizers as guests arrive, help serve buffet, bus dirty dishes and glasses. Arrange furniture back in living room at end of party.

9/21	Steve Higgenson	Kitchen Assistant	3:00 P.M./9:00 P.M.	$12/hour

Responsibilities: Meet Chef Cheryl at location and help unload van. Start grill. Grill swordfish steaks halfway, finish in rental oven, sauté green beans for chafers, carve beef tenderloin on the buffet, help clean up and break down buffet and temporary kitchen. Drive to commissary and help Cheryl unload van after party.

Step Five: Your Marketing Plan

Creating an image for your company, attracting new customers, and establishing referral business are the essence of marketing. In this section of your business plan, you need to commit to paper all your strategies for increasing your exposure within the community and for drumming up business.

Advertising and Promotional Ideas

Provide time and cost estimates for the twelve-month operating agenda you provided in step four. (See chapter 6 for additional ideas.)

A useful exercise (and a necessary one if you're creating a business plan as a formal document designed to appeal to loan officers or investors) is to include a sample ad for the Yellow Pages online. If you plan on running any other ads, illustrate them in this section and specify the schedule and costs involved as well. Also consider whether direct mail is for you. A simple postcard with a recipe can work wonders; detail how many cards you plan to send out and at what cost, and include a sample.

If you have a celebrity client or well-known relative, seek out a way you can utilize his or her visibility to help market your business. Include in your business plan letters of recommendation or thank-you letters you've received on clients' letterhead.

This section should also describe the networking you plan to do in your community and any other ways you hope to garner new business.

Long-Term Strategy

Keeping your business going over the long haul is the name of the game. To do that you need to consider the marketing steps you'll be taking two or three years from now to keep customers calling.

Chapter 6 discusses long-term strategies. Once you've chosen those that appeal to you, describe them and the costs involved in this section.

Pricing and Services

What services you intend to offer and how much you intend to charge for them are both part of your marketing plan. Stress the service or services you will be able to provide for your clients that are different from anybody else's in the marketplace today. Perhaps you cook without salt and use only fresh herbs from a local organic garden. Say as much. After all, offering products like everyone else's won't help you stand out.

Most new businesses fail in the first year from underpricing their products. As you consider what to charge for your product and services, remember that.

Step Six: Creating a Menu

A menu is the strongest marketing tool you have, yet most caterers never print one up. Making up menus as you go along to suit clients' desires has become the norm. Such an approach is certainly creative, but it's also costly. Perfecting a number of dishes can save you time, money, and mistakes. Plan from the start to design menus for profit and success, and include menus in your business plan. Make sure you describe each dish well enough so that people will be hungry simply reading about them. Personalize your menus by including locally grown sustainable items or highlighting products your area is known for. (See chapter 6 for more information on designing winning menus.)

This is the section of your business plan where you'll also want to describe your plans for making and marketing a signature item. For example, my partner made the best lemon ginger cake in Los Angeles. The more I sold, the more clients wanted. Describe your plans for your signature item and indicate your profit margin.

If your business plan is intended to open doors for you, let your reader know that you intend to review your menus, food-cost percentages, and profit margins every six months.

Step Seven: Crunching the Numbers

This section, filled to the brim with financial data, is where you discuss the nuts and bolts of your business. Being realistic about "the numbers" is your only chance of survival and long-term success.

With personal computers, accounting programs, and some good advice from a friendly accountant, financial statements are easy to create and understand. After all, financial statements are nothing more than simple arithmetic. Don't let unfamiliar terminology scare you off. It's harder to make perfect soufflés for one hundred guests than it is to balance a budget.

A standard business plan includes the following:

Balance sheets: Compile a list of your assets and liabilities. Assets include all cash, party deposits, accounts receivable (contracted future money), and an inventory of the value of everything physical that makes up your company—food products, equipment, even the leasehold on your kitchen. Liabilities include accounts payable (the amounts you owe to purveyors) and any other debts you have to pay each month.

Total up each column, subtract liabilities from assets, and you have your equity, or your company's net worth.

Income statements (also called profit and loss statements or P&Ls): You'll need to create two different P&Ls for your business plan. The first one is a monthly analysis of income and expenses. Using an actual month's sales and expenses, figure out the day-to-day cost of running your business.

Your second P&L should project your income and expenses over the next twelve months. Take into account as many variables that might affect sales as you can: national holidays, taxes, harsh weather, religious days. An example: November is notoriously bad for caterers. People stay home for Thanksgiving and cook their own turkey. Everyone is getting ready for Christmas and saving his or her entertaining dollars for December. And November's weather can't be trusted, so brides steer clear. (If you need some data on industry trends or national figures to help with your projections, contact the National Association of Catering Executives for valuable statistics. Call 410-290-5410; write NACE Headquarters, 9891 Broken Land Pkwy., Ste. 301, Columbia, MD 21046; or visit them online at www.nace.net.)

Cash flow statements: Here you compare the amount of cash coming in with the amount of cash going out. Make out twelve statements, one for each month. Be sure to include bills you pay only on a quarterly basis.

As you project your cash flow, remember that deciding on what terms you'll bill your clients is essential. It is standard business practice to collect a deposit for at least half of the event bill when you sign the contract. As a convenience to my clients, I get the balance in full five days before their party. Then with the excitement of the day, they don't have to do bookkeeping. Of course, the initial deposit must be enough to cover all your out-of-pocket costs.

Island Style BBQ

Tropical Fruit Display with
Coconut Dipping Sauce
Jerk Rubbed Pork Skewers with
Pineapple Mint Salsa

Bibb Lettuce, Mandarin Orange,
and Red Onion Salad
Vegetable Sauté
Hawaiian Rolls with Honey Butter
Green Onion Fried Rice
Grilled Boneless Chicken Breast
Teriyaki Beef Tenderloin

$21.00 per person

California Lite

Vegetable Crudités with Salsa
Oysters on the Half Shell

Cold Poached Salmon
Sliced Turkey Breast
with Mushroom Dressing
Sourdough Flutes

Pasta Primavera
Asparagus Vinaigrette

$29.00 per person

Italian Renaissance

Mushroom Caps Stuffed with
Spicy Turkey Sausage
Caesar Salad

Breadsticks and Ciabatta
Spinach Cheese Ravioli in Basil Marinara Sauce
Quartered Roasted Chicken with Rosemary

Zucchini and Eggplant Parmesan
Sliced Melon and Lime

$23.00 per person

Mexican Fiesta

✥ ✥ ✥

Ceviche in Blue Corn Tortilla Cups
Crudité Baskets
with Black Bean Dip

Spicy Chicken Enchiladas
Steak Fajitas with Guacamole and
Grilled Onions
Cheese and Salsa Quesadillas
with Cilantro Sour Cream

$24.00 per person

Steak and Lobster Club

✥ ✥ ✥

Spinach Crab Buttons
with Spicy Mustard
Limestone Lettuce Salad
with Lemon Zest Vinaigrette

Filet Mignon (carved at the buffet)
with Creamy Tarragon Horseradish
Half Australian Lobster Tail
with Citrus Drawn Butter
Trio of Green Beans, Red Potatoes, and
Red Bell Pepper in Garlic Aioli
Parkerhouse Rolls

$45.00 per person

Terrace View Buffet

✥ ✥ ✥

Jumbo Alaska Shrimp and Stone Crab Claws with Cocktail Sauce
Pesto and Warm Brie Wrapped in Puff Pastry
Toast Points and Water Crackers
California Mesclun Salad
Roasted Prime Rib with Creamy Horseradish
Poached Norwegian Salmon with Dijon Mustard Cream Sauce
Baby Red Potatoes in Garlic Olive Oil
French Green Beans
Dinner Knots and Sweet Butter

$36.00 per person

Step Eight: Projections for the Future

There's a saying in catering that you're only as good as your last party. Referrals based on your good reputation are the mainstays of continuing success. You listed your strategy for ensuring repeat and referral business as part of step five. In this section, project how those plans will translate into dollars. Be sure to chart how much growth you expect in the next few years and also what you anticipate in the way of challenges.

I closed my own business plan this way:

> Living in the country's trendiest city keeps me on my toes about changes in America's lifestyle. I know that keeping current on the public's eating habits is a full-time job. And in the last thirty years, I've been able to predict needs and supply what my clients have asked for.
>
> As the national economy changed and the decadent eighties came to a close, I didn't need a crystal ball to know that the nineties and the following decades would be a time during which I would be selling and producing greater value for the client's dollar.
>
> I've told my clients for years that it's easy to build a beautiful buffet with lots of money, but it takes talent to make a fabulous presentation with no dollars and a ball of string. What I offer every client is my desire to anticipate challenges and enjoy the opportunity to meet them head-on. I never say it's going to be easy, but creating memorable, exciting, and profitable parties is plain, old, wonderful fun.
>
> My favorite referral and compliment came from former senator John Tunney: "Denise is a phantom, she moves fast, her staff is beyond trained, and the fund-raiser went so smoothly, I'm still not sure she was there!"

INCOME

Gross Sales	$32,833
Cost of Labor	5,875
Cost of Food & Beverage	7,875
Cost of Transportation	650
Total of three = Cost of sales	**14,400**
Gross Profit	**$18,433**

OPERATING EXPENSES

Rent	$1,500
Utilities/Phone	550
Owner's salary	3,500
Payroll/Benefits/Taxes	3,350
Advertising/Promotion/Website	500
Accounting/Legal	400
Office supplies	300
Linen service	200
Insurance	630
License/Taxes	250
Depreciation	250
Interest	195
Equipment maintenance	230
Miscellaneous	400
Total Expenses	**$12,255**
Net Profit before Taxes	**$6,178**
Net Profit as a Percentage of Gross Sales	18.8%

Sample Cash Flow Statement

	January	February	March	1st Quarter

EXPENSES

	January	February	March	1st Quarter
Food	_____	_____	_____	_____
Staff	_____	_____	_____	_____
Insurance	_____	_____	_____	_____
Rentals	_____	_____	_____	_____
Other Expenses	_____	_____	_____	_____
	_____	_____	_____	_____
	_____	_____	_____	_____
TOTALS:	_____	_____	_____	_____

INCOME

	January	February	March	1st Quarter
Deposit	_____	_____	_____	_____
Balance	_____	_____	_____	_____
Other Income	_____	_____	_____	_____
	_____	_____	_____	_____
	_____	_____	_____	_____
TOTALS:	_____	_____	_____	_____

Business Books, Software, and Online Resources

Books

The Consultant's Manual, Thomas L. Greenbaum (Wiley, 1994)

Dig Your Well Before You're Thirsty, Harvey Mackay (Currency Books, 1996)

Don't Sweat the Small Stuff, Richard Carlson, PhD (Little Brown, 1997)

Home-Based Business for Dummies, 3rd edition, Paul and Sara Edwards and Peter Economy (For Dummies, 2010)

101 Ways to Promote Yourself, Raleigh Pinskey (Avon Books, 1999)

Secrets of the World's Top Sales Performers, Christine Harvey (Adams Media Corporation, Publishers, 1990)

The Seven Habits of Highly Effective People, Stephen R. Covey (The Free Press, 2004)

7 Steps to Fearless Speaking, Lilyan Wilder (Wiley, 1999)

Stephanie Winston's Best Organizing Tips: Quick, Simple Ways to Get Organized and Get On with Your Life, Stephanie Winston (Fireside, 1996)

Success Is a Choice, Rick Pitino (Broadway Books, 1997)

Successful Time Management for Dummies, Dirk Zeller (For Dummies, 2008)

Time Management from the Inside Out, 2nd edition, Julie Morgenstern (Simon & Schuster, 2004)

True Success, Tom Morris, PhD (Berkeley Press, 1995)

Software

These companies have extensive product lists. Call and ask for additional information on the various business software they sell.

Business Resource Software:
Plan Write
2013 Wells Branch Pkwy., Ste. 305
Austin, TX 78728
(800) 423-1228 / Fax (512) 251-4401
www.brs-inc.com

Jian:
Biz Plan Builder
20 Sunnyside Ave., A#333

Mill Valley, CA 94941
(650) 254-5600
www.jian.com

Palo Alto Software:
Business Plan Pro
(800) 229-7526
www.paloalto.com

I ordered the new thirty-five-page color brochure from Jian to see what this smart company was up to. I am impressed. Talk about making the operations of your business easier! All you have to do is fill in the blanks. What software program haven't they thought of? The catalog showcases Business Basics, Employee Manual, Marketing, Publicity, Loan Builder, and even Safety Plan Builder with specific information for food service.

Jian has been updating this useful software for nearly twenty years. Call the number or visit the website for more information.

Online Resources

The US Small Business Administration (www.sba.gov) has guides that will take you through all the steps required in starting your business. From creating a business plan to buying equipment and hiring employees, the SBA has easy-to-follow instructions for every aspect of small business start-up. Read as many of their tutorials as you can. There is also advice from guest experts and bloggers.

04

The Legal Aspects of Your Catering Business

Although every new business owner makes mistakes, there are certain areas where you really don't want to have a misstep. In this chapter we'll discuss when to call an attorney, why you have to have insurance, and how you can protect yourself and your clients with contracts, as well as the costs, responsibilities, and obligations you have to your employees. In addition we'll cover employee management techniques, rules for good employee-employer relations, and ways to document each relationship in your business.

Why You Need a Good Attorney

As we've already seen, an attorney can be helpful in setting up your company or helping you write a partnership agreement. An attorney can also help you negotiate and understand your lease when you rent or share a kitchen and help you verify ordinances governing the use of the property. In older leaseholds local ordinances have often been ignored, and new tenants find themselves in violation of zoning laws and thus unable to conduct business legally. You want to know your rights as a tenant and your landlord's legal obligations to you. The safety of your company and any employees you may have depends on it.

Though it may seem expensive to talk to an attorney, I think of it as preventive medicine. I don't want my business to get sick from laws I don't know about.

As our catering business grew, my partner and I worked with our attorney regularly. As our parties became more complex and expensive, the one-page agreement we first used grew into a several-page contract that protected our clients and us from events beyond our control.

An attorney taught me to discuss with clients any potential problems that might arise during the planning of an event. He taught me to make notes and document what I promised in the weeks of pre-party planning. Both these measures helped avoid unpleasant surprises.

Staying informed of current legislation on employer-employee relations is also your attorney's job. Whether you have one employee or twenty, you'll need to update your information constantly. Just ask your attorney about new legislation as well as workers' compensation and unemployment insurance.

Insurance: Can't Live with the Premiums, Can't Live with the Risk

New caterers often complain to me that they can't afford to buy insurance and pay the premiums. I tell them they can't afford not to. In fact, you should budget for it from the start. Consider what would happen if your kitchen caught fire in the middle of party preparation. How would you replace equipment? Fulfill your contract? Insurance protects existing assets and provides a continuous future for your company.

Listed here are the essential types of insurance with which to start. Discuss these with your attorney. Then sound out several companies and agents about coverage and rates. Look for insurance companies that specialize in restaurants and caterers. A local chapter of the National Restaurant Association can help you with a referral list. Be aware that there are additional types of policies available to you as your business grows.

Two examples: Business interruption insurance covers your fixed costs and expenses if a fire shuts down your business. Salaries to employees, taxes, and utilities, as well as the profits you are losing, can also be covered. There is mortgage insurance if you own your building and want to insure payment of the mortgage in the face of catastrophe.

Start-Up Coverage

If at first all your storage is at home, check to see if you can upgrade your existing tenant's or homeowner's property insurance. Get the broadest available coverage. This policy can cover fire losses, vandalism, wind damage, smoke damage, explosions, and even malicious mischief.

Product Liability Insurance

Don't even think about serving food to the public without product liability insurance protection. The coverage protects you and pays your client damages in the event that the food you serve is or becomes contaminated. Your company can even be sued for serving someone else's contaminated product. Know your purveyors and insist that their product is also insured.

What if a bride wants you to serve a wedding cake made by her best friend? The friend is going to make this cake in her home, and she has no product insurance, no licensed and legal business, and no board of health permit. What do you do? You explain to the bride that she, personally, will have to sign a liability waiver with your company, giving up her rights and her guests' rights to any legal action against you in the event of food poisoning or contamination. Her other option, of course, is to buy her wedding cake from a licensed and insured bakery or from you.

Serving the public food is an enormous responsibility. It should never be taken lightly.

Public Liability Insurance

Public liability insurance covers injury to the public. A customer or client falls down during a party and gets hurt. You could be sued. You want to buy the biggest policy you can afford. Find out about purchasing one-day coverage for individual events involving unusual situations.

I once had a bride and groom arrive by helicopter. The owner of the property wanted additional coverage for them to land in his backyard. I couldn't blame him. My client paid for the day rider fee.

Workers' Compensation Insurance

This type of insurance covers employees in case of injury at work. Catering is a high-risk business. Kitchen work involves knives, fire, and heavy lifting. Chances of accidents are greater in this business than in, say, libraries. Speak to an attorney to find out exactly what your financial and legal obligations are in your state.

In California it is illegal to operate any business with employees without workers' compensation insurance. Check with your state's industrial relations department to find out what requirements you must adhere to.

In every state, under common law, employers are required to provide employees with a safe place to work. They are also required to train employees to be competent and safe coworkers, to provide the safest tools for employees to handle, and to warn employees of existing dangers such as fumes from certain chemical cleaners or exposure to pesticides (poisons) on a continuous basis. If you fail as an employer to protect your employees, you are risking a lawsuit and damages.

Written Agreements and Contracts

With the first phone call to any client, you are creating a contract. Whether or not you want to put it in writing is your business, but trust me, it's easier to keep track of the dimes and dollars involved in catering finances with a written agreement. A written contract is an enforceable document.

From my previous life as a real estate agent, I brought to my catering career my habit of documenting every conversation about business. In real estate you're taught "to get it in writing" because an oral contract will not hold up in court if a problem arises in closing a transaction. So for me it was natural to write down every detail of an upcoming event, making sure that all parties indicated their agreement by signing. When other caterers tell me they have never needed a contract, I assume they have not staged lavish, expensive parties or worked with corporate clients. A corporation planning an employee bash for 250 achievers or parents spending $25,000 on a wedding want to know what they have paid for and what they are going to get.

It makes no difference to me whether my client's bill is for $500 or $50,000; I want to provide everything as promised because I want my clients to feel they got their money's worth and to tell their friends about me. In return I need to know that my client will pay me what we agreed, that I will get the money on the dates we decided (the better to manage my cash flow), and that we both intend to do what we promised in good faith.

Take a look at the sample contract that follows, on page 65. Not only does it keep track of everything you need to remember and have promised, but it provides an entire script if you are new at selling and closing a deal. (Before you use it, however, be sure to run it by your attorney.)

Let's say you have had one or two conversations with a client and pitched your ideas over the phone or by e-mail. Write that information in the spaces provided. Start at the top. Fill in all the other blanks with your client. By the time you get to the signature at the end, this party is starting to take shape.

The more preparation and organization you put into party planning, the smoother the party will run. By showing your client your business skills from the beginning, you are building a basis of trust, assurance, and professionalism.

Every contract decision in catering boils down to how much it will cost, so get this information right from the start. Put the costs in the contract, and no one will be surprised later.

Elements to Cover in a Catering Contract

- Date and day of catering
- Location of catering
- Minimum guest count for menu pricing
- Date of notification for final guest count
- Exact time your catering work starts and ends
- Fire-safety floor plan and seating arrangements
- Final menu selection and price per person
- Description of service and labor quotation
- Staff schedule
- Approximate additional costs/subcontractors
- Deposit money and payment schedule for balance
- Cancellation policy and refund of deposit
- Anticipated total cost
- SignaturesError! Bookmark not defined

An example: A new client calls and says she can spend $30 per person. Does she mean on food alone? Or is she assuming that $30 will cover everything, including rentals, food, taxes, and staff? A good contract will make the point clear.

Contracts are made up of three parts: offer, acceptance, and consideration or money. Protect yourself and your clients by detailing these parts and the agreement between you.

Working with Subcontractors or Suppliers

What happens if the fish your purveyor supplies turns out to be tainted and your clients' guests get sick? Or if the disc jockey rigs up the music system in such a way that a guest trips over a cord and breaks a leg? So that you're not held responsible, insist that each supplier or subcontractor sign an agreement holding you harmless against any losses or claims made by your clients because of the supplier's own negligence or oversight. I'm sure it doesn't surprise you to learn that you will want to consult an attorney for the appropriate language here.

In general, it pays to make sure that the subcontractors you work with are licensed and insured and that any employees they send to work with you are covered by workers' compensation. After all, if it's the disc jockey himself who trips over the speaker cord and breaks a leg, you want his employer to take care of him.

Employees

When you started your home-based catering business, you became your own boss. As you take on larger or more complex parties, you might find it necessary to hire kitchen assistants, waiters, or bartenders to help you produce your events. Now you are someone else's boss. If this is your first time as a boss or manager, I offer a reading list (see page 76) geared to minimizing "people" problems and maximizing employee potential.

In my consulting business the biggest complaint I hear again and again is "I can't find any good helpers." Well, if party after party, year after year, you have the same problems with personnel, the real problem is you, not your help. You need to be a great manager to have a great staff.

Good management practices create good employees. Think about your own personality and what makes you work to your full potential. Think about jobs that you adored or disliked and bosses that you hated or respected. What were important issues to you when you were an employee? Your own work record offers you insights into human behavior and guidelines to be the kind of boss you respect.

Here are some points to keep in mind as you work toward building a winning team:

- Are you providing your employees with everything they need to do the job well (equipment, supplies, etc.)?
- Have you made your expectations clear to your employees (arrive on time, wear clean uniforms, be courteous to guests, etc.)?
- Have you made job duties clear to all employees (roll silver in napkins, uncork wine, zest lemon peels, assemble dessert trays, etc.)?
- Do you treat your employees with courtesy and respect?
- Do you encourage comments and suggestions from your employees? (Do you use their ideas when they're better than yours?)

- Do you give employees an honest assessment of their performance in a positive way (encouragement, positive reinforcement)?
- Do you offer praise and compliments when deserved?
- Do you apologize when an apology is owed?
- Do you thank your employees for the talent and support they bring to the team?
- Do you solicit an evaluation of your performance from your employees?
- Do you pay your employees promptly?

In your successful catering company, a shared vision or team spirit must prevail. All good teams need a coach or strong leader who sets the tone and policy.

Hiring versus Leasing Employees

Hiring employees can be an exercise in paperwork, even if you use them only occasionally. You need to think about payroll taxes, social security taxes, unemployment insurance, and workers' compensation. A reasonable alternative for the home-based caterer is to use employment services that send out temps. Here in Los Angeles several personnel services have chefs, waiters, and busboys on tap. You determine the size of the staff you need, and the company sends them out in uniform. You pay an hourly fee for each. The fee is higher than what you'd pay if you hired each person directly, but you write just one check to the personnel company and it handles the payroll, employee taxes, and workers' compensation. Using this kind of service as you grow may well save you cash. It will certainly save the time you'd otherwise have to spend interviewing people and puzzling over mounds of paperwork.

Employees versus Independent Contractors

I happen to prefer hiring my own employees, and I've perfected a system for screening them, as you'll see later in this chapter. Going to the extra trouble is worth it to me because it's the best way I know to build team spirit. You may end up feeling the same way. If so, know that if you hire waiters, bartenders, kitchen help, or other help yourself, even on a very occasional basis, it's not a good idea to try to avoid paying taxes by claiming that they're independent contractors. For someone to qualify as an independent contractor, he or she must work without supervision, supply his or her own materials, be considered an expert in his or her field, and work at his or her own pace. Once you tell someone when and where to show up and how long to work, that person is an employee. Talk with your attorney and your accountant for more information about exactly what your obligations are.

Client name _____

Title _____

   Company _____

   Address _____

City/State/Zip _____

Event date _____

Start time _____ End time _____

Guest count _____ Minimum guarantee _____

Final count _____ By date _____

We request the final guest count and payment balance three days before your event. Menu price (per person) is based on your minimum guest count. If the minimum count goes down, we may reprice your menu. If your count goes up after you have given us the final count, we will be happy to accommodate you as best we can.

Location _____

Contact name _____ Telephone _____

Directions _____ Travel time _____

Location rules/restrictions _____

_____

Special insurance requirements _____ Cost $ _____

Tent _____ Permits required _____

Cost $_____

Does the location provide for day deliveries the day before the event and for early staff arrival?

_____

Check the location features that apply: ☐ Parking available ☐ Staff changing room ☐ Bathrooms

Security service _____ Cost $ _____

Type of event _____ Theme/decor _____

Cost $_____

Table size _____ Number of chairs _____

Rentals and linens quotation $ _____ Sizes _____

Date ordered _____ Date confirmed _____

Special equipment _____

Cost $ _____

Menu (based on the minimum guarantee) _____

Time each course will be served _____

Price per person $ _____ Disposables per person $ _____

Bar and wine selections _____

Price per person $ _____ Bar setup/Supplies $ _____

Soft drinks and water $ _____ Type of service _____

Special instructions _____

Number of staff _____

Party managers _____ Chefs _____

Waiters _____ Bartenders _____

Kitchen assistants _____ Delivery driver _____

Labor quotation $ _____ Uniforms/costumes $ _____

SUBCONTRACTORS

Florist _____ Parking valet _____

Telephone _____ Telephone _____

Federal ID number _____ Federal ID number _____

Certificate of insurance _____ Certificate of insurance _____

Signed loss and damage waiver on file _____ Signed loss and damage waiver on file _____

Photographer _____   Entertainment _____

Telephone _____   Telephone _____

Federal ID number _____   Federal ID number _____

Certificate of insurance _____   Certificate of insurance _____

Signed loss and damage waiver on file _____   Signed loss and damage waiver on file _____

In case of guest overages:

Authorized credit card number _____   Approved limit $ _____

Anticipated total cost: $ _____

18% service charge* $ _____

8.25% state sales tax $ _____

Grand total $ _____

Upon acceptance we require a 50% deposit of the entire bill

Deposit $ _____

Balance due $ _____   Date _____

Caterer shall not be liable for any damage in the event that performance shall be delayed or prevented by fire, flood, riot, strike, labor dispute, or act of God. Caterer reserves the right to subcontract any or all of its obligations hereunder.

Should customer cancel the event for any reason whatsoever, customer shall be liable for all out-of-pocket costs sustained by the caterer.

Caterer does not assume or accept any responsibility for damages to the location, loss of personal articles, or broken or unreturned rentals.

Accepted by _____   Date _____

Caterer _____

* Optional for small parties or parties where all you do is drop off the food, but highly recommended for parties of any complexity. See Chapter 5 for more information on pricing goods and services.

Food Fanatics
P.O. Box 351088
Los Angeles, CA 90035
Phone: 310-836-3520
E-mail: me@DeniseVivaldo.com

Catering Agreement

In consideration of the services to be performed by FOOD FANATICS ("Caterer") for the benefit of
_____ ("Client") at the event scheduled for _____,
200___ ("Event") as set forth on the attached invoice ("Invoice"), Client agrees to the following terms
and conditions:

1. In order to reserve the date of the Event, Client must deliver a signed copy of this Agreement to
   Caterer along with a Deposit ("Deposit") or payment as follows:
   (a) If the Agreement is delivered to Caterer more than seven (7) days prior to the Event, Client
       shall deliver to Caterer, along with the Agreement, a Deposit equal to 50% of the invoice
       amount. The balance is due and payable no later than the 7th day prior to the Event.
   (b) If the signed Agreement is delivered to Caterer seven (7) or fewer days prior to the Event,
       Client shall pay the entire invoice amount when the signed Agreement is returned, plus a
       surcharge equal to 30% of the Invoice amount (the Invoice amount plus such surcharge being
       hereinafter referred to as the "Adjusted Invoice Amount").

2. At least seven (7) days prior to the Event, Client agrees to inform Caterer of the number of persons expected to attend the Event and to pay for the amount confirmed or the actual number in
   attendance, whichever is greater. If the actual number in attendance is greater than the amount
   confirmed, Caterer cannot guarantee that adequate food will be available for all persons in attendance. If the actual number in attendance is more than 20% less than the number confirmed,
   Caterer reserves the right to increase the price per person.

3. If Client fails to pay any payments when due prior to the date of the Event, this Agreement may
   be canceled or rejected by Caterer. Client agrees that Caterer shall not thereafter be obligated to
   provide any services hereunder. In such case, or if Client shall, for any reason whatsoever, cancel
   this Agreement, Client acknowledges that it would be impossible to fix the actual damages resulting from such cancellation, and Client therefore agrees that Caterer may retain (a) 50% of the
   Deposit (if this Agreement was delivered to Caterer more than seven [7] days prior to the Event)

or (b) 25% of the Adjusted Invoice Amount (if this Agreement was delivered to Caterer seven [7] or fewer days prior to the Event), in each case as liquidated damages and not as a penalty, which represents a reasonable estimation of fair compensation to Caterer for damages incurred by Caterer resulting from such failure to pay, or cancellation, by Client.

4. Client agrees to indemnify and hold harmless Caterer for any damage, theft, or loss of Caterer's property (including, without limitation, equipment, plates, utensils, and motor vehicles) occurring at the Event that is caused by persons attending the Event.

5. Caterer shall not be responsible for inability to provide food or other services due to inclement weather or acts of God (including, without limitation, fire or earthquake).

6. In the event attorneys' fees or other costs are incurred to secure performance of any of the obligations herein provided for, to obtain damages for breach thereof, or to obtain any other appropriate relief, whether by way of prosecution or defense, the prevailing party shall be entitled to recover from the losing party reasonable attorneys' fees and costs incurred herein. This Agreement contains all the terms and conditions agreed upon by the parties hereto with reference to this Event, and no other agreements not specifically referred to herein, oral or otherwise, shall be deemed to exist or to bind either of the parties hereto.

7. Event must be at least five (5) hours in duration.

AGREED AND ACCEPTED:

Client   FOOD FANATICS
            Caterer

By: _____   By: _____

_____
Signature

_____
Print Your Name

_____
Date

Event Quotes

Client's name _____

Billing address _____

City/State/ZIP Code _____

_____

_____

Directions _____

Expected number of guests _____

_____

Theme/occasion _____

_____

Food/Menu/Bar _____

Ice delivery _____

Personnel _____

_____

time _____

18% Service charge $ _____

Flowers/decor $ _____

Rentals $ _____

Subtotal $ _____

Sales tax $ _____

TOTAL $ _____

Deposit $ _____

(required to hold date)

Office phone _____

Home phone _____

_____

Party location _____

_____

Guaranteed _____

_____

Parking _____

_____

_____

Function date _____

Function

_____

_____

_____

_____

_____

_____

Miscellaneous

Photographer

Music

Valet

Security

Labor Practices

Laws and regulations regarding state labor practices can be found online under your state government services. In California, for example, the state's Labor Commissioner's Office has information on wages, hours, and working conditions on their website www.dir.ca.gov/dise.

As an owner-employer you need to be aware of the current minimum wage. You need to pay for every hour worked by an employee. You have to know how many consecutive hours and days determine overtime pay. You have to know how many breaks an employee is entitled to in one shift and when an employee is entitled to a meal and rest facilities. You need to keep a copy of these orders available for any employee or post a copy where it is easy for employees to read.

Each person you hire to help run your business goes out into the marketplace and is a reflection of you. Choose your help carefully. In chapter 2 we discussed hiring family and friends. Well, as your business grows, you will want to develop a larger network from which to choose.

Where to Look for Great Staff

- Other caterers

- Waiters at your favorite cafe

- Local culinary students from hospitality programs

- Personnel directors of hotels or conference centers for referrals to their unused applicants

- Theater or performance groups (actors make great waiters)

- Personnel service agencies

- Hospital or rest-home kitchen employees

- City or county employees for moonlighting on weekends

- Hungry college kids

- People who love to cook and entertain but have never had a job outside the home

There are no shortcuts to building a terrific team. It takes time to interview and get to know a prospective employee. You spend valuable time and money to create a staff to help you run your business efficiently.

Tip: Never hire anyone you haven't interviewed at least three times. You start to see the person behind the interview facade only after the third time.

Applications/Job Interviews

Standard employment applications are available in stationery stores, or you can call your local restaurant association. State and federal laws govern questions that you can legally ask job applicants.

On page 74 is an example of an application I adapted after years of experience. I learned to ask pertinent questions about food-related talents. Not only does it save me time in the first interview, but it gives me a feel for the applicant's talent and expresses my high expectations at the very beginning.

After prospective employees have filled out the application, start the interview process. Following are some questions you might want to ask:

1. Would you be interested in working for me in a professional relationship as a paid employee?
2. Will you and I be able to be honest and up front with each other?
3. I respect your opinion. I'd like your input about how you see me as a manager. After we have worked on our first event, would you be willing to give me such an evaluation?
4. What are your strongest attributes?
5. Your weakest?
6. I am developing a party-procedure list for all my employees. I want your honest reaction. We need to make another appointment to go over it. When would be convenient for you?
7. What kind of referral do you expect from your last boss?
8. Do you have any concerns about our working together?
9. I've written out a job description for you. After you've read it, please initial it and ask me any questions you might have.
10. Why are you applying for this job?
11. I start all employees at $_____ per hour. After three parties we meet again to discuss pay. Does this suit you?
12. (optional) Let me tell you why, as a friend or family member, I would like you to work for me.

Job Descriptions/Policy Manuals

Once you have hired someone, make it easy on yourself and your employee. Write out a job description and have the person read it. Then both of you edit it. When the two of you have established a comfortable range of job responsibilities, explain that you will use this piece of paper as a tool to help measure job performance and as a basis for raises.

A written job description offers a set of boundaries and guidelines that should answer any questions a new employee has and helps eliminate mistakes. New bosses are often guilty of the "if-only-my-employees-could-read-my-mind" syndrome. Remember that you hired a waiter, not a psychic.

In addition, if you as an employer are not satisfied with your employee's job performance, a job description serves as a written reference to amend or document grounds for warnings, suspension, or termination.

When you have decided what kind of behavior you expect from all your employees, regardless of their position or job description, tell them. Write your policies down. Give everyone a copy, and have each employee initial it. With these policies in writing, employees are at much less risk of disappointing you or themselves.

As a matter of good record keeping, prepare folders for each employee. You will need to document every promotion, pay change, tax change, or change of address made when someone is in your employ. The employee folder is open to the employee for inspection at any time. Letters of recommendation or a complaint should also be put there.

Sample Job Description for Servers

General duties and responsibilities:
- set up tables and chairs
- put down table linens
- set tables
- put out salt and pepper shakers
- keep ashtrays emptied
- keep water glasses filled
- serve courses
- bus tables between each course
- serve wine/take drink orders
- collect and count table linens
- break down tables and chairs

Application for Employment

Job you are applying for:	Date:
Social Security Number:	Telephone:

Name:

Address:

Employment history (food service only):

List three references with phone numbers:

Days/times you are available for work: Weekdays   A.M. or P.M.   Weekends   A.M. or P.M.

Please answer and evaluate yourself with the following: Excellent = E   Good = B   Average = A

Do you have experience opening champagne or wine?	_____	Do you know buffet service?	_____
French service?*	_____	Russian service?*	_____
Do you know how to carry a waiter's tray?	_____	Do you know how to pass appetizers?	_____
Do you have busing experience?	_____	Do you have food-prep experience?	_____
Do you know how to cut a wedding cake?	_____	Do you know how to set up a buffet?	_____
Do you know how to carve meat on a buffet?	_____	Have you ever carved a turkey?	_____
Do you have food-garnishing skills?	_____	* French (or English) service is the presentation of each course plate; Russian service is platters served person to person by the waiters.	

Tell me in a paragraph about any other skills you have and why you think they would be helpful in a catering job.

Please answer: If you saw another employee stealing from me or my client, what would you do?

Employee File Checklist

Employee name: _____ Employee number: _____

Date hired: _____ Position hired for: _____

Rate of pay: _____

The employee listed above has received the company policy manual, job description, and position training manual. The employee has also been briefed on safety awareness as concerns the position hired for within this firm.

_____

This employee's file includes:

☐ W-4

☐ Performance appraisals

☐ Application

☐ Application questionnaire

☐ Company policy

☐ Employee handbook sign-off

☐ Job safety awareness

☐ Sanitation sign-off

☐ Alcohol awareness sign-off

☐ Copy of Certified Food Handler Certificate

☐ I-9 has been received, with photocopy of IDs, and is in the I-9 file.

☐ Uniform has been issued
   Date: _____

☐ Uniform returned
   Date: _____

Emergency information: _____

Telephone number to call: _____

Person to contact: _____

Relationship to employee: _____

Notes: _____

_____

_____

Becoming a Great Manager Booklist

Building Trust: A Manager's Guide for Business Success, Mary Shurtleff (Crisp Learning, 1998)

Coping with Difficult People, Robert M. Bramson, PhD (Dell, 1988)

Dealing with People You Can't Stand: Revised and Expanded Third Edition, Dr. Rich Brinkman and Dr. Rick Kirschner (McGraw-Hill, 2012)

How to Make Meetings Work, Michael Doyle (Berkley Trade, 1993)

How to Win Friends and Influence People, Dale Carnegie (Pocket Books, 1998)

Leadership and the One Minute Manager, Kenneth H. Blanchard and Patricia and Drea Zagarmi (William Morrow, 1999)

Managing from the Heart, Hyler Bracey, Jack Rosenblum, Aubrey Sanford, and Roy Trueblood (Dell, 1993)

Practical Intuition for Success, Laura Day (Harper Paperbacks, 1999)

Self Leadership and the One Minute Manager, Kenneth H. Blanchard, Susan Fowler, and Laurence Hawkins (HarperCollins, 2007)

Success Is a Journey: 7 Steps to Achieving Success in the Business of Life, Jeffrey J. Mayer (McGraw-Hill Trade, 2000)

Take Yourself to the Top, Laura Berman Fortgang (Tarcher, 2005)

10 Steps to Empowerment: A Common-Sense Guide to Managing People, Diane Tracy (William Morrow, 1992)

Thinkertoys: A Handbook of Creative-Thinking Techniques, 2nd edition, Michael Michalko (Ten Speed Press, 2006)

13 Fatal Errors Managers Make and How You Can Avoid Them, W. Stephen Brown (Berkley Books, 1995)

True to Yourself: Leading a Values-Based Business, Mark Albion (Berrett-Koehler Publishers, 2006)

The Work at Home Balancing Act, Sandy Anderson (Avon Books, 1998)

Employee Policies

- You are responsible for your own clean, pressed uniform.

- Keep shoulder-length hair tied back at all times.

- Jewelry should be kept to a minimum. If your ears are pierced, small stud earrings requested.

- Political badges should not be worn while at work.

- Wear only black socks and shoes.

- Keep fingernails short and clean (no heavy/dark polish).

- No chewing gum or smoking on the floor of the party.

- There is no excuse for being late.

- No eating or drinking except at scheduled breaks—never on the floor of the party.

- No drugs or alcohol before or during your shift.

- No more than two waiters may congregate on the floor of the party.

- No employees are allowed to take any food or beverages off the property.

- Never use offensive or inappropriate language with clients or coworkers.

- If you are hurt or injured, please report to your supervisor.

- Maintain a professional and positive attitude at all times.

05

Setting Prices, Estimating Quantities, and Writing Proposals

The biggest mistake most new caterers make is underpricing the food they sell. They get into this habit because they are used to cooking for family and friends for free and without worrying about labor costs or overhead. Any profit seems grand if you see food as your only expense.

Of course, food isn't your only expense; even if you're not shouldering the costs of an elaborate storefront and a permanent staff of six, you need to factor in your time in setting new menu prices. But that's not all. Before you arrive at a final price for a party, you also need to take into account the staff costs; price of flowers, decor, and entertainment; the cost of supplies; and your overhead.

How to Price Your First Menus

Since many caterers start their business the day they land their first job, they don't really have enough experience to know how much it costs or how long it takes to make various dishes. The more catering you do, the faster you will become at menu pricing and food production. Time is your earning power. You must learn to measure it and charge accordingly. The following information will help you do just that.

The cardinal rule of accurate pricing is simple: Use a calculator and fill out a menu pricing form (see page 85) for every item.

Don't guess on your menu prices. Don't assume you know how much products cost without verifying the prices with your purveyors. Prices on products change from season to season, week to week. Do your calculations carefully. Recalculate and, if necessary, reprice your menus every three months. Your investment in time will pay you back in dollars.

For your first menus it's wise to choose six different themes to show versatility. One might be an American Barbecue, another your fabulous fried chicken billed as a Southern Sunday Dinner, another your Italian Pasta Collection, another an Asian Celebration, and so on. Be sure the menus reflect your niche and the research you did on your competition. To control costs and make life easier in your kitchen, try to sell these complete menus (as opposed to specific dishes) whenever possible. Remember that perfect menus are flavorful, colorful, nutritionally balanced, varied enough to appeal to a wide range of tastes, and in step with current food trends.

It is also smart to add a disclaimer to the bottom of your menus: "All items and products subject to availability."

When it comes to pricing your menus, it doesn't matter if they're for complete dinners, buffets, deli planners, or drop-off picnic lunches—the process is the same. Calculate every menu price per person, and make it clear when you quote the price to your client that it is for food only. Party waitstaff, decor, soft drinks, disposables, and rentals are all separate costs.

Don't take the shortcut of pricing your menus to match or beat your competition. Their prices don't tell you whether they're making any money. You want to compete, but you also want to be profitable.

Here's what is involved in setting menu prices:

- Analyze your food costs. List every ingredient in the dish on your menu pricing form. Determine the amount you are going to serve per portion and the exact cost of that amount. Add up the total cost for each dish.
- Divide the total cost by your target food-cost percentage to arrive at a price. In order to ensure profit, I like my food cost to run between 28 and 34 percent of my menu price, although I've been known to get it down to 22 percent.

Start by breaking each item down into the proper number of ounces per serving. (To arrive at a per-ounce cost, divide the price per pound by sixteen ounces.)

After pricing every menu you design, document the individual dishes with recipe cards. If you wish, you can buy computer programs that multiply recipes for whatever size yield you need. You can also buy catering software to help you in the beginning with food-cost percentages and estimating food quantities. (See sidebar on page 106.)

For the long-term growth of your reputation, it's important to be able to duplicate every product consistently so that you can guarantee quality standards job after job. The busier you get, the likelier it is you'll delegate preparation tasks to others. Just make sure that you test your recipes yourself before you pass them on.

Food Trends

You should know current food trends and share them with your clients. Trends can suggest different ways to serve the same old food or new ingredients and flavors to incorporate into your menus.

People are getting more adventurous in their eating, and a **tasting menu** is a great way to introduce them to new foods. A tasting menu offers choices, and we Americans love our choices. Almost any menu can be turned into a tasting menu by serving smaller portions of more dishes. Who wouldn't be charmed when presented with three mini desserts?

Southern food is enjoying a comeback. And why shouldn't it? It's comfort food at its best. Remove some of the guilt by serving it as a tasting menu or pared down to appetizer size for a cocktail party. See page 214 for my Southern Picnic menu.

Street food is any food you can hold in your hand and eat standing up. It's characterized by being simple, basic, and usually highly flavored. Many recipes in your repertoire can probably be altered to serve in this way.

Special diets are a bigger concern than ever, and a caterer that can supply menus for these diets will be way ahead of the competition. If you are knowledgeable enough, offer vegetarian, vegan, gluten-free, lactose-free, or low-fat menus. Do your research so you can offer inventive menus, not just tofu meat-replacements.

Simple, fresh food is more popular than ever; play up the uniqueness of your ingredients. There is a variety of wonderful and easy-to-cook grains available. Use them alone or mixed with other grains or rice to make interesting and delicious pilafs and salads.

"Location, location, location" isn't just true for real estate; it's also a nice selling point for caterers. Do you have any **local products** that would help sell your menus? Anything from grass-fed beef to Aunt Sue's Homemade Strawberry Jam—it's all in the way you sell it.

Chart A

Average Per Person Portion Size

Hors d'oeuvres (mix of hot and cold)

Before a meal	6 pieces
One hour hors d'oeuvres party, no meal	8–10 pieces
Two hour hors d'oeuvres party, no meal	10–12 pieces

Platters (before a meal)

Fruit	4 ounces
Cheese	2 ounces
Crackers, breadsticks, crostini	4 pieces
Crudités	4 pieces
Dips, dressings	1 ounce

Entrees (plated)

Poultry, meat, or fish, boneless (single selection)	6 ounces
Poultry, meat, or fish, boneless (multiple selections)	3 ounces
Pasta (main dish)	7 ounces
Pasta (first course)	3 ounces

Side Dishes

Vegetables	4 ounces
Rice or other grains	3 ounces
Potatoes	5 ounces
Beans	2 ounces
Pasta	2–3 ounces
Green salad (weight of greens only)	1 ounce
Salad dressing	1 ounce

Sauces and Gravies	2 ounces

Desserts

Cake, tart, or pastry	1 slice or piece
Pudding, mousse	4 ounces
Ice cream	5 ounces
Cookies	2 pieces
Bite-size dessert assortment	4 pieces

Purveyor Bid Sheet

Date _____ Name _____

Product _____

Unit/Size/Weight _____

Vendor/Salesperson #1	Vendor/Salesperson #2	Vendor/Salesperson #3

Days to place orders _____

Terms _____

Delivery date and instructions _____

_____

_____

_____

Notes:

For example, my partner and I were asked to make fifty lemon bundt cakes for another caterer. (We priced each cake at $12.00 after dividing the $1.89 raw product cost by our target food-cost percentage of 24 percent.) Because we owned only ten bundt pans, we multiplied the recipe by ten and decided to bake five batches. After the first batch, we knew the conversions were correct, and we were able to leave the recipe card with a prep cook to make the remaining forty cakes. I continued making cold calls on the phone, and my partner worked on the corporate lunch we had scheduled for the next day.

Calculating Your Kitchen Labor

You'll need to keep track of the number of hours it takes you or someone you hire to shop and prepare any food in your kitchen. The more complicated the plate, the higher the labor, and the higher the sales price.

The higher the guest count, the lower your kitchen labor percentage (wages divided by sales price) is likely to be. Simply put, you can fix food for a hundred guests in the same amount of time it takes you to fix food for fifty guests. (See Chart B on page 90.)

Whether you're cooking a menu or a single dish, document on the recipe card or your menu pricing form the amount of time it takes, the exact yield, and the level of expertise it takes to produce. If you find that your labor costs are amounting to more than 15 percent of the menu price, consider raising your prices—or choose simpler recipes.

How to Estimate the Right Food Quantities

The second most common problem for the new caterer is making either too much food or not enough. This can be as deadly to your business as underpricing your menu.

Many factors play into the amount of food you need to allow for each guest. For years I have managed to make just the right amount of food party after party by taking the following factors into account.

Sample Menu Themes

Day at the Circus

Hamburgers • Corn dogs • Peanuts • Popcorn • Cotton candy
Carrot curls • Animal crackers • Ice-cream bars

South of France Picnic

Red potato salad • Rare roast beef with Dijon mustard
Baguettes with sweet butter • Marinated haricots verts in
champagne-shallot vinaigrette

Western Roundup

Three-alarm turkey chili with corn bread • BBQ tri-tip • Mashed yams
Roasted potatoes • Garden vegetable salad

Edge of Thailand

Chicken satay with peanut sauce • Spring rolls • Cucumber salad
Pad thai noodles • Sizzling rice soup • Sautéed lobster in black beans

Chinese Marketplace

Szechuan chicken • Black mushrooms and beef stir-fry • Shui mai
Pot stickers • Shrimp fried rice • Sautéed vegetables

Viennese Dessert Buffet

Bite-size napoleons • Cream puffs • Éclairs • Linzer tortes
Chocolate truffles • Orange Florentine cookies

South American Fiesta

Pork empanadas • Carne asada • Tamales • Soft chicken tacos
Grilled vegetables • Flan

Rockin' Fifties Soda Bar

Hot fudge sundaes • Banana splits • Root beer floats
Egg creams • Strawberry shakes

Anniversary Dinner Plate

New York steak, 7 ounces @ $9.99 per pound	=	$4.37
Baked potato, 5 ounces @ 99 cents per pound	=	$ .31
Green beans, 4 ounces @ $1.99 per pound	=	$ .50
Sautéed mushrooms, 6 ounces @ $3.49 per pound	=	$ 1.31
Butter, 2 ounces @ $4.29 per pound	=	$ .54
Sour cream, 1 ounce @ $2.49 per pound	=	$ .17
Condiments: olive oil, spices, fresh garlic	=	$ .47
TOTAL COSTS:		**$7.67**

Calculate: $7.67 divided by 34% food cost = approximately $22.50.

$7.67 divided by 28% food cost = approximately $27.50. That's your target range.

If your food-cost percentage is 34%, that means you're spending 34 cents out of every dollar on food, which leaves you 66 cents for kitchen labor (about 15%), overhead (variable based on monthly sales—see Chapter 7), and profit.

SAMPLE MENU ITEM PRICING FORM

Menu Item			Date	
(1) Ingredients	(2) Unit	(3) Unit Cost	(4) Portion	(5) Portion Cost
		$		$
		$		$
		$		$
		$		$
		$		$

Cooking condiments $ _____

Total cost $ _____

Desired food-cost percentage   _____ %

Menu price $ _____

Gross profit (menu price minus food cost) $ _____

I first met Rudy Miick when we were both hired as consultants on a start-up restaurant project. His professionalism, sheer joy for the business, and generous spirit in sharing his knowledge impressed me then and still does. Rudy is on the board of directors of the Foodservice Consultants Society International and holds degrees in organizational psychology, organizational management, and human resources.

Rudy brings more than thirty years of operational management and consultation experience to every project. His work covers food-service turnarounds and new project development, including restaurants, ski resorts, and country clubs across the United States.

If you have questions for Miick and Associates, call them at (303) 413-0400 or check out the Web site at www.miick.com.

The Main Ingredients in Your Food-Cost Recipe

BY RUDY MIICK, FCSI

Maintaining consistent food cost is one of the most difficult tasks in daily management of a food-service establishment. However, in my more than twenty-five years of experience, regardless of concept, I have found this not to be the case. So, "How do I maintain my food cost through seasonal ups and downs?" There are four primary steps to monitor food cost. They are simple and effective. I'll address two of the four steps here to give you guidance. These steps will also provide an anticipatory approach to your management style. Let's take a look:

PURCHASING BUDGET

Regardless of concept or size of your catering business, you can develop a purchasing budget.

Here's how:

A. Define the ideal food cost for your business.
    Let's say your "target" choice is a 30% food cost.
B. Simply multiply the "target" food cost by your projected food sales for a month.
    You end up with your monthly purchasing budget. As an example, at our test catering company, Savory Treats, we target a 30% food cost on monthly food sales of $70,000.

Recap:

30%	"target" food cost (goal)
$70,000.00	projected food sales for the month
30% x $70,000.00	is $21,000.00
$21,000.00	is our purchasing budget for the month
$21,000.00	divided by 4.25 weeks = $4,941.18
$ 4,941.18	is our purchasing budget per week

This is an ideal case, but "My actual sales may vary up or down, what do I do then?" If sales are up, your purchasing budget should go up; if sales are down, then the purchasing budget should go down accordingly (if your inventory is at the correct amount; see "The Right Inventory," below). The secret is to establish a likely budget, then track it daily. Accrue your total to the week, then month to date. Then tie the budget to your inventory. You will hit your goal. Bravo!

THE RIGHT INVENTORY

"How do I tell if I have the right amount of inventory on hand?" Most caterers carry too much. Consequently, owners have their money on the shelf, rather than in the bank. So, what's the right amount? Many professionals will tell you to have a week's to two weeks' inventory on hand. You won't hear that from me! My experience is that most food-service operators should "turn" a food inventory (or "roll" your inventory) 1.25 to 1.3 times a week.

You will find that the 1.3 turn ratio is typically equivalent to 3 days of your purchasing budget. Using our example above, the ideal inventory would be

$4,941.18	weekly purchasing budget
$4,941.18	divided by 7 days' weekly operation
$705.88	is the daily purchasing budget
$705.88 x 3 = $2,117.64	ideal food inventory for $70,000 in food sales monthly

It is rare that businesses have the ideal amount on hand. Yet when food operators work to achieve the goal, waste, shrinkage, and costs go down. Subsequently, cash in the bank and profit go up. The secrets:

BUY only what you need. Buy for discount only if you are strong financially.

DO your inventory weekly. Make inventory a good business habit, not a neglected event. Tie your purchasing budget to your inventory.

SUMMARY

Is your inventory higher than it should be? Reduce your inventory by reducing your purchasing budget. That is, buy less and use up on-hand inventory. Back to our examples. You may find that your inventory is $3,500 high. By reducing your purchasing budget $700 weekly, from $4,941.18 to $4,241.18, you will use up any excess product on your shelves and be at an "ideal inventory" in five weeks.

Aggressive, yes. Effective, absolutely. This process is not theory; it works. Try it! Meanwhile, enjoy your profit!

The Age Group of the Guests

The older a group is, the less its members tend to eat. Envision the amount of food that athletic teenage boys might eat in an afternoon compared with the amount that a group of retired women might consume.

The Guests' Lifestyle

Will the guests be primarily singles or couples? Singles usually come to a party thrilled to be getting a home-cooked (and free) meal. Couples are likelier to have food in their refrigerator, especially if they have kids. As a result, couples eat less.

The Style of the Party

Will people be seated comfortably at tables? Or will the party be a stand-up buffet in a packed room where it's impossible to elbow your way back for seconds?

Rule of thumb: For a buffet, plan to bring one and a half times the amount of portions per guest of each menu item. For a sit-down meal, bring 10 percent more than the guest count (and know that guests eat twice as much bread at a sit-down dinner).

Daily Food-Cost Sheet

Employee name _____

Day _____

Date _____

PURCHASES

Purchases total today:	$	_____
Food waste		_____
Other costs		_____
TOTAL COSTS	$	_____

SALES

Sales total today	$	_____
Comps		_____
Employee meals		_____
TOTAL SALES	$	_____

FOOD COSTS

$$\frac{\text{Food cost today}}{\text{Food sales weekly}} = \underline{\hspace{3cm}} \quad \underline{\hspace{3cm}} \text{ \% Food PC today}$$

$$\frac{\text{Food cost week to date}}{\text{Food sales week to date}} = \underline{\hspace{3cm}} \quad \underline{\hspace{3cm}} \text{ \% Food PC WTD}$$

$$\frac{\text{Food cost period to date}}{\text{Food sales period to date}} = \underline{\hspace{3cm}} \quad \underline{\hspace{3cm}} \text{ \% Food PC PTD}$$

Chart B

Estimated Shopping and Kitchen Prep Time

Guest count: 50 to 100

Type of Work	Estimated Hours
Continental breakfast	1½
Cheese/crudités platters	2
Box lunches	3½
Three passed hors d'oeuvres	4
Appetizer stations	6
Two entrees	6
Plated dinner service	6–7

The Time of the Party

Is the party scheduled for a time normally associated with a full-fledged meal? Guests may not eat before they come, in which case they'll be starving! Or will it be in the middle of the afternoon, when guests will already have eaten? In the latter case, you can probably get away with serving less food. It's a good idea to let guests know on the invitation if they are getting a meal.

The Nature of the Party

You need to know the guests' motivation for being at the affair. Is it a business lunch where workers only want to show their faces and leave? In that case they may well skip dessert. Or is it a wedding—say an Italian wedding like mine, where the guests ate for three hours, took a break, and then went back to work on the buffet some more?

Clients' Concern about Running Out of Food

I have had clients express so much concern that they'll run out of food that I have brought backup products to relieve their fears. I sell it to them with the understanding that I probably won't serve it. They can have it for the next day, with reheating instructions, but it is not my policy to refund any money.

Say that you're hired to put on a fiftieth wedding anniversary party (see the anniversary plate on page 85). The first thing you should ask your client is the age group of the guests. If you know that all ages will be represented, make the portions average size. If you find out that most of the guests will be in their seventies, cut down the steak portion to seven ounces. In my experience older people eat smaller portions, drink very little, prefer decaffeinated coffee, leave before it gets dark, and want to take dessert home with them. (Be sure to bring foil or extra paper plates and napkins so that they can wrap the desserts.)

On the other hand, say you find out that the majority of guests at the anniversary party are the couple's grandchildren and their friends from college. Not only can college boys devour a sixteen-ounce steak standing up, but they'll want to wash it down with plenty of beer and tequila shooters. The party takes on a different tone entirely.

When I figure portions, at the end of my calculations, I up them 10 percent to cover my employees and an extra guest or two. (In this part of the world, it's understood that staff will have a chance to eat once they've served the guests.) If a client orders an extravagant entree like live lobster from Maine or extra-thick lamb chops, the food cost is too high to buy extra portions "on spec." Instead I state in the proposal that I'll do my best to accommodate last-minute guest increases, but if the guest count grows in the last twenty-four hours before the party, the menu price might well increase, because I will be scurrying around to find comparable lobster and lamb chops retail at the last minute (I may even have to pay someone to go shopping for me). Of course, with a menu of Maine lobster or lamb chops, I don't expect to have my staff eat the leftovers—instead I bring them chicken breasts or pasta.

Quoting Other Party Costs

If you're to fill out a contract for each party, as I recommended in chapter 4, you'll want to make sure you know how to quote the other costs involved.

Estimating Waitstaff

Five important factors determine how much help you'll need to hire for any job or party. Answer these questions with the information you have gathered from your client, from visiting the location, and from working with your staff breakdown worksheet.

- How far is the party from where you park and off-load?
- What kind of menu and what type of service are required?
- What ratio of help to guests will your clients pay for?
- How many stories are there at the location?
- Are you using china and glasses or plastic disposables?

Disposables

The amount of paper and plastic products, foil pans, garbage bags, and cans of Sterno you use at each party will astound you, but you can pass on the cost of these items directly to your client.

I ask either my rental company (which sells disposables by the case) or a wholesale party goods store to give me a price quotation, which I mark up by 50 percent. To arrive at a per-person cost, I divide this number by how many people will be at the party.

Floral, Decor, and Subcontractors' Services

Remember that any extra services your clients request are just that—extras. Musicians, florists, specialty desserts, or decor are services you have the expertise to provide. It takes more of your time to coordinate this kind of party or event, so you charge for it.

It's standard in the industry for a caterer to add on an additional 15 to 20 percent to the subcontractors' invoices. This markup covers the phone calls, paperwork, and time you spend organizing.

The Art of Bidding and Writing a Proposal

As a caterer you will often be called on to write proposals and bid for jobs. In your proposals you will describe your menu, name your price, explain your schedule of payment, and enclose a cover letter telling the client why he or she should choose you. Creative, well-written proposals are perhaps the best sales tools around. Call or sit down with your client and ask him or her the following questions to elicit the information you need. Write down the answers on a client inquiry sheet that you design yourself. In this way you'll have a report of what your client wants and what you suggested, even if it takes your client three months to decide.

- Am I the only caterer with whom you are working? If not, whom else are you approaching? I'd like to know my competition.
- Are you giving each caterer the same budget? If not, why? (Sometimes a company's reputation precedes it. A client may hear you are cheaper and want to prove it.)
- For whom is the party being given? Is it social or corporate? What is its purpose?
- What are the date and time of the party? (Remember that seasons and time of day dictate food choices and quantities. Holidays mean different pay scales for staff and may interfere with delivery of produce and props.)
- Where will the party be held? (You will want to look at kitchen facilities at that location and also determine what types of rentals may be needed. Be sure to get the name and phone number of someone at the location.)
- What's your budget? (Needless to say, the answer to this question determines your whole approach and should allow you to gauge whether the client is realistic or asking you to spin your wheels.)
- What sort of party do you have in mind? Casual or elegant? Cocktail or buffet? Sit-down dinner? Exhibition cooking with food stations? Dessert only?
- What do you want the party to look like? Do you have a color scheme in mind? Have you selected invitations yet? (Suggest ideas and current trends. If you are taking down this information over the phone, make an appointment to review your portfolio of party pictures with the client. You will want to be able to ballpark both design and floral costs.)
- What sort of menu do you have in mind? (Try to sell a menu you do well and know is profitable. If you have another party the same day or week, try to sell the same menu to save food and minimize labor costs.)

Event Planning Worksheet

STAFF BREAKDOWN

Event #: _____   Event Date: ___/___/___   Event Name: _____   Page _____

Setup Time: _____   Food Service Hours: _____   Breakdown Time: _____

| Shift | | NUM | POSITION/TITLE | Regular | | | Overtime | | |
IN	OUT			HOURS	RATE	TOTAL	HOURS	RATE	TOTAL
			Field Manager		30.00			45.00	
			Manager		28.00			42.00	
			Assistant Manager		25.00			37.50	
			Captain (bar, floor, kitchen)		22.00			33.00	
			Kitchen Manager		28.00			42.00	
			Chef		28.00			42.00	
			Cook		22.00			33.00	
			Grill		22.00			33.00	
			Kitchen Assistant		18.00			27.00	
			Driver		25.00			37.50	
			Display Attendant		25.00			37.50	
			Attendants		18.00			27.00	
			Display Cook		22.00			33.00	
			Floor		18.00			27.00	
			Bartenders		25.00			37.50	
			Dishwashers		18.00			27.00	
			Party Manager Meeting		15.00			22.50	
			Assistant Manager Meeting		15.00			22.50	
			Kitchen Manager Meeting		15.00			22.50	
			Display Attendant Meeting		15.00			22.50	

Regular Total: _____   Overtime Total: _____

Estimated Regular & Overtime Total _____

Travel Time Pay: _____ Staff @ _____ = _____

Parking/Shuttle Charge: _____

Staffing Fee: _____

Total Labor: _____

Chart C

Waitstaff

TYPE OF PARTY	GUEST COUNT	STAFF
Cocktails	1–100	1 bartender 1 bar back
Cocktails with cold appetizers	1–100	1 bartender 1 bar back 1 waiter
Self-serve buffet	1–100	3 waiters 1 chef 1 chef's assistant
Sit-down dinner	1–20	1 waiter/1 buser 1 chef

Make your proposals thorough and precise. If the client is nervous about entertaining or about hiring you, this detailed party plan will put him or her at ease.

Your proposal may have to outshine the bids of the older, more established caterers, so write it as though the client has never been to a party and knows nothing about you and your fresh, fabulous food or your impeccable eye for detail.

Your bag of tricks has to include glowing prose. Even if it's only cheese and crackers, make it the most interesting cheese you ever bought. Talk about where the cheese comes from. What kind of special crackers are they? Aim for something like this: "Wooden crock of aged English Stilton surrounded by ripe Bosc pear slices, fresh mint, red grapes, toasted baguette rounds, whole-wheat crackers, and graham biscuits served on antique silver trays with red brocade linen."

Don't fall into the trap of thinking you won't be able to compete with the big guys. Many home-based caterers or even part-time caterers are selected over established companies on the merits of a well-written proposal.

I stopped e-mailing proposals to my clients. I like a person-to-person appointment where we go over every line and I answer questions on the spot. I want to sell my ideas. I take the proposal with me and mention I will return with changes. I do not give them a written copy of the proposal until we sign a contract. I got tired of clients sharing my ideas with other caterers and then asking my competition to match them it. Your expertise, creativity, and ideas are all you really have to sell.

Now try the exercise I give students in my catering classes:

The dean of the film school at a local university calls you and tells you that he wants to throw a party to fete the winners in a student film competition. He tells you that he's getting bids from two other caterers and that all three of you have worked for the university before. If you're interested in doing the party, you'll need to e-mail him your proposal within three hours, as his committee meeting is early the next morning.

Denise Vivaldo
Food Fanatics Special Events

October 15, 2014

Dear Dean,

Thanks for calling Food Fanatics Special Events for a proposal to cater "The Bright New Stars of Tomorrow." The enclosed proposal was designed to suit your needs and please your guests.

Budget: I understand that the university has $5,000 for this party and not a penny more. We need to establish a maximum guest count. Some 500 people for $5,000 is $10 per person. If this count goes up, you will need to pay me an additional $10 per person. For this amount Food Fanatics Special Events will provide setup, breakdown by my staff, rentals and display pieces, decor, and food. You will provide students to help my waiters. You said that the wine, water, and ice are being donated. Would you like an estimate of the quantity needed?

Usually about two-thirds of the guests invited will attend. Ask guests to RSVP by the Thursday before.

The dean prefers to give you carte blanche on decor and menu so long as you stay within his budget of $5,000. To round out the picture, you elicit the following information from him:

Name of party: THE BRIGHT NEW STARS OF TOMORROW

Date: Monday, November 15, 7:00–10:00 p.m.

Location: Director's Guild, Hollywood (location donated)

Guest count: 500 to 600 people

Guest profile: Students, instructors, patrons, and celebrity alumni

Budget: $5,000 plus tax

Here's the actual proposal I wrote when the dean of the UCLA film school came to me with just such a party in mind:

MENU

We talked about cheese and crackers to go with the wine. Since the party is after dinner, I'd like the menu to include a variety of cookies, brownies, lemon bars, and dessert cheeses. My chef will garnish the display with red and green grape garlands and whole strawberries. Do you want coffee and tea service?

TIME

Your invitation should ask guests to arrive on time at 6:45 p.m. Guests will be escorted directly to the screening rooms by student filmmakers. The three shorts will end at about 8:30 p.m.

My staff will be in place to open the wine bar and food stations at 8:15 p.m. The double doors to the party room will be open as the guests descend the stairway. Portable spotlights will guide them to the door, compliments of the theater art department.

You might want to reconsider your rule of "no breaks during the screening." I know you hope to keep on schedule without breaks, but if you don't have them, the ladies' restrooms will be jammed between 8:30 and 8:45 p.m.

It would be nice to have two of your department staff volunteer to be bathroom monitors (replace tissue, wipe counters, etc.). I admit this is not a glamorous job, but it is essential.

How to Stay Profitable When You're Working with a Fixed Price

You may find, as I did with this party, that a client prefers to give you a fixed price. Don't agree to take the party on until you've determined that you can do it profitably.

On page 101 you'll find the budget worksheet I filled out before writing the above proposal. This helped me decide whether or not to take the job.

A budget worksheet gives you the financial parameters you need to stick to if a given job is to be profitable. It forces you to estimate every last expense in advance so that you know exactly what you're getting into.

My advice is to get right to the budget when discussing a job with a prospective client. I believe that being honest and not wasting my time or the client's shows how professional I am. Your budget worksheet should help you avoid making promises you can't afford. Often a client doesn't want to pay as much as you want to spend. If

LAYOUT

As the guests walk in, drinks will be on three 8-foot-long tables draped in white linen with black metallic overlays. The wine and water will already be poured by your volunteer wait-staff. Pouring wine and water ahead of time makes it easy for guests to pick up a glass and cocktail napkin on the way to the buffet tables.

Two separate but identical serpentine (S-shaped banquet tables) food displays, each 16 feet long, will be placed perpendicular to the windows to make a dramatic statement. Besides giving guests room both to eat and to socialize, the placement of the buffet allows maximum flow.

THEME AND DECOR

I called the film historian on campus and asked if I might borrow props. She is happy to oblige with five miniature replicas of movie cameras. I also envision sparkling gold stars floating from the ceiling, stacks of antique tin film canisters, the camera replicas, and ribbons of film.

My three waiters will wear white tuxedo shirts, black slacks or skirts, and gold bow ties.

You might like the envelopes of your invitations to be sealed with small gold stars.

you have your entire budget worked out, you'll be in a much better position to come up with a creative solution that meets both your needs and those of your client.

Remember: Budget worksheets are for your use only; they're not something you show a prospective client. The amount of money you make is your business.

Two days after I e-mailed the proposal, the dean called to say that we got the job. Except for the actual day of the event, most of our work was done. We were happy to accept. By working with a budget worksheet, you too can eliminate surprises and enable yourself to plan cash flow, profit, and your future.

On page 103 is an example of a simple, straightforward proposal written by a former student of mine, Donald King. He and his partner, originally a professional pastry chef, met in a cooking class and their company was launched.

PARKING

Please give me the name of the valet parking service you normally hire. Valet service must arrive at 6:30 p.m. Dress is black-and-white formal attire.

LOCATION

I have called the manager of the Director's Guild, who faxed me the location guidelines. My company meets all the insurance requirements. I asked for a floor plan of the lobby, kitchen, and party areas.

PAYMENT

We request 50 percent ($2,500) of the payment upon acceptance of this proposal. The balance, $2,500, will be due three days before the event.

Don't hesitate to call me with questions or changes. I look forward to hearing from you. Thank you again for thinking of Food Fanatics Special Events.

Very truly yours,
Denise Vivaldo

Closing the Deal

Now that you know how to set prices and write a proposal, it's time to learn a few tricks about closing catering deals.

- Sometimes it pays to really stand out from the crowd. Good catering is not so different from good theater—in both you create an effect. In my town caterers outdo themselves to come up with creative ways to present their proposals. One caterer I know told me how she submitted a proposal for the film premiere of *Charlie,* a film based on the life of Charlie Chaplin: She arrived hopelessly caught up in film with the proposal speared on the end of her cane. She got the job. You don't have to be a wild extrovert to succeed at this. Another home-based caterer I know convinced an Italian airline to serve her cookies on board by sending them a proposal, hand-written in calligraphy, that was tucked into a basket shaped like a boot. The basket was stuffed with her cookies and wrapped in the colors of the Italian flag.

- Be firm but flexible. Set the business ground rules about deposit money and guest guarantees, but be ready for changes from clients. After reading a proposal a client may be excited about working with you but may want to go in another direction entirely. Be prepared for changes, and you'll be able to take them in stride.

- Have a backup plan ready. Clients like to think that they have options. For instance, one client decided out of the blue that she didn't want a three-piece band. I quickly came up with the cost of a disc jockey and suggested that she allocate the money she saved to an ice-cream sundae bar. She appreciated how quickly I was able to suggest an alternative—and she loved the idea of a sundae bar.

- Make good use of your digital photographs, letters of recommendation, and videos. Show your client what you can do for him or her with a visual presentation. A dazzling portfolio or short video on your iPad of a recent party is proof positive that you do a good job. You should also make sure that you ask satisfied clients for written recommendations. Do it right after the party when the client is flushed with success. You'll get a great letter that you can use to wow prospective clients.

- No matter what happens, be professional: Never knock your competition. Instead prove to the potential client that you're even better suited for the job.

Dean's Party Budget Worksheet

Food	$1,112.00
Beverage (to be supplied by client)	– – – – –
Labor: kitchen	$80.00
setup/site	$342.00
Rentals	$201.00
Decor	$100.00
Facility rental (waived)	– – – – –
Transportation	$75.00
Disposables	$100.00
Additional labor: proposal hours	$96.00
Unpacking and cleanup labor	$160.00
TOTAL ESTIMATED COSTS	**$2,094.00**
Income	$5,000.00
Gross profit	$2,906.00
Overhead (15 percent)*	–$435.90
NET PROFIT	**$2,570.10**

*See Chapter 7 for information on calculating your overhead percentage.

Menu portion per guest	Cost	Quantities		
1 chocolate brownie	$ .45	brownies	500	pieces
3.2 ounces whole grapes	$ .16	grapes	100	pounds
1.72 whole strawberries	$ .31	strawberries	6	flats
1 lemon bar	$ .55	lemon bars	500	
1 oatmeal raisin cookie	$ .25	oatmeal raisin cookies	500	
1 orange zest cookie	$ .25	orange zest cookies	500	
1 graham cracker biscuit	$ .04	graham cracker biscuits	576	
½ ounce whipped raspberry cream cheese	$ .065	raspberry cream cheese	6	pounds
1 taste of warm Brie with toasted almonds	$ .142	Brie	6	(1 kilo each)
		nuts	3	pounds
1 piece of baguette	$ .019	baguettes	20	
TOTAL	**$2.24**			

Labor

By purchasing brownies and lemon bars from the same bakery, I can get a good deal. That leaves me only the cookies (purchase frozen dough) to bake, grapes to wash and put back in box, strawberries to wipe with damp cloth. I also need to chop nuts, slice baguettes, whip cream-cheese mixture.

Kitchen prep:	cook—8 hours x $10.00	=	$80.00
Setup/site:	waiters—15 hours x $10.00	=	$150.00
	chef—8 hours x $12.00	=	$96.00
	party manager—4 hours x $24.00	=	$96.00
Proposal fee:	4 hours x $24.00	=	$96.00
TOTAL LABOR COSTS:			**$518.00**

Rentals

Six 8-foot tables @ $13.50	=	$81.00
Twelve banquet cloths @ $10.00	=	$120.00
TOTAL:		**$201.00**

Decor

Free from university. The archives historian will deliver to Director's Guild. Film cans and film are free from studio near my house. Black metallic overcloths cost about $200 new. This is the third time I have sold this decor this year. I charge $100 and pick up some profit.

Transportation

Van rental (including insurance, tax, and gas)

TOTAL:	**$75.00**

Disposables

Garbage-bag liners, 1,000 cocktail napkins, plastic wrap, 600 5-inch paper plates, 100 plastic knives for Brie, aluminum pans to carry leftovers home, 750 small plastic cups no bigger than 5 ounces.

TOTAL:	**$100.00**

Another Bite

May 5, 2005

Jane McDermott
The Miller School at UCLA
500 Westwood Plaza
Los Angeles, CA 90095

Proposal

RE: Event: Board of Director's Meeting - Breakfast & Lunch
Date: Saturday, June 4, 2005
Location: Regent Dining Room
Budget: $1,600.00 including tax
Guests: 40

Menu: Please see attached menus.

Bar/Liquor: N/A

Rentals: N/A

Staffing: (5-hour minimum Industry Standard)
      1 Event Planner/Chef - $25.00 per hour
      1 Chef Assistant - $18.00 per hour
      Staffing Cost: $215.00

Food Cost: 40 guests - Breakfast & Lunch
      $28.00 per person $1,120.00

Service Charge: (usually 17%)
      (10% on food and staff to stay within budget) $133.50

Sales Tax:
      (9.25%) $121.15

Event Estimate: $1,589.65

We request 50% ($794.82) of the payment upon acceptance of this proposal to secure event date. The balance, $794.83, will be due three days before the event.

If you should have any further questions, please do not hesitate to call. I look forward to hearing from you soon. Thank you again for thinking of Another Bite.

Best regards,
Donald King

Food Fanatics Catering

P.O. Box 351088, Los Angeles, CA 90035

Tel: (310) 836-3520, Fax: (310) 836-3422, E-mail: dvivaldo@earthlink.net

Dear Mr. and Mrs. Meyer,

It was a pleasure meeting with you yesterday. Below is my suggestion for your menu with an estimated amount. Please look it over and get back to me.

Proposal for:	Full-service dinner
Client:	Tony and Jackie Meyer
Date and time of event:	April 27, 2006, 6:30 p.m.
Address of event:	1877 Meadow Lane, Cheviot Hills
Contact phone number:	(310) 555-1234
Number of guests:	50

Menu

Appetizers (passed):	Herbed Shrimp on Skewers
	Goat Cheese Tartlets
	Crab-Stuffed Endive
	Prosciutto Pinwheels
Salad course:	Baby Spinach, Roquefort & Toasted Walnuts in a Champagne Vinaigrette
Main course:	Tenderloin of Beef with Creamy Horseradish Sauce on Crispy Potato Pancakes served with Honey-Orange Glazed Baby Carrots and Haricot Verts
Dessert:	Poached Bosc Pears in Cabernet Sauce with Vanilla Bean Ice Cream and Amaretti Cookies
Beverages:	Coffee, Tea, Bottled Water, Wine

Schedule

4:30 p.m.	Arrival at location for setup
6:30 p.m.	Guests arrive. Hors d'oeuvres passed until 7:30 p.m.
7:30 p.m.	Dinner served
9:00 p.m.	Dessert served
10:00 p.m.	Kitchen cleanup finished

Cost Estimate For 50 Guests

Appetizers @ $15.00 per person:	$750.00
Dinner @ $37.00 per person:	$1,850.00
Dessert @ $7.50 per person:	$375.00
Wine, 15 bottles white, 15 bottles red, @ $12.00 per bottle:	$360.00
Other beverages @ $3.50 per person:	$175.00
Dinnerware, flatware, water glasses,	
wine glasses, coffee cups/saucers @ 12.00 per person:	$600.00
Tables and chairs @ $5.00 per person:	$250.00
Tablecloths and napkins @ $3.50 per person:	$175.00
Flowers 8 @ $20.00:	$160.00
Servers and kitchen help	
1 bartender @ $20/hr for 7 hours:	$140.00
1 bar assistant @ $18/hr for 7 hours:	$126.00
4 waiters @ $20/hr for 7 hours:	$560.00
4 busboys @ $15/hr for 7 hours:	$420.00
2 chefs @ $25/hr for 7 hours:	$350.00
1 kitchen assistant @ $18/hr for 7 hours:	$126.00
SUBTOTAL:	$6,417.00
15% F&B charge	$962.55
SUBTOTAL:	$7,379.55
8.25% sales tax:	$608.81
ESTIMATED TOTAL:	**$7,988.36**

As soon as I receive a deposit of half the estimated total I will consider the reservation firm. Please let me know the total number of guests 72 hours in advance. The price for food is based on a total of 50 guests and will change if the total number of guests change.

Thank you for the opportunity to provide you with a very memorable event!

Sincerely,
Denise Vivaldo
Owner

From Computer Software to the Internet: High-Tech Help for Caterers

In this high-tech age, computers can boost the creativity and efficiency of anyone in the home-based catering business. Over the years I've come across an increasing number of computer products and resources designed especially for caterers. While they tend to be expensive, I've included a sampling of a few of them. Many software companies offer free trials of their programs. This is an excellent way to test out which program is right for you.

ChefTec Software by Culinary Software Services, Inc., is designed by an executive chef and a staff of programmers for food-service professionals. It's more than a home caterer needs but useful if your business grows to include an off-site location and employees. ChefTec lets you customize management reports and print out recipes, organize monthly inventory procedures, generate ordering lists, and maintain your par levels. Store, scale, and size an unlimited number of recipes; instantly analyze recipe and menu costs by portion or yield; update prices and change ingredients in every recipe with the touch of a button. ChefTec allows you to cost an entire function or catering job in minutes; generate accurate catering bids; add pictures of plate layouts; and calculate nutritional values for recipes and menu items. You can also print out nutritional facts labels. Call (800) 447-3334 for information, or visit them online at www.culinarysoftware.com. Culinary Software Services, Inc., 1900 Folsom St., Ste. 210, Boulder, CO 80302.

CaterPro for Windows catering management software by CaterPro Software has a straightforward point-and-click interface; will generate revenue and production reports, packing lists, labels, and to-do lists; and will automatically update price changes. It has a staff scheduling function, and comes with a video user guide. For more information contact them at: CaterPro Software, 1174 Stone Pine Ln., Lincoln, CA 95648. You can call and request a demo CD at (800) 606-1597, or request one online at www.caterprosoftware.com.

Total Party Planner by Computica offers a free fifteen-day trial of their software. Features include: quickly build custom event menus, per serving or itemized pricing options, track client and delivery details, and automatically generate professional proposals and invoices. It also categorizes and assigns non-menu event items such as delivery, rentals, and floral, in addition to generating packing lists, payment histories, and accounts receivable reports. You can enter recipe data, and it includes a flexible, searchable database. See their website for more information: www.totalpartyplanner.com. You can write or call them at: 11126 Air Park Rd., #201, Ashland, VA 23228; (866) 636-4062.

CostGuard is a food costing tool that allows you to get pre-cost information based on most current food costs. Standardized recipes mean greater consistency, better food costs, and more satisfied customers. CostGuard converts recipes to larger and smaller yields and automatically generates production sheets, prep lists, orders, etc. You can get reports on recipe pricing, ingredient cross-reference, and recipe cross-reference. You are able to search recipes and print reports using your own customized categories. For more information visit their website at www.costguard.com, call (888) 325-6937, or write to At-Your-Service Software, Inc., 450 Bronxville Rd., Bronxville, NY 10708.

CATERPLUS OnSite by Caterware, Inc., was designed by caterers and software developers as a comprehensive business solution for catering professionals. CATERPLUS OnSite offers account management, performance tracking and reporting, event management (cost and price tracking, event creation, etc.), and list management (accounts, contracts, reports, staff information, statements, tasks, venues, etc.). CATERPLUS Classic is designed for the needs of the off-premise operation, offering all of the same great features as OnSite, without the Venue Reservations Module. Visit Caterware's website for more information at www.caterware.com or call (800) 853-1017.

MasterCook Deluxe by ValuSoft (www.valuesoft.com) is a low-cost menu managing database that will produce nutrition labels based on your recipes. Also available on Amazon.com.

There are some free online resources, like Recipe Center (www.recipecentersoftware.com). This nifty program organizes your recipes and creates shopping lists from them. It also automatically changes quantities. They sell a professional version but offer the streamlined version for free. It also allows you to access their world-wide database of recipes.

Also free is the Nutrition Data website (www.nutritiondata.com). This site is devoted to calculating the nutritional content of food. Not only does the site give you the nutrition label, it also gives you a graphs and charts such as the Nutritional Target Map, Calorie Ratio Pyramid, Nutritional Balance, Protein Balance, Estimated Glycemic Load, and Inflammation Factor.

For free information on all things culinary, visit the Chef2Chef website (www.chef2chef.net). They have articles, recipes, online communities, food blogs, and a huge listing of farmers' markets in the United States and Canada. Check out their Top 100 page to find out the top 100 recipes, wines, beers, culinary websites, cookbooks, restaurants, and culinary instructors.

06 Sales and Marketing

It doesn't matter how great a caterer you are if only a handful of people know it. Creating an image for yourself and telling the world about it are what marketing is all about. Marketing is mandatory as you set up your home-based business, important as a long-term strategy, and absolutely necessary to ensure continued success. Your goal every day should be to find new markets for your products and services. As a beginner, appreciating the importance of constant promotion and continuous marketing is your first step in attracting customers and building an image. Fortunately, marketing your company doesn't have to be expensive or difficult. It takes only planning, creativity, and resourcefulness—talents you already have.

Remember that you are what makes your catering company different from every other catering company. In the final analysis you're selling not only parties but yourself. You're the most effective marketing tool your company has. Start thinking of how to sell yourself even before you open your business. What do you plan to do that's different, unusual, or essential? What knowledge, ideas, or contacts do you have that will help you sell yourself and your company? If you will spend the time it takes to learn and track effective marketing techniques, you'll find that your ideas, suggestions, and creativity turn into business.

Your next step is talking to the people closest to you to generate some good old-fashioned word-of-mouth advertising. Ask your church group if they have a designated caterer for celebrations after christenings. Might your temple have a referral list of caterers for planning a bat or bar mitzvah? What about your spouse's law office—who coordinates the parties to entertain clients or find new associates? How about groundbreaking or new-building parties from the general contractor who lives next door? What about client leads from your real estate agent for housewarmings? Or would he or she like to buy gift baskets of your pasta sauces for new clients?

I first started teaching cooking classes to attract clients to my home-based catering business. I wrote and taught classes such as "Perfect Party Recipes for the Holidays" and "Easy Turkey Dinner and Trimmings for a Crowd." By reading a local newspaper, I discovered that the food editor ran a free column about cooking classes each Thursday in the food section. I constantly sent her information about upcoming classes. My credits read, "Denise Vivaldo, partner, Food Fanatics Special Events." Not only did the listings produce business, but many of my students became clients.

Check the society page of your local newspaper every week and start to get involved in community activities. The more people you know, the more people who will get to know you and the services you can provide.

Sell, Sell, Sell

I had a strong background in sales when I opened my home-based catering business. During the years I spent working in a real estate firm, I went to seminars on sales techniques, classes on public speaking, and training programs for those who want to hone their competitive edge. I learned to make offers, sell, and negotiate. I needed these same skills to open my own business. When you're a caterer, the client "offers" you the chance to handle his or her party, you "sell" your version to the client, and the two of you then negotiate.

I do think that caterers have an advantage over real estate agents when it comes to sales: Everyone loves to talk about food. An example: cold calls. People are instantly interested in talking about throwing a party, even with a stranger; but they're not always comfortable with a discussion about selling their home. It's also easier to "upsell" clients in catering—in other words, to get them to spend more money and think in grander terms.

Of course, not everyone switches into catering from sales, but whatever your background, know that the ability to sell your food, your ideas, and your services is an absolute necessity in this business. If you have never made a cold call or bid and closed a deal or walked up to a stranger and offered to sell your services, consider taking a course on developing your sales technique.

Set specific goals for yourself to help develop your skills: one cold call every day, at least three introductions to new people every week, five promotional packages with cover letters to good leads each month. Fortunately, you'll find that loving what you do makes selling your services much easier. This chapter is designed to help you, too, by supplying you with marketing tips and techniques. Simply choose those that feel the most natural to you.

And remember this cardinal rule in sales: Never take no for an answer; just rephrase the question.

Defining Your Niche

To define your niche you need to know your area's demographics, research the competition, and decide what kinds of clients (and catering) appeal to you.

You gathered a lot of this information when you wrote the market analysis portion of your business plan. Studying it will help you market your business successfully and target the clients you want to reach.

To get a fix on what your prospects are, you'll need to size up the different types of catering going on in your marketplace. Is there a lot of catering or only seasonal work? Are the other caterers in your town busy or strictly part-time? What clients do you think you'd be most suited to? Do you imagine yourself preparing elegant dinner parties on the weekends or delivering box lunches to offices five days a week?

These days catering can be divided into three categories: social, corporate, and community affairs. The needs of the client differ in each case.

Social Catering

Here we're talking about weddings, anniversaries, bat or bar mitzvahs, sweet-sixteen parties, and other occasions that people plan to celebrate once in a lifetime. I call these the emotional, "hand-holding" events of life. Families may have set aside money to pay for these occasions for years, and whether the economy is weak, strong, or indifferent, traditions like these are likely to go on.

When it comes to celebrating milestone events, caterers are entrusted with more than the food: They're expected to provide memories as well—no small task. In many instances the client may never have used a caterer before (now you know where the hand-holding comes in).

If social catering is a niche that interests you, create channels to get your name around. Find out which churches or rental halls are booked for weddings or receptions in your town and leave cards and menu packages with the managers. Contact every baker that makes wedding cakes and see if you can develop a referral system. Introduce yourself at bridal-wear and rental shops. Many times the bride shops for her dress first, before choosing the caterer, and a reference from the shop owner can be an introduction for you.

Telephone Inquiry Sheet/Contact Ledger

Date _____

Customer referred by _____   Call taken by _____

Organization _____

Name _____

Address _____

City/State/Zip _____

Phone _____

Party location _____   Date of party _____

Number of guests _____   Party hours _____

Purpose of party _____   Start _____ End _____

_____

What was discussed/questioned/suggested:

Company information/Menus _____   Faxed _____ or mailed _____

Additional services requested:

Beverage _____   Flowers _____

Rentals _____   Valet _____

Entertainment _____   Security _____

Cake _____   Photographer _____

Vendor Referrals:

1. _____

2. _____

3. _____

Follow-up _____

_____

First callback date _____   Action _____

Second callback date _____   Action _____

Third callback date _____   Action _____

Date booked _____   Future follow-up call date _____

Inactive _____   Why? _____

Comments:

Corporate Catering

Daily breakfast meetings, snack baskets, and lunch boxes are viewed as time-management techniques in today's business world—they cut down on the time people spend out of the office. Caterers are often called on to deliver food to offices for executives' use or for management training seminars. And nearly every corporation throws an annual holiday party where a caterer's services may be desired.

Corporate catering is much less personal than social catering. Most of the time, in-house company party planners have budget guidelines and limited time to spend on setting up the catering. They are shopping for price and convenience. You may not meet the corporate party planner you're working with until the day of the event. His or her decisions will be made based on your website or menu package. The transaction can be handled through the e-mail, over the phone, or by fax. Arranging these caterings takes less of your time.

If you know the business world already, the corporate niche might appeal to you. Target corporations by calling their head offices and asking for the name of the person who handles their special events or meetings. With the correct contact name, you have the opportunity to direct information about you and your business to the people with decision-making power.

Community Affairs

The third catering market is community affairs. This includes catering local fund-raisers, charity auctions, or perhaps a town's library opening. I charge these customers the same as private clients, because my costs are the same. Occasionally, however, I'll donate a gift or service in order to gain some free publicity.

For example, once I contacted the local American Heart Association regarding its annual February bake sale and volunteered to work on the coordinating committee. I was appointed chairperson. I contacted fifteen bakeries and five caterers, all of whom were willing to sell their product at cost to the committee and donate time to the fund-raiser. My idea for the theme was "Our Town's Generous Sweetheart Table." All my costs for decor were approved for reimbursement, and I donated my time. I designed platter-size red hearts for all the baked goods and garlands of white doilies to dress up the tables. When the cookies and cakes arrived, we marked up the goods for sale, waited on the customers, and made a considerable profit for the Heart Association. Along with the other caterers and bakeries, I received publicity in the local newspapers and on radio spots, and our names appeared on big banners all around town.

As a home-based caterer, you have more flexibility than a caterer whose overhead is high, which means you can move into the market you're most comfortable with first. Most caterers work in all three niches. It keeps their businesses well rounded financially and covers all leads to client exposure.

Choosing a Name and Logo

The name of your company may be the first words potential clients ever hear about you. For this reason your company name should be memorable and indicate the services you provide. I think it's helpful if it reflects your personality as well.

Choosing a name is a big step that requires careful consideration. Here are a few pointers to keep in mind:

- Make the name simple to pronounce and easy to spell. If it's long or complicated, people won't repeat it, out of fear of sounding foolish.
- Look online to see what your competition is named. How do you respond to those names? Do they make sense? Which names stand out from the crowd?
- Compile a list with the competition's names and twenty potential names for your company, and ask your family, friends, purveyors—anyone you can engage in conversation—which names they like and why. Call these same people back three days later and ask what names they remember.
- Be careful not to pick a name too similar to that of another company in town. If you do, you'll end up with a lot of wrong numbers, lost mail, and confused orders.
- Consider using your own name as part of your company name: Alison Stone's Corporate Catering, for example. If you do, you may not have to file a fictitious-business-name statement with your locality.
- So-called fictitious or assumed business names—in other words, names without your own name in them, such as Party Planners or Devilish Desserts—should be registered. Call your local chamber of commerce or county courthouse for more information on registering your business's name. Most localities have a list of all fictitious business names registered in the area, so that you can check to make sure you're the only person using a particular name.

Many people think that filing a fictitious-name statement will protect their use of a trade or fictitious name. It will not. Generally, filing a fictitious-business-name statement in most localities will allow you only to open a bank account under that name.

To properly protect a trade name, a trade search must be done, which includes a search of business directories, phone books, and rosters of professional organizations. Companies exist that will conduct name searches, but it is easily done online in most localitits.

It's not essential that you have a logo, but doing so helps to establish a professional image. If you can't design one yourself, try contacting student graphic designers from a local art school. Work with a designer to bring your ideas to life and offer them the opportunity to showcase their talents.

Another option is to use one of the logos available from printers who do business cards; or check out independent shops with in-house graphic designers, many of whom will work with you on a logo at reasonable rates. Remember that a successful logo needs to accentuate your style and your name; it also needs to grab people's attention.

Take the time to choose your company name and logo wisely. It's the first step in building your reputation.

Designing Promotional Pieces

Your business card is your first promotional piece. When we were just starting out, my partner found a great printer who suggested that we print on both sides of our business cards. It was a terrific idea. We used the back of the card to describe our commitment to fine foods and perfect service in a single paragraph. Clients ended up quoting to their friends from the paragraph. (We, in turn, sent a lot of clients to this smart printer.)

Once your cards are printed up, think about your second promotional piece. Inexpensive pens or small note pads are popular. (Women will keep them in their purses forever.) Look online for companies listed under "merchandising" or "promotional products." Their online catalogues contain thousands of inexpensive novelties you can buy imprinted with your name.

Another inexpensive promotional item would be a refrigerator magnet with your logo and phone number on it. Ask the manager of your favorite retail appliance store if you can stand out in front one afternoon with a basket of magnets and pass them out to foot traffic. Better yet, ask the store manager if you can set up a card table with cookies, lemonade, and a guest book.

Your goal is to get your name out to the public. I never leave a restaurant without leaving a 30 percent tip and two business cards underneath it. Good waiters are trained to sell, and often they come into contact with a hundred people in a shift. Make your services known to everyone: the most successful members of your chamber of commerce, the president of your homeowner's association, the mayor's secretary, the director of your town auditorium or convention center, and the general manager of your local news station. One of the best ways to do this is to buy a listing in the Yellow Pages. When people look for caterers, they still often begin with the phone book. Remember that the listings are in alphabetical order, so make sure that the name of your business doesn't relegate you to the end of the list.

A Yellow Pages ad should include the following information:

- business name and phone number prominently displayed
- address
- a brief description of what your business offers
- motto or trademark services statement
- logo, if space permits
- specialty, if you have one
- length of time in business, if appropriate

Here is a sample Yellow Pages ad:

ASTRO FOODWORKS AND DESIGN
catering services since 1984

Our creative menus and elegant setup and design
will make your next

WEDDING	COCKTAIL PARTY
SPECIAL OCCASION	GRAND OPENING
DINNER PARTY	and more . . .

a memorable experience.

1234 City Avenue • Los Angeles, CA • 555-1234

When you select purveyors, give them eye-catching sweatshirts or hats with your logo to wear around town. Replace them when they look faded. Call your local sign shop and find out what it would cost to get your name and logo replicated on a plastic decal or magnetic panel for your car doors or van side panels. Think marketing wherever you are. You'll come up with plenty of new ways to get your name around.

As your business grows, you can take your company philosophy, style, and success and broadcast it with a brochure. A brochure doesn't have to be expensive—it just has to be attention getting. To keep costs down you can use a single 8½ x 11 piece of colored paper folded into thirds so that it fits inside a business envelope. Design each section separately. You might give your company's name, address, phone number, and logo on the front; a short description of the company inside; and some quotes from satisfied customers on the back.

Write and design every marketing or promotion piece so that it's easy to read and understand. You can keep costs down by hiring local graphic design students or by composing it yourself on a computer. If you're feeling inspired, you might even make one-of-a-kind brochures using construction paper, pressed herbs, and calligraphy. Every time you mail out a brochure or any other promotional piece, make sure to follow up with a phone call. There's no better way to make a good impression.

Making Your Menus Part of Your Marketing Program

Your passion for food and your skill for entertaining are the natural resources you bring to your business. One of the best ways to broadcast your passion and skill in what you do is to use your menus as marketing tools. Design your menus to showcase your style, talent, and knowledge. If your clients could cook like you, they wouldn't need to hire you. Make sure you show them you're an expert.

Menus can function as information packets or as great direct mailers. My partner and I once booked fifteen parties in a matter of days by using our menus as the centerpiece of a direct-mail campaign. We had a target to hit when we designed the piece; we wanted to sell parties of a hundred people, strictly buffet, for Sunday afternoons over the next eleven months of the new year. We sent the piece out on January 12 (for the first week of the month, people are still recuperating from last year's parties). We used our existing client list and also addressed 400 envelopes to families in our neighborhoods.

We divided an 8½ x 11 piece of paper on the computer into four boxes, each highlighting a different season's menu priced from $18 to $32 for complete dinners based on one hundred guests. The format encouraged clients to think about having a party at any time of the year.

On the reverse side of the paper, we printed tips for the hostess: Have one big party this year to pay back everyone you owe; invite people over you never get to see away from work; ask every neighbor you don't know—make it a big block party. We explained why having the party on Sunday afternoon was nicer for guests with children and how it enabled them to make it a family day. We also said it was nice for single people to have something to do on Sunday, not just Saturday night. We told the hostess that our menu had been priced to reflect the fact that Sunday isn't as busy a catering day as Saturday. To keep costs down even more, we suggested using disposable plates for appetizers and desserts. We even gave them a suggested bar list with the approximate dollar amount we thought they would spend at the liquor store. We also advised them not to clean until the day after the party. Once one hundred people arrive, who can tell whether or not the floors are spotless?

We enclosed a stamped postcard asking them two simple questions: Would you like us to call about booking a party? If so, would you prefer paying all at once or in three or four easy payments?

We didn't spend money on typesetting. Instead we used a special font on the computer. We printed 500 menus at a speedy press and stuffed each one in an envelope with two business cards. We received thirty-four phone calls and booked fifteen parties. It cost us six hours of our time, $200 in stationery supplies, $230 in stamps, and $35 in business cards.

Of course, we reaped plenty of referrals from that one mailing, and one party led to another. We even received one phone call from a woman saying she got our number from the employee bulletin board at work and asking if she could buy baskets of cookies for Christmas.

Make your menus part of a long-term marketing strategy. Send out new menus—quarterly or seasonally or whatever you budget for—and keep doing so. Even if you don't get feedback right away, people enjoy the chance to stay informed.

Sample Four Seasons Menu

❀

Spring

Fennel-sprinkled Parmesan sticks
Poached salmon with fresh dill mayonnaise
Green beans and mushrooms
sautéed in herbed butter
Endive and radicchio salad
Strawberry-rhubarb pie

✦

Fall

Mixed antipasto
Osso buco braised in wine
Roasted new potatoes
Escarole salad with red onion and black olives
Charlotte aux Poires

Summer

Cold purée of spinach soup with crostini
Veal scallops dressed with lemon and parsley
Glazed carrot rounds
Garden salad with balsamic vinaigrette
Pears and cherries in custard tarts

❄

Winter

Crudités platter with warm artichoke dip
Sausage-stuffed trout
Tricolored roasted peppers
Roasted red potatoes with rosemary
Chocolate mousse with zest of orange

Standing Out from the Crowd

It isn't enough simply to come up with a snazzy name, logo, and brochure (though it surely helps). You also need to distinguish yourself from other caterers in your area. Let me tell you what worked for me when I opened my home-based catering business.

After I had catered a half-dozen parties, I called clients, guests, purveyors, and staff workers and asked them all the same question: What, if anything, made my parties distinctive? They all said the same thing, as if they had been reading from a script. The food was great, but the presentation was spectacular. With that I had my hook. From that point forward I made sure that every buffet table, every flower arrangement, and every appetizer tray my guests saw looked spectacular.

Show-stopping displays became my trademark. Early on in my career, I worked with a couple who wanted to get married in a week. The bride wanted to serve nothing but seafood, caviar, and champagne. She had already called two other caterers, who said it couldn't be done on such short notice and who hated the menu besides. I not only told the bride I could do the job in seven days but also came up with a wonderful way to present her menu.

With such a limited menu, I felt that the food served at the reception had better be the finest in the world. With the bride and groom's blessing, I bought the biggest shrimp (eight to a pound) from Louisiana, the finest Maine lobster tails, and the most succulent Alaskan king crab claws. I ordered an exquisite mermaid ice sculpture in whose outstretched hands I placed an enormous tin of Iranian beluga caviar. Using cookie cutters, I turned toast points for the caviar into shells, sea horses, and fish. Sprays of white orchids and a blue light box underneath the ice sculpture completed the buffet. A couple of waiters in black tuxedos served French champagne. The display was a knockout, and my labor costs were agreeably low.

This presentation of rare seafood and champagne made the guests feel as if they were attending a once-in-a-lifetime party, just the feeling the bride wanted to convey. The wedding worked so well that I booked three parties from it.

In your search for your hook, study the marketplace ads, menus, fliers, and brochures sent out by the competition. What are they doing to make themselves stand out from the crowd? Are you impressed or not? If you are, call and compliment the caterer on his or her brochure or business logo and ask who came up with such a clever idea. Also ask whether the piece created more business. Remember: The whole point of any marketing you do is to increase the growth of your business.

Keeping a Portfolio

Don't forget to take pictures of every event you cater and every product you produce. Arrange your photos in a slideshow on your smartphone or tablet. Use these images on your website and in your social media postings.

Show a slideshow of parties to clients the next time you're trying to sell yourself and your services. Include images of menus, letters of recommendation, and awards.

Ideas to Help You Sell Yourself as a Pro

THE PROFESSIONAL'S APPROACH	THE AMATEUR'S APPROACH
Be firm with client when necessary; stick to the terms of your proposal and budget	Try to accommodate the client's every wish (the "customer is always right" syndrome)
Come up with creative solutions to problems	Say "It can't be done"
Document the party from proposal to checklists to employee records to follow-up notes	Rely on your memory to organize the party, as well as answer questions that may arise months after the party
Take pride in your industry	Speak disparagingly of your competition
Make sure you stand out from the crowd; promote your talents	Rely on word of mouth to boost your business
'Fess up to your mistakes	Blame anyone else—even the client!—for snafus
Plan every detail ahead of time	Deal with things as they arise
Send thank-yous to clients, purveyors, suppliers, etc.	Never say thank you

My own portfolio is bursting with pictures of celebrities I've catered for, newspaper clippings covering the events with descriptions of my menus, and even a film clip from a Thanksgiving scene where I appeared as the caterer on a highly rated television show.

An effective portfolio can be worth thousands of dollars in additional sales. Once I was working with a British event planner representing a Swedish manufacturer who was planning a reception for a Japanese dignitary. They all wanted a traditional American barbecue.

I submitted one barbecue menu with three different presentations: One party used paper plates and checkered tablecloths, the second party relied on a swimming pool location and Hawaiian shirts, and the third was a Wild West Hoedown. It was no contest—all because I had fabulous pictures of a Western Hoedown I had staged the year before. After seeing the images of covered wagons, hay bales, waiters as gunfighters, and waitresses as saloon girls (and me dressed as Miss Kitty from the television show *Gunsmoke* . . . yes, I am that old!), the client was more than willing to increase the cost of the party for the additional decor.

Your portfolio offers proof that you can deliver your ideas and creativity.

Portfolio Photography 101

If you *don't* have good photos of your food and your events, you will put yourself at a serious disadvantage. With a little practice and a nice camera on your phone, you can take pictures that will get you work.

Take photos of your parties from all angles. Include close-ups of food, decor, and table settings to put the wider shots of your parties into perspective (look at any entertaining magazine for examples). Take a few photos of the party being set up; this invites viewers to participate. If your photography skills aren't great, just use the nicest ones.

Find the time to take a few pretty close-ups of your food. Nothing sells food better than beautiful photography. Limit the number of images for each party— one photo of each menu item is more than enough.

Putting Together a Promotional Kit

Promotional kits are handy for two reasons: They can help you land new clients, and you can use them as press kits to gain free publicity for your company from food editors, magazines, and radio shows.

My online promotional kit, on my website, denisevivaldo.com, consists of my résumé, biography, client list, press clips on my parties, articles written about me, copies of food shots I've styled for magazines, and menus I've created, plus a demo reel, my picture, and information about any services I am trying to sell. Potential clients can just click a link and find out about classes, trips, or tours. The site is available 24/7, so even when I'm busy or my office is closed, the information is available. The whole "package," or informational site, is designed to put a prospective client at ease by showing that I know every aspect of the business and can solve any problems that crop up because I've done it all before.

In addition to the online promotional kit, I've printed out the materials to send to various radio stations, suggesting that they interview me. Twice program managers have called, and I've been able to plug special events I was coordinating for civic groups. My promotional kit has also helped me book appearances on almost one hundred television food shows.

I began sending my press kit to people who produce infomercials. I started after I got a call from a public relations firm representing a new bread machine. The firm had heard of me from the local cooks' bookstore. They were looking for a chef to complement their celebrity cook, who didn't know how to make bread. The idea was to show my hands in close-up shots. I didn't get the job, but the experience made me aware of a whole new market.

As you put together a promotional site or "kit" to help you launch your business, consider what you want the public to know about you. Is it that you were a designer before you became a caterer and you can't help but bring that attention to detail with you? Or should you tell them that you are the great-granddaughter of the original baker in your town? Or perhaps that you collect antique copper molds and cooking utensils and often use them in your food displays? Create a package promoting your talents. You may not have much of a track record yet, but you can still offer new ideas and beautiful menus. If you can draw, create renderings of parties you hope to stage or dishes you hope to prepare. Add a few paragraphs about who you are and what you like to do. Include a recent picture. Be sure to show any community service awards you've received and any volunteer work in which you might be involved. You don't have to reinvent the wheel; just grease the one you have.

By adding a press release, you can use this same kit to approach local food editors and managers of radio food programs. You can make their jobs easier by supplying a list of questions to ask you or a well-written interview that you are glad to let them print.

Appetizers

✴ Menu 1

California Mini Pizzas

Chicken Sausage Stuffed Mushrooms

Baskets of Crudités

Choice of 2 Dips:

French Onion, Black Bean, Gorgonzola, Salsa, Green
Onion, Ranch, Hummus

Seasonal Fruit Trays

Imported Cheese Board with Crackers

Spinach and Cheese Phyllo Pastries

✴ Menu 2

Spring Rolls and Potstickers with Plum Sauce

Crab Puffs

Apricot Brie in Puff Pastry

Smoked Salmon Display:

Mini Bagels, Red Onions, and Cream Cheese

Petite Kaiser Roll with Black Forest Ham

Sesame Chicken Skewers with Peanut Sauce

Crudité Baskets with Salsa and Black Bean Dip

Fresh Fruit Skewers

✴ Menu 3

Angel Biscuits with Proscuitto and Garlic Aioli

Spicy Chicken Empanadas with

Cilantro Sour Cream

Salmon Cheesecake

Torte Milanese with Artichoke Hearts

Crab Meat and Scallop Mousse

Chicken Satay with Peanut Sauce

✴ Menu 4

Spinach Buttons with Spicy Chinese Mustard

Mini Quiche Lorraine

Mascarpone and Basil Torte

Roasted Garlic Crustades

Smoked Salmon Display

Beef Satay with Peanut Sauce

Vegetable Won-Ton with Chili Oil

Taquitos with Guacamole

✴ Menu 5

Hot Artichoke Mousse in Hawaiian
Bread Bowl

Seafood Display:

Oysters, Shrimp, Steamed Clams,

and Green-Lip Mussels on Crushed Ice,

Cocktail Sauce, Tabasco, and Lemons

Caviar with Buckwheat Blinis

Chinese Chicken Salad Lettuce Leaf Tacos

Skewered Spinach Tortellini with Pesto Sauce

Broccoli Frittata Squares

Miniature Beef Wellington

✴ Menu 6

Baskets of Crudités with Artichoke Mousse

Warm Crab and Cheese Dip with
Blue Corn Chips

Chicken Pecan Skewers with Curry Sauce

Spinach Tortellini with Pesto Sauce

Salmon Pâté with Water Crackers

Lobster Seviche in Tortilla Cups

Guacamole Torte

Exotic Fruit Display

Sliced Tenderloin of Beef (carver optional)
with Petite Kaiser Rolls

How to Write a Press Release for Pickup

Written correctly, effective press releases can catch the attention of the media and generate more coverage for your business than an ad ever would—at a substantially cheaper price. Editors and producers prefer to receive releases that follow a standard format so that they don't have to hunt for the pertinent information. Make their jobs easier by including the following components in your next release:

■ Before you start, make sure you have something newsworthy to say. You don't want to waste the media's time with information they don't care about. Send them news they can use.

■ Audience, audience, audience. Watch the tone and style of your writing to make sure it works for your audience. Journalists want to see factual information. Save your opinions for the editorial page.

■ Indicate the release date. If the release is applicable starting immediately, write "For Immediate Release." If the release should not be used until a later date, write "Hold Until xx/xx/xx" or "For Release on Halloween."

■ Include your contact information flush right on the same line as the release date. It should include your name, phone number, and e-mail. Bold the word "Contact" to make it easy to find on the page.

Contact: Martha Hopkins, (254) 644-3505
martha@terracepartners.com

■ Write a catchy, to-the-point headline. Center and bold the text for a standardized format. Sometimes the title is the only thing an editor will read. If you don't get her attention here, your release may go straight to the trash.

■ List the city, state, and current date at the beginning of the first sentence.

■ In the first paragraph, get straight to the point and answer those five important journalistic questions: who, what, where, why, and when. It needs to have timely, immediate information.

■ In the second paragraph, you can go into more detail about your business, your new offer, your event, or whatever you're announcing. To add credibility, quote the owner, client, or another reliable source.

- In the final paragraph, you can provide general information about your business such as "Terrace Partners is a boutique packaging and publishing firm specializing in cookbooks. They are based in Texas." You can also repeat contact information here and important deadlines.

- To indicate the end of your release, center three number signs (###) below the last paragraph.

- Format the entire press release in Times New Roman (or another easy-to-read font) in 12-point type. Make sure to double-space the text for easy reading.

- Spell-check and proofread. Nothing will catch the eye of an editor faster than a typo. Take the time to read your work carefully, rewrite anything that's confusing, and correct any errors.

Writing articles yourself is an excellent way to get free publicity. And the higher your profile, the more opportunities will come your way. When I wrote and published an article titled "How My Expensive Culinary Degree Has Paid for Itself" in a trade paper, the dean of a local university asked me to sit on the advisory council for their hospitality/food-service program. I accepted the position, which gives me great statewide exposure by means of the press releases they send out.

Drumming Up Business

As a caterer you have the ultimate marketing weapon at your disposal: the ability to stage incredible parties with wonderful food. Put your expertise to use on your own behalf. You might plan an open house in your own home, in your commercial kitchen, or in a local park. Send invitations to everyone you know: friends, any clients, the news media, or even politicians in your town. Serve spectacular desserts and coffee. If you're outside, supply tables for other merchants to place product displays or brochures and encourage networking. Place a huge calendar in the middle of your buffet table with plenty of colored markers. Invite guests to schedule their own appointments with you to discuss their catering needs in the year ahead.

It's also good to make your services available to local charities. Most charities need caterers to help plan and orchestrate food fairs and wine-tasting events.

Catering a charitable event is an excellent way to have 1,000 people discover you and your business in a single evening.

It also pays to become recognized as a food expert in your field. Volunteer to be a speaker for clubs and schools. Prepare talks such as "Global Influences on Our Food Supply" for the environmentalists in town, "Cheap Eats in Your Neighborhood" for the singles looking for meeting places, or "Healthy Foods from Around the World" for local travel agents. You never know when one of these speaking engagements will land you a paying job. For example, as an officer of the California Culinary Academy Alumni Board, I often speak at the CCA's career recruitment days. One year a representative of a nationwide department store heard me and called me up the next day to offer me a job as a consultant coordinating celebrity-chef demonstrations throughout Southern California.

The point is to give of yourself, enjoy, and get your name out there.

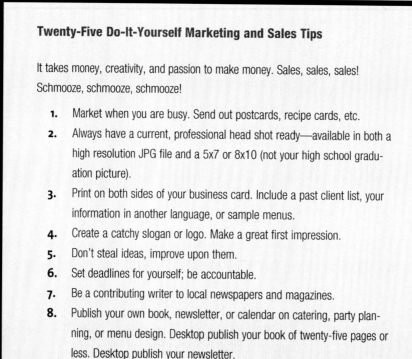

Twenty-Five Do-It-Yourself Marketing and Sales Tips

It takes money, creativity, and passion to make money. Sales, sales, sales! Schmooze, schmooze, schmooze!

1. Market when you are busy. Send out postcards, recipe cards, etc.
2. Always have a current, professional head shot ready—available in both a high resolution JPG file and a 5x7 or 8x10 (not your high school graduation picture).
3. Print on both sides of your business card. Include a past client list, your information in another language, or sample menus.
4. Create a catchy slogan or logo. Make a great first impression.
5. Don't steal ideas, improve upon them.
6. Set deadlines for yourself; be accountable.
7. Be a contributing writer to local newspapers and magazines.
8. Publish your own book, newsletter, or calendar on catering, party planning, or menu design. Desktop publish your book of twenty-five pages or less. Desktop publish your newsletter.

9. Send personal, handwritten thank-you notes. Remember to enclose your business card and a set of pictures of your client's event.

10. You are an expert in your profession . . . become a guest speaker or lecturer at your local city college, the chamber of commerce, women's groups, or SCORE.

11. Teach a class that makes you the star.

12. Have an 800 or 888 toll-free number—this takes the distance away.

13. Create a monthly e-mail newsletter.

14. Have a professional voice-mail message.

15. Conquer the chamber of commerce.

16. Hire a professional graphic designer—barter or trade services.

17. Give interviews or opinions on local radio.

18. Give referral fees.

19. Have a webpage and e-mail. Monitor webpage hits and update frequently.

20. Don't be difficult to contact—have a cell phone. Tell your clients it's okay to text you.

21. Write press releases of parties, staff promotions, book signings, and classes you've taught. E-mail your releases to industry magazines, small local newspapers, past clients, and potential clients.

22. Conduct a publicity stunt, one that makes you look good and is for the good of your community. Research upcoming fund-raising events to contribute your talents to. Make sure the local media knows about the event and your involvement.

23. Always maintain current and good references.

24. Make sure your portfolio is up-to-date, neat, and organized. Include photographs of events, photographs of yourself with celebrities or VIPs, menus, and thank-you notes from clients. Set your portfolio in a slide-show format and include it on your website.

25. Hire or barter with a film or art student from your local college to videotape the planning, prepping, and production of a major catering job. Use voice-over narration and music to explain and add interest.

Marketing with a Website

Why Is It Important for You to Have a Website?

- Potential clients are more likely than ever to do an initial search for services online. Being found on the Internet will give you an advantage over your competition.
- Through your website, clients can become educated about your business and get answers to many of their questions. In turn, this will help to cut back on the number of phone calls you receive with simple inquiries.
- People have more confidence in, and prefer doing business with, someone that they know something about. Inform visitors about your business, of your community involvement, the products and services you offer, and of your experience.
- There is potential for your website to become a resource of information for the public. By supplying helpful tips and articles that are relevant, you will gain repeat visitors.

Website Content

Your website need not be complicated. It is better to be clear and simple than to go on and on and confuse potential clients. Start with something simple:

Gina Papetti
Catering for special events and for every day

Menus customized to your needs and preferences.

Organic seasonal foods are my specialty!

Delicious food prepared by an experienced and talented professional.

Call for more information:
310-555-0123

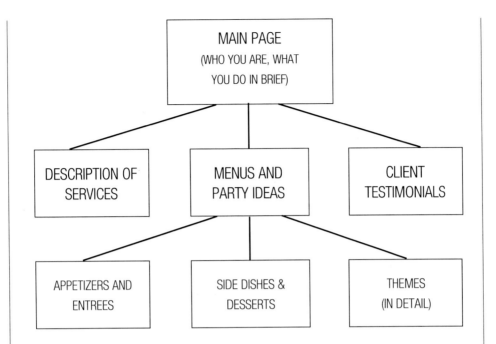

Once you've established a website address and put up the first page, you can add more information as you go along.

Include photos of your food (only if the photos make the food look good!) and previous events, stock photography, or clip art. Images add interest to your pages but only if they are relevant. Don't include numerous photos of children, pets, motorcycles, or anything that will detract from your message—which is to sell your catering services.

Remember to make it easy for visitors to your site to get the information they need. Don't make them search all over your site for your e-mail address and phone number.

To Be or Not to Be Your Own Designer

If you are computer literate and have a good sense of design, you can build a nice-looking site using the free website builders (and sometimes free website hosting) offered by many e-mail or Internet service providers. Earthlink and Comcast both have free site builders. Another source for free web-building templates and assistance are web-hosting sites like GoDaddy.com, JustHost.com, PowerWeb.com, HostMonster.com, FatCow.com, SuperGreenHosting.com, and WebHostingPad.com.

If this isn't one of your talents, then you will want to have somebody design and install a site for you. Contact a local design school to hire a student, or look for nice websites online and get the webmaster's name. Ask for referrals. Don't hire anybody without seeing his or her work first. Hire somebody local and you may be able to barter your services.

Where Your Website Lives

There are thousands of places that will host your website, but the most convenient place could be your own Internet provider. Check with them first. Many Internet providers give you complimentary or low-cost website space.

Getting Hits

Your website isn't doing you any good if nobody can find it. Here are tips for getting hits whether you or somebody else is doing your site:

- Hustle for links

Your site can be ranked higher in search results if many links lead to it. Have anyone and everyone you know link to your site. Offer to put a link on your site to their site.

- Submit your site to multi-database pages

It is best to use a multiple-database submission service such as SubmitIt! to save you the time of contacting each search service separately.

- Key words

Put in key words that are repeated in the text of your site: "caterer, experienced caterer, Los Angeles, party planning, event planning," etc. Search engines rate your site higher the more often the key words show up in the actual text of your site.

Getting Referrals and Repeat Business

Referrals and repeat business are the name of the game in catering. When a satisfied client presells you to a colleague or a friend or calls you up to cater another party, you save time, money, and resources. Referral and repeat business are proof positive that you're building a reputation.

One of the best ways I know to get referrals and repeat business is to stay in touch with former clients. A good way is to write your own newsletter. A personal computer and $99 worth of software are all you need to produce a professional-looking document. I also use Constant Contact, an online marketing site (www.constantcontact.com; 866-876-8464). There is a free trial offer, period templates to choose from, and experts to help you. I picked a simple format, which allows my office to produce the newsletter in-house and keeps my company's name in front of my clients on a monthly basis. We send out pictures and recipes of food we have created. The newsletter generates a lot of correspondence. I suggest you write a few paragraphs about an event you've just catered, together with a recipe column and news on food trends. If you're feeling ambitious, you can always include reprints of articles (be sure to get permission from the original publisher). E-mail this newsletter to your client list as well as to local corporations, PTA groups, weight-control clinics, and doctors' offices in the area you want to target.

If a newsletter isn't the jam on your peanut butter sandwich, plan to send out a new menu postcard each month, or a recent party photograph, or a food treat to old clients and to anyone you'd like to have as a new client. Send food updates, holiday wishes, or entertaining tips; it's up to you. Or just pick up the phone and say hello.

If you need to light a fire under old clients to help you find new clients, consider offering them a referral fee: 5 or 10 percent of the net profit from any party you book as a result of their leads.

Advertising

When it comes to establishing your home-based catering business, I recommend that you get as much free publicity as you can before you think of running any ads other than a listing in the Yellow Pages.

An ad in the Yellow Pages is probably the best ad you can buy. Some people still use phone books, and the Yellow Pages have an online presence. Other types of advertising you might consider are radio spots (can be highly effective), sponsoring a Little League team (maximum goodwill), billboards (not as expensive as you think), ads in neighborhood newsletters (big bang, little bucks) or city magazines (big bucks, questionable bang), or a website (the possibility of major exposure).

Search out every online listing of local caterers and make sure you are on it. Do you have a culinary specialty that would interest particular groups? Do these groups post recipes? Contact them and find out if you can submit some of yours. Always include a nice photo. Always, always write simple, clear, easy-to-follow recipes (see

Ways to Write Clear Recipes, page 142). Always, always, always proofread your recipes before sending.

Devote time to posting on social media sites like Facebook, Twitter, Tumblr, and Pinterest. Create a LinkedIn profile and keep it updated. Let people know what you've got coming up and what jobs you've just finished (get permission from your clients before you use their names). Make it brief and upbeat, and include a few photos.

A blog can have a huge impact on your business if you do it right. Think of it as a way to expand upon your social media postings. If you think of your website as a brochure for your business, a blog is a peek into the life of your business. A blog offers you the space to include more photos (see Ten Tips for Making Food Photos Appetizing, page 137) and even links to your videos (which you can post for free on YouTube). You can post as much or as little as you want, but make a schedule to post every week or two.

Keep your blog posts short and sweet to retain your readers' attention; don't make them scroll down too far to get to the bottom or they will stop reading! Include a recipe and short anecdote, and mention upcoming events. Insert a few beautiful photos. My rule of thumb is the more frequently you send out advertising e-mails, the shorter those e-mails should be.

E-mail Marketing Services

All of the e-mail marketing services below offer services for a monthly fee based on the number of subscribers to your newsletter.

- AWeber—www.aweber.com
- Campaigner—www.campaigner.com
- Constant Contact—www.constantcontact.com
- iContact—www.icontact.com
- JangoMail—www.jangomail.com
- Mail Chimp—www.mailchimp.com

Ten Ways Not to Get Referrals or Repeat Business

1. Assume that your clients will give out your name for referrals without your asking them.
2. Take satisfied clients for granted and assume they'll never find another caterer.
3. Forget to write a thank-you note for a referral or favor a client did for you.
4. Don't compliment a client for solving a problem for you.
5. Make a client wait for an answer.
6. Don't apologize for a mistake you made.
7. Forget who is paying you.
8. Take yourself too seriously. You are not a rocket scientist; you are a caterer.
9. Hire staff and think you can teach them to be polite to your clients. Hire polite and considerate people to start with.
10. Think that problems are never your fault but always the client's fault.

My two problems with traditional advertising are these: How do I know I will reach the market I want, and why is it so expensive? I've had only moderate success when paying for advertising. An ad costs me $350 to $500 in my local paper, and if I book only one party, that's not a good return on my money. For $500 I can host a soiree at a swanky hotel suite, invite twenty VIPs, serve them superb Cabernet with my warm pesto Brie for an hour, and walk away with thirty to forty qualified leads for clients.

I suggest that you inform yourself about advertising by research, study, and inter-actions with professionals in the field. You can call up sales representatives from your local newspapers, magazines, radio stations, and Internet providers and have them show you the sales growth they track on successful accounts. Ask for a list of their satisfied clients. Or get in touch with professionals in your area who handle public relations and advertising. Ask them for a complimentary proposal of the services they would provide for you or the ads and placement they think you need. If you decide to go ahead, be sure to negotiate a campaign you can afford.

The Best Free Resource: The SBA

The Small Business Administration has a wealth of information for all types of small businesses. There is a page on their website (www.sba.gov) called Starting and Managing a Business.

- Starting a Business:
- Thinking About Starting a Business
- Create Your Business Plan
- Choose Your Business Structure
- Choose & Register Your Business
- Obtain Business Licenses & Permits
- Learn About Business Law & Regulations
- Finance Your Business
- Explore Loans, Grants & Funding
- Filing & Paying Taxes
- Choose & Register Your Business
- Choose Your Location & Equipment
- Hire & Retain Employees
- Managing a Business:
- Leading Your Company
- Growing Your Business
- Exporting
- Running Law Regulations
- Getting Out
- Business Guides by Industry
- Health Care
- Forms

To keep costs down, maybe you can trade a service or share expenses with other accounts they handle. Or how about collaborating with a rental company or the local wedding chapel for a spring ad?

However you decide to do it, advertising will keep your name in front of the public. Your goal is to have people know that your company is living, breathing, and ready to do business.

Tracking Your Success

As you generate new business, ask clients how they found you. Was it the magnets? The open house? The newsletter? Your blog? The ad you ran in the hospice magazine? The speech you gave on Career Day at your child's school? The story the food editor wrote about you in the local food pages? Keep track of your promotional ideas and stick with those that pay off. Before long you'll have the pleasure of seeing your business grow by leaps and bounds.

07

Using Photos and Recipes Effectively to Sell Your Home-Based Catering Business

Appetizing food photos and well-written recipes engage readers and tell a story about your food, your style, and your expertise. To get photos and recipes worth sharing, you'll need to approach them from your viewers' perspective. People are busy; don't make them work at understanding what they are looking at. Make your photos simple and colorful and your recipes brief and easy to understand.

Photos

Before whipping out your camera, or even making your food, decide what you want to accomplish. Do you want to create interest in one of your catering menus? Are you celebrating a season, an occasion, a type of food? Make sure your photograph isn't cluttered with irrelevant elements that distract the eye.

Will the photo be used large or small? The smaller the photo, the simpler the elements should be. Who are your intended viewers? Where are they from, and what would they find interesting? Would they be put off by photos of upscale food? Or would they be put off by anything as pedestrian as comfort food? A June newsletter featuring an incredible wedding cake will have a completely different look and feel than a web page featuring barbecue recipes.

I teach food-styling classes as well as catering across the United States. My career keeps growing. But, truly, my entire platform is food presentation. One of the food-styling workshops I teach is marketed to caterers, bloggers, and personal chefs. My goal is to make any artwork you put on your blog or website, in a newsletter, or on a recipe card look appealing.

Below are some cheap tricks for anybody to apply to his or her food photos. When I catered exclusively, I never had enough money in my budget to hire a professional photographer. That's why I learned to do it myself.

Whenever you cater an event, make an extra dish and set it aside to photograph during a lull or after you have served your guests. Keep sauces separate and greens undressed. Cover the food with several damp paper towels to prevent it from drying out. Arrange your entire menu on a counter or polished table. Use your smartphone, digital camera, or iPad to take a picture.

Learn easy photo-editing techniques with free apps. Not only is it fun, but you will have marketing pieces of your food at your fingertips!

Ten Tips for Making Food Photos Appetizing

1. Undercook your food. Food loses moisture as it cooks and shrinks as it cools. Cook food only long enough so that it no longer looks raw. You can always color too-light areas or apply heat with a kitchen torch, such as one you would use for crème brûlée.

2. Have an extra of what you're shooting so you can fill holes, prop up, or replace anything that doesn't look good. For example, make two grilled chicken breasts—one to photograph, one to use for patching.

3. Make sure your prep is meticulous. Go through the product and get rid anything wilted, old, or unsightly. Cut, chop, and slice precisely.

4. When designing a plate, consider color (contrasting or complimentary), texture, and balance.

5. Create elevation and movement. Prop pieces up from the back to create definition. Make a hidden base under food to hold it in place, using shortening, damp paper towels, cosmetic wedges, or even mashed potatoes.

6. Plan for the use of garnishes. Have appropriate herbs, lemons or limes, or extra ingredients to use if needed.

7. Know that cool food photographs better than hot food. Make cool or room temperature food look hot by adding moisture and shine. Brush with oil or mist with spray oil. You can also spray your food with water or brush with a little corn syrup.

8. Use any available light. If needed, use a shiny sheet pan, a white cutting board, or a hand mirror as a reflector for added light.

9. Study food photographs you like. What do they have in common?

10. Less is more. Appreciate how the camera's eye is different than your eye. You don't need to have a sliced mushroom in every square inch of your food to know that it contains sliced mushrooms; one or two will get your point across without making the image messy.

A Caterer's Food-Styling Kit

You can improve your photos by using professional food-styling equipment and tricks. Keep these items in a small tool bag and have them with you whenever you cook:

- Butane kitchen torch-top with fuel
- Purchase the inexpensive top that fits onto eight-ounce butane canisters (the same canisters used in portable burners) to quickly cook food surfaces, melt cheese, or brown fatty areas.
- Corn syrup

   Brush corn syrup onto the surface of meats to emphasize highlights and shine. Stir into thin sauces to add body or into thick sauces to thin down.
- Cosmetic sponges, wedge-shaped

   Use sponges to prop up food and adjust the angle for your camera. Use small pieces of sponge to lift and separate similar elements that look flat in photos (like pancakes).
- Cotton balls

   Give stuffed foods lightweight structure. Pull cotton balls apart a little bit and fill the center of omelets and burritos to keep them from collapsing.
- Cotton swabs

   Use cotton swabs for cleaning those tiny, hard-to-reach places.
- Denture cream

   Denture cream, like Polygrip or Fixodent, is designed to stick surfaces together in a warm, moist environment, making it a perfect glue for food. I use it to solve all kinds of food problems, including fixing broken pieces of meat; gluing pita bread together; holding fillings inside sliced items like stuffed meats, burritos, and wraps; and keeping slippery items in place.
- Fruit Fresh

   Fruit Fresh is an anti-oxidizing agent that keeps foods from browning. It also revives wilted greens and herbs.

- Heat gun or paint stripper

  It may look like a hair dryer but it gets much, much hotter. Use a heat gun to melt cheese, warm food surfaces, or even brown small areas of food.

- Kitchen Bouquet

  Kitchen Bouquet is a gravy browning agent made from caramelized vegetables. It can be used to color all kinds of foods and liquids. Add a tiny bit at a time to darken sauces or brush onto meats. Dilute it with water (about six parts water to one part Kitchen Bouquet) and store in a small spray bottle; spray lightly over meats and poultry to darken. Gravy Master is another popular brand.

- Museum Wax, Quake Hold, or Florist Clay

  Use these to hold items firmly in place. Sometimes that fork just doesn't want to stay on the rim of the plate—put a small bead of Museum Wax underneath the fork and it won't move.

- Rubbing alcohol

  Rubbing alcohol dissolves fat and grease. Dip a soft paintbrush in rubbing alcohol, then wipe very gently across the surface of a cut cake to remove excess frosting. The rubbing alcohol will evaporate in a few minutes and the cake will look perfect. This trick also dissolves the white fat that rises to the surface of cooked fish. Just remember to keep cleaning the fat or frosting off your paintbrush.

- Spray oil

  Lightly spray foods to add shine. This works for nearly everything except greens. Oil on greens looks greasy and makes them wilt very quickly. Spray oil will also make food look moist and hot long after it has cooled down and dried out.

- Small paintbrushes

  Have a dozen in a variety of sizes. I buy the cheap sets from discount and craft stores. They work great, are easy to replace, and I don't worry about ruining them.

- Spray bottles

  Have small (two- to four-ounce) bottles filled with water and browning spray. Browning spray works on most proteins; water refreshes the look of greens and, if you're close enough to see it, adds droplets of water to raw vegetables.

- Squeeze bottles

  Use these for precise placement of sauces and liquids.

- T-pins

  These work great to secure things together, like the slices of a spiral cut ham, wayward pasta, or layers of a sandwich.

- **Toothpicks**

  Use these like you would use T-pins, or use in place of your fingers to move stuff around and to keep food in place.

- **Vaseline**

  Use this to glue broken food together. Only use Vaseline on room temperature or cooler foods—it liquefies if it becomes too warm. Combine Vaseline with crumbs of food to patch holes.

- **Windex**

  Spray Windex on cosmetic sponges or swabs to remove smudges and mistakes from plates and glasses.

Recipes

There are a couple of rules to keep in mind when writing recipes. It doesn't matter how much or how little cooking experience your audience has, you should be as clear, consistent, and brief as you can. Follow a standard recipe format beginning with a title, header, and serving size, followed by ingredients and directions.

Titles

Use a title that is descriptive but not too long. Cinnamon Coffee Cake doesn't give very much information; Grandma Bea's Cinnamon Crunch Raisin Coffee Cake with Caramel and Fresh Blueberries is exhausting; but Grandma Bea's Cinnamon Crunch Coffee Cake is nice.

Headers

Headers are where you can expand upon the ingredients, origins, ethnicity, and preparation notes, or insert your personality, sense of humor, and memories. A header can be placed before a recipe or between the recipe name and the ingredients.

Serving Size

Serving sizes should be kept to four or six servings unless you are giving a recipe for cookies, sauces, or other items usually made in larger batches.

Ingredients

Always list ingredients in the order they are used in the directions. If an ingredient is used twice, put both usages on the same line.

It makes no difference whether you use "tablespoons" or "tbsp." as long as you are consistent. If you shorten "tablespoon" to "tbsp.," you should also shorten "pound" to "lb." and "ounce" to "oz."

When using a packaged amount of an ingredient, like canned whole tomatoes, specify the package or can size: "1 (28-ounce) can whole tomatoes."

If an ingredient needs to be at room temperature (or warm or chilled), state this in the ingredient list: "1½ cup unsalted butter, at room temperature."

Be specific when listing ingredients that are available in different varieties, like milk (whole, low fat, nonfat?). Include garnishes in your ingredient list.

Directions

Be specific, simple, and clear. List steps in the order that you prepare them. (See "Ways to Write Clear Recipes," page 142, for excellent recipe writing tips.) End recipes with serving instructions: "Let cool 5 minutes before slicing and serving." Or "Spoon sauce over top and serve immediately."

Recipe Example

Tangerine Spinach Salad
Makes 6 servings

This colorful, fresh salad has pistachio nuts, dates, and a slightly sweet dressing that complements the spinach. This recipe can be doubled or tripled, and the dressing can be made up to two days ahead if refrigerated in an airtight container.

Ingredients

1 (5-ounce) package baby spinach
⅓ cup olive oil
2 tablespoons seasoned rice vinegar
½ teaspoon salt
¼ teaspoon ground black pepper

2 tangerines, peeled and segmented
6 dates, pitted and sliced
⅓ cup thinly sliced red onion
¼ cup shelled pistachios
4 ounces crumbled feta cheese

Directions

Place spinach in a large bowl. Place olive oil, vinegar, salt, and pepper in a medium bowl and whisk until creamy. Pour over spinach and toss to coat. Add remaining ingredients, tossing to coat. Serve immediately.

Ways to Write Clear Recipes

There is no one better than writing and editing everything culinary than Dianne Jacob. She is the author of Will Work for Food: The Complete Guide to Writing Cookbooks, Blogs, Reviews, Memoir, and More. The suggestions below are from her fun and informative blog, www.diannej.com/b.

- Writing is rewriting, as the saying goes, and that applies to recipe writing too. When I'm editing recipes for clients, whether individuals or publishers, part of my job is to line edit. That means rewriting to make the instructions clearer.

- Line editing requires constant vigilance. I tighten, choose the most specific word, clarify, and strive for elegance. There's a fine line between spelling everything out and not being too obvious. Sometimes I vote for the reader and common sense instead of more explanation.

- Avoid mixtures. This kind of instruction makes me crazy: "Mix together two mixtures with a mixer, and then mix the mixtures together in a mixing bowl." First of all, there are six uses of versions of "mix" in one sentence. That's just nuts! If you keep referring to "mixtures," your reader has to go back and figure out which ones you're talking about. And trust me, you never want to mix up your reader. Substitute specific words or terms for a mixture, such as batter, custard, wet ingredients, and dry ingredients. And for heaven's sake, don't add more "mix" words to make your sentence even more confusing.

- Set aside "set aside." I don't like overused terms, especially superfluous ones. Here's an example: "Prepare a pan. Set aside. Combine the apples and sugar. Set aside. Prepare the mixture. Set aside." Stop setting things aside. Just go on with your recipe.

- No need for two words that mean the same thing. You don't need the word "in" for these examples: "Add in the cold water." "Gradually add in the flour." Just add it.

- Trim, trim, trim. Verbosity is one of the most common problems for editors, and I've got plenty of examples:

- "Roll out the dough with a rolling pin." What else are readers going to roll it out with? Stick with "Roll out the dough." Similarly, "Place the cookies 2 inches apart from one another" works just as well by eliminating the words "from one another."

- Replace the sentence "Transfer to the refrigerator to chill" with the word "chill."

- No need to say "Place in the oven" when just "bake" or "roast" works fine.

- There's rarely a reason to tell people to remove food from the oven either.

- No need to top with a topping. "Spread the chocolate topping on top of the cake." Hmm. I'm either getting rid of top or topping, since both don't work in one sentence. I changed it to a sauce. A chocolate topping and a chocolate sauce are similar enough.

- Things don't begin to happen—they happen. There's usually no reason to say, "When the soup begins to boil." Nothing is lost if you just write "When the soup boils."

- Write like you talk. I like recipes that read the way that someone talks. No one ever says, "To a large oven-safe sauté pan, add the butter and melt it." Besides, starting a sentence with an action verb is livelier. So try "Add the butter to a large oven-safe sauté pan and melt it over medium-high heat."

- No permission needed. No need to let or allow objects to do things, such as "Allow the cake to cool" or "Let the soaked beans sit on the counter overnight." For the first sentence, the word "cool" is sufficient in its entirety. For the second, "Soak beans overnight at room temperature" is sufficient and specific.

- Don't state the obvious. If you end a recipe with "Serve hot, cold, warm, or at room temperature," what's left? There is no other way to serve it. I deleted the sentence. Since the writer had no preference, there's no need to mention it.

- I'll leave you with a good one, on the same theme. I found this line at the end of an ice cream recipe: "Serve frozen."

08

Crunching the Numbers

When you're putting together your first event, it may seem easier to gather your receipts, pay as many expenses as you can by personal check, and figure out the rest the morning after. This is not a good idea, because it may tempt you to leave everything for later. Before you know it, you won't be able to take a step without treading on bills and invoices, and what is worse, you won't know the economic health of your business in any objective way.

I recommend that instead of letting things pile up or running your business by the seat of your pants, you make an appointment with a good accountant. Read this chapter to acquaint yourself with your options and then work with your accountant to arrive at a bookkeeping system that will help you manage your business, which is the whole point of a bookkeeping system. Not only does it help you operate your business in a professional manner, but also it allows you to keep track of your income and expenses in such a way that you can analyze where your business is going. Is it hard to do? Absolutely not, so long as you do it every day. It takes me an average of eight minutes a day!

One of my friends spent her first year in business without using any particular system. She paid her purveyors' bills as soon as she received them (never thinking she might negotiate more favorable payment terms and thus hold on to her money longer), extended credit to her clients (a terrible idea, and one designed to put you out of business), and never had enough information on hand to anticipate cash flow. Then, at the end of the year, she invested in a computer bookkeeping program. "It's changed my life," she said to me. "I had no idea how much money I was spending on anything. For example, I spent way too much on new equipment, considering my income. [Your accountant will tell you that you can deduct only a maximum of $10,000 for equipment purchases, without amortization, as a direct expense, so it really doesn't make sense to purchase, as opposed to lease, more.] I also paid top dollar for a lot of the food I bought. Had I realized how much produce I was buying from one particular purveyor, I might have thought to negotiate a better price." The new bookkeeping program she's been working with keeps her business in the black and gives her access to an incredible amount of useful information.

Making Good Use of Your Accountant

Unless you are already an accounting whiz, I suggest that you sit down with your accountant as soon as possible to discuss the following five issues:

Record keeping. As a caterer, you will need to keep track of your equipment (some inevitably gets lost, broken, or abused), your inventory of food stock (if you do have a kitchen and keep stock on hand), your labor, your consumables (paper, streamers, decorations, and other disposables), your dishware, your rentals of both equipment and locations, and so on. This chapter discusses a variety of ways to keep track of all these important bits of information, from manual bookkeeping to bookkeeping by computer. Your accountant, who should know the scope of your business as well as you yourself do, is in an excellent position to advise you on which system will work best for you.

Establishing a chart of accounts. To keep accurate books you must have a consistent set of categories to put individual items of income and expense into. This set of categories is called a chart of accounts, and it should accurately reflect your day-to-day business activities as closely as possible. Moreover, you should set it up well before you pay your first dollar to launch your new business.

First, set up a checking account to be used only for your catering business. Next, consult your accountant for help in setting up a chart of accounts. You'll find a sample basic chart of accounts in the sidebar on page 149. As you can see, there are separate categories under food costs for staples, poultry, fish, and so on. This level of detail allows you to track your various costs as part of an overall effort to determine which items are the most profitable. Unless the items are broken down into meaningful categories, you won't have the information you need to analyze your expenditures or to cut better deals with vendors.

Say that after six months in business you notice that people are buying much more fish from you than chicken or meat. The trend is easy to see because "fish" is a separate item in your chart of accounts. Armed with this information, you can say to your fish vendor, "Hey, I've spent $500 [or $1,000 or $5,000] with you over the past six months. That's quite a bit of money. How about cutting me a discount any month I spend more than $100 [or $200 or $1,000]?" Without this information you'll be at a disadvantage. In fact, you may lose parties to other caterers in your market area who have been able to cut better deals with purveyors based on their analysis of their own chart of accounts.

Understanding the difference between cash-basis and accrual-basis accounting. Until several years ago it was popular, and legal, for many businesses to use a type of accounting called accrual basis. This method accounts for income and expenses not as they are paid for or received, but against the job or party to which they are allocated. For example, let's say that you had a party in January of 2014 and were paid a deposit in December of 2013. That income would not, under the accrual-basis method, be legally "received" by you until after the party in January 2014. Likewise, the monies you pay, either in December 2013 or January 2014, that are directly attributable to that party would not be "received" or "spent" according to your books until after the party in January 2014.

Obviously this was a popular way for many small businesses to not pay taxes on money they received until the following tax year, so in 1987 the US Congress closed the loophole for most people who were using it, such as small businesses. Most small businesses, even small corporations, must now use cash-basis accounting, and most must—unless there are extremely good reasons that your accountant will use to convince the IRS—be on a calendar-year basis. This means that unless your accountant devises some way for you to avoid it, you will have to declare income when you receive it and also deduct expenses when you pay them, and your "tax year" for your business will have to be the same as your "personal" tax year: January 1 through December 31. It is still important, however, to understand the concept of accrual-basis accounting for your budgeting purposes.

For example, let's say you have that big party on January 14, 2014, and you know you will have to buy a lot of food and pay for a lot of expenses a few days before the party; yet you've received a big deposit on December 3, 2013 and you know you'll be taxed on that even though most of it really won't be your net income—it will go for event expenses. What do you do? Probably it would be a good idea to take as much of that money as possible and prepay as many of the event items as possible. Often your location fee will be refundable, except for a small nonrefundable deposit if you cancel within ten days. If you prepay the location expense in December, you have shifted out much of the deposit you received, and if your event is canceled or postponed more than ten days before January 14, you can still get your money back from the location; you did not have to bear the tax expense on your deposit either. These are techniques that a good accountant will teach you, and the more experienced you become, the less often you will have to call him or her to ask how to handle a particular thorny situation.

Understanding the difference between gross and net profit. Generally your gross profit on an event is what you make on an event after paying the expenses allocated specifically to that event only. So it is obvious that if you get paid $10,000 for an event and it costs $2,000 for a location, $2,000 for food, $1,000 for labor, and $1,000 for other supplies that went into that event (for a total of $6,000), you have made $4,000—or have you? What about your car, your equipment rental, and your other overhead? When you deduct these later costs, you get to "net before tax profit." Then you still have taxes to pay before you get to the money you keep to live on.

For you to stay in business, it is essential that you know the amount of your overhead; and if you are just starting, you must be able to project the amount of what your overhead will be. Otherwise you will not end up with anything at the end of the year. Overhead items include the expenses you pay to stay in business that cannot be assigned to one specific event. Examples of these are rent, equipment lease payments, labor costs that are not hourly such as secretarial support, professional fees such as accountants and lawyers, insurance, the cost of the use of your vehicles, and the amount of any purchased equipment such as computers and kitchen equipment.

It is important that you make sure there is enough "gross profit" to cover a "pro rata" share of your overhead. This pro rata share of overhead that is assigned to each event is often what people tend to forget to include in figuring out what they need to charge to break even. These expenses are just as real as the costs of food, waiters, and location. Your accountant will assist you in determining this figure, but there are two basic ways to approach it.

One, probably the one you will start with, is on a calendar basis: You add up all of your overhead for the year (including your estimated taxes and an estimate of what you need to pull out of the business to live on), divide the total by twelve, and the result is a monthly amount of money attributable to overhead. If you have two parties in one month, you add to each event's out-of-pocket expenses one-half of your monthly overhead. If you have six events in one month (lucky you), you need only to be sure that you add one-sixth of one month's overhead to break even.

A different method is a dollar percentage. You and your accountant add to each dollar of direct-event expense a markup percentage that includes your margin for overhead, plus taxes, plus net profit (the amount you intend to pull out of the business). This is harder to arrive at, but standard industry markup figures do exist. The problem with both of these methods is that they assume regular future business and do not necessarily take into account your start-up costs.

Your accountant will be invaluable in assisting you with this very critical calculation. Remember, if you add on too much, you will not be competitive; if you add on too little, you will not have enough money to pay the actual costs of running your business. Computer programs such as Quicken or Microsoft Money, which are discussed on page 152, can assist you with these calculations. For example, assuming that you have entered the appropriate information on your expenses, you can use Money to calculate your overhead expenses as a percentage of your total expenses.

Taxes. Taxes, as the old saying goes, are inevitable. When you are in business for yourself, they are also confusing. What your employer used to take care of, you must now take care of yourself. Suddenly you find yourself paying quarterly estimated taxes on your income, your own social security tax, sales taxes on your goods and services, and withholding and social security taxes on your employees' income.

Because taxes vary from locality to locality, be sure to check with your accountant to find out exactly what your responsibilities are. In the United States we generally pay on an honor system; the government expects us to keep track of our transactions, report them accurately, and then have the money on hand to pay

Possible Business Deductions

Accounting fees	Depreciation expenses	Office supplies
Advertising	Dues to industry groups	Partial entertainment
Attorney's fees	Gifts	Portfolio materials
Automobile use	Home office	Rent: kitchen
Bad debts	Insurance	Salaries, bonuses,
Conventions and	Interest	and commissions
trade shows	License fees	

the relevant taxes in a timely fashion. This is where a lot of small businesses get in trouble—their owners do not plan well and do not have the money on hand to pay their taxes when due. The government can, and often does, assess interest and penalties and may even take your possessions. In fact, you can even be thrown in jail! As a preventive measure, you must work out a plan with your accountant for paying your taxes on a timely basis.

This is an area where you can't afford to make a mistake. For example, if you have employees who require withholding (be sure to check with your accountant, as you may need to withhold money even for waiters you use only a couple of times a year) and you fail to withhold the appropriate taxes, you can quickly get in arrears and then in serious trouble. The same is true for sales tax or your own estimated taxes. If you have put in enough hard work to make a net profit and you have not prepaid your own taxes, you could be liable for a penalty plus interest. A small business can quickly be buried by tax liabilities like these.

This book will not, and cannot, address the tax issue in more detail (except to list the types of deductions a caterer ought to keep track of—see sidebar below), because taxes vary widely from location to location and the tax laws are constantly changing. Consult your trusty accountant without delay.

Accounting Systems

Several types of accounting systems are currently in use: manual systems, professional bookkeeping companies, computer software systems, and the "I have no system until I panic at the end of the tax-reporting quarter" system. For obvious reasons, try to avoid the latter.

The manual system has several points in its favor. First of all, it is the least expensive to acquire. Examples of this system are the "one-write" and "pegboard" types of devices that incorporate ledger cards with the checks you write. Each time you write a check, you put the appropriate ledger card under it, and a carbon copy of the check amount is made on the ledger card. You will have one ledger card for each bookkeeping account listed in your chart of accounts. For instance, when you write a check for your monthly business telephone bill, you would put the "telephone and messenger" ledger card under the check so that as you write the check, the same information is recorded on the card. If you do this faithfully, you will always have accurate, up-to-date information about what you have spent for each category in your chart of accounts. A good source for these systems is NEBS business forms, and

Sample Basic Chart of Accounts

	JANUARY	FEBRUARY	MARCH	FIRST QUARTER TOTALS
INCOME				
Prop rental income				
Food income				
Entertainment income				
Design income				
Consulting income				
TOTAL INCOME				
EXPENSES				
Auto expense				
Books				
Cleaning				
Uniform rental				
Rental of kitchen				
Rental of event location				
Permits				
Equipment lease				
Telephone				
Utilities				
Kitchen salaries				
Office salaries				
Taxes				
Insurance				
Advertising				
Entertainment				
Food costs				
Fish				
Meat				
Poultry				
Produce				
Staples				
Other				
Prepared food costs				
Desserts				
Appetizers				
Juices, mineral water, soft drinks				
Other beverages				
TOTAL EXPENSES				
NET PROFIT (LOSS)				

they can be reached at (800) 225-6380 or on the web at www.nebs.com. NEBS also has a nice assortment of invoices and other forms.

There are drawbacks to this system, however. You must total it manually; in other words, you will not have a current total unless you manually add the items on the card each time. If you write one check to cover items that ought to be on several accounting cards, you're in trouble. For example, if you write a check to a purveyor who sells you both fish and meat and you have separate accounts for fish and meat, you will have a hard time splitting the amounts. Because it is a manual system, it does not have anywhere near the speed and flexibility of a computer, which, if time is money, is worth a fortune in savings.

Another option is to use a professional bookkeeping service. These companies come into your workplace periodically (or you drop off your checkbook at their offices) to input your check register into a computerized accounting system, which will then give you and your accountant the information you need in the appropriate format. These companies can also handle payroll and deposits to the appropriate taxing agencies. Another advantage of using one of these services is that you can call and speak to someone who can explain things to you, which can be reassuring when your business is in its infancy. Another plus is that you pay as you go. There is little or no initial investment, and there is no need to learn computer programs. So if you are easily frustrated and want to leave the bookkeeping expertise to others, you can hire someone to take care of your books for you.

The disadvantages of using an outside service to do your bookkeeping are (1) you are dependent on others to give you access to the information you need about how your business is running, (2) in the long run an outside service is more expensive, and (3) you will have no real incentive or opportunity to become acquainted with the ins and outs of computers and how they can make your life easier and more efficient.

Computers save so much time that, in my opinion, it is a very serious error in business judgment not to use them. Some of you may have been using the excuse that you're a chef, an artist who is "too creative for such mundane things" (I know, because I used this excuse myself for many years). Nevertheless, if you have been afraid to learn how to use business accounting software or have not yet had the chance, my advice is: "Get over it—fast!" A computerized business system allows you to generate checks and have that information automatically entered into your accounting system. Some of these systems will even keep track of your estimated taxes, create detailed reports, allow you to view spending histories, and track payments on invoices. The cost savings in bookkeeping and accountants' fees are phenomenal. The only drawbacks to a computerized accounting system are (1) the initial cost of the hardware and software and (2) your "learning curve" in studying how to use the programs. I recommend that you spend about $500 to $1,200 for a computer system plus $50 to $200 more for some accounting software, and thus enter the modern era of information access.

Buying Computers and Software

There are two major types of consumer computer systems currently available: Windows-based PC systems and Apple systems. They both have their good points, and you can most likely use whatever computer you currently own. Windows-based systems are somewhat less expensive, but Apple has a friendly user interface. I recently changed our systems over to Apple and I do find them easier to operate. Having said that, PCs are used much more often in the catering business, and many specialized catering software programs will work only on a PC.

I suggest getting a laptop or notebook computer, and if it is your first one, you might want to get a well-known brand with a well-developed support system, such as Dell, Samsung, or Lenovo. Notebooks and laptops are designed to be light and transportable, which means you can take them with you from job to job, location to location, and then home again. They can weigh three pounds or less and are just as fast and can hold as much information as the larger, non-portable desktop computers. For example, you can get an entry-level notebook computer for under $400.

You will also need a printer. I've been using Hewlett-Packards for years and am very happy with them. These ink-jet printers cost between $100 and $200 and print all the letters, invoices, accounting statements, and other information you will need to print beautifully. They are also compatible with most major brands of computers and most major software programs.

Word Processing Programs. For word processing I recommend that you use Microsoft Word, which includes not only a spell checker but also a grammar-checking program.

Accounting Programs. In my opinion, when it comes to bookkeeping software, Microsoft Money Plus Home and Business, Intuit QuickBooks, AccountEdge, and

Peachtree are all excellent programs that will allow you to track all of your income and expenses by the categories you choose. You can keep track of your income and expenses per job as well as per time period. If you elect to use their check-writing functions, these programs will fill in checks that you buy specifically for your printer.

Once you're up and running, these programs will generate cash flow reports, income statements, balance sheets, and much more. They track payables and receivables, print payroll checks, and generate invoices.

Invoicing

Some people are shy when it comes to invoicing. You can rest assured that many clients will gleefully take advantage of this. As I've said before, be sure to get at least a 50 percent deposit when you sign a contract. If your client has a hard time giving you a deposit, he or she will be worse when it comes time to collect the balance. I have developed a rule of thumb: Never, ever spend any of my own money for someone else's event; that is what the deposit money is for. The easiest way to get burned is by "last-minute manipulators." This is the name I give to people who tell you that they need you for a last-minute rush job the day after next and they can't possibly give you a check at the time because they are out of checks, and the president of the company is on vacation, and the checks are cut only on Wednesday out of the accounting office, or some such story. You can bet dollars to doughnuts that if you ever get paid, it will be weeks or months after the event and after many angry calls by you.

Also be sure to get the entire balance owed you three, four, or five days before the day of the event, because this is the last time that you will have effective leverage with your client. Collecting all the money before the event is strictly good sales technique and policy. You can do this in a professional manner by letting your client know that these are the only terms you work with. You'll be happy to do the work for them, but because you will lay out a lot of time, talent, knowledge, and your reputation to make their party happen, you feel that the goodwill must flow both ways

The Artist versus the Businessperson: Why So Many Caterers Fail

Someone once said that the greatest thing in the world is to have the freedom to do what you love to do. Why didn't Mr. Someone just come out and say the greatest thing in the world is money? You may be great at what you do, love what you're doing, have lots of talent, new friends, and business booked, but if you are not making a profit, your company is not going to last. If you continue not to make a profit, your catering business is a hobby, and an expensive one at that.

Far too many people in catering love what they are doing but overlook the obvious fact of life that they have to support themselves—until ugly reality knocks at the door or comes in the mail. You need vision, drive, enthusiasm, and faith to succeed, but I suggest that you do not mislead yourself into thinking that these merits alone will sustain you. You need to be very practical and make your business work within a financial framework. Once you are on solid financial ground, you can feel secure that you have created a company that will sustain you artistically as well as financially.

Catering can be lucrative, exciting, and fun. Is there anything wrong with being a rich artist?

09

Setting the Stage for a Successful Party

Before you do anything, make sure you have a signed contract or proposal from your client, a minimum guest guarantee, and half the cost of the party in your hand. Put every party on paper. Invent a system of checklists to use for every one. Checklists make your preparations disaster-proof.

Before the Party

You've worked out a theme with your client. Now get set to roll up your sleeves and make it happen.

Get estimates and references; interview subcontractors for job bids as designers, florists, entertainers, and photographers. This is what full-service catering is all about. It's standard practice to mark up all support-service fees by 10 to 20 percent and include the cost in your bill. You need this cushion to reimburse your company for time, telephone calls, expertise, and coordinating skills.

It's well worth your while to use your best sales techniques to convince your client to buy these services from you. Even if clients hire these services themselves, you still end up as coordinator. Why? Because the caterer is the party's ringmaster. All these other services depend on how and at what time you serve the food.

At the very least, charge a coordination fee. Clients will understand if you explain the time you must spend on their event. Don't give away time or ideas. They are something you provide for a fee, just like quality food.

You will need to have signed contracts or agreements with all the subcontractors you use, and you will have to provide them with deposit money to reserve their time. It is important to stay in touch with them through the months of preplanning. Don't assume they know what you or your client expects. Each party is different.

Two weeks before each party, I send/e-mail an information sheet, "Information You Should Know Before the Party," to all subcontractors. I follow through with a phone call to verify that they've received it, and I ask them to review it with me by phone. This information includes the exact location of the party and how to get there, the amount of time they are expected to put in, and the time they should arrive for setup. I add instructions about where they can park, what they should wear, and where they can change clothes if necessary. I let them know whether or not the client is paying for them to eat, too. I remind them that drugs of any kind are illegal. I ask if they'll need a closet with a lock to secure any additional items and whether they have insurance for their equipment—and for themselves—in case the host's insurance doesn't cover them.

While I'm writing up this information, I make a separate list for myself:

- Order an extra tablecloth for the disc jockey's card table.
- Bring extra black duct tape to secure the photographer's cables and light cords.
- Check to see that the buffet tables are strong enough to support the designer's props.
- Bring cosmetic sponges and facial tissue for blotting the makeup of the costumed servers.

Greening Your Party

- Use potted flowering plants, herbs, or even vegetables for your centerpieces and tabletop decor. Grasses and succulents can also be used beautifully. Arrange on risers, in baskets, or place together in larger pots to achieve the look you want. Wrap containers in inexpensive fabric and tie with a ribbon so guests can take home as a party favor.

- Rent real dishes and napkins instead of using disposables.

- Highlight a specific local product or ingredient on your menu.

- Set up separate waste containers for recyclable items, clearly marked to make it easy for your guests. Every little bit helps!

Two weeks before each party, I send/e-mail an information sheet, "Information You Should Know Before the Party," to all subcontractors. I follow through with a phone call to verify that they've received it, and I ask them to review it with me by phone. This information includes the exact location of the party and how to get there, the amount of time they are expected to put in, and the time they should arrive for setup. I add instructions about where they can park, what they should wear, and where they can change clothes if necessary. I let them know whether or not the client is paying for them to eat, too. I remind them that drugs of any kind are illegal. I ask if they'll need a closet with a lock to secure any additional items and whether they have insurance for their equipment—and for themselves—in case the host's insurance doesn't cover them.

While I'm writing up this information, I make a separate list for myself:

- Order an extra tablecloth for the disc jockey's card table.
- Bring extra black duct tape to secure the photographer's cables and light cords.
- Check to see that the buffet tables are strong enough to support the designer's props.
- Bring cosmetic sponges and facial tissue for blotting the makeup of the costumed servers.

Mistakes happen if you don't double-check and put everything in writing. At one party, a black-tie affair, we were expecting a three-piece jazz combo, but the musicians arrived dressed in Hawaiian shirts with conga drums! At another party a wedding cake was delivered to the wrong restaurant, and I had to carry five tiers of spun-sugar bridges, fountains, and figurines through heavy traffic on a busy street. One time flowers arrived so late that we passed them out as good-bye gifts to departing guests.

My worst mistake was hiring a photographer who smoked in the bathroom, set off the smoke detector, and brought out the local fire department. I had to evacuate 300 guests and my entire staff five minutes before dinner was to be served and keep them out until the firemen discovered the culprit in a stall in the john.

Rule of thumb: Make it easy on yourself and others by discussing your expectations for their performance days before the event.

Organizing Your Time and the Party Setup

If you didn't have time to visit the location at the time you wrote the proposal, go now. Preview the site at the same time of day that the party will be held. Are there parking restrictions at this time? Traffic? Barking dogs? Garbage cans waiting for pickup? Are there adequate lights, safe walkways, temperature changes, or strong winds? Will you need a security guard to watch gifts or to keep out party crashers? Do you have the cell phone number of every person involved with the party for emergencies? Do you know the closest hospital? If you rent a van, is there a place to park it, with easy access to the kitchen? Where are you going to seat the guests for dinner? Is the location on different levels, and will you need a set of walkie-talkies to keep in touch with your waiter three flights up?

You can kill two birds with one stone by meeting the representative from the rental company you're working with at the same time you do the site inspection. Ask him or her for suggestions and help with your logistical problems. Most rental companies will draw up blueprints or layouts free of charge. They can draw details of seating to scale as well as buffet arrangements or temporary kitchen facilities. No matter how small the party, get professional input before you even move a couch to make room for a single table. Rental companies are successful because of referrals and repeat customers. They'll do the little jobs in the hope of getting bigger ones.

After your site inspection, build a comprehensive rental list. If your client decides that he or she wants a dance floor or a tent in the backyard, a rental company will handle such special needs.

For one wedding I catered, the hostess ran out of room in her backyard as the guest count grew. I called a rental company, and they covered the swimming pool with wooden scaffolding and Astroturf. Another fifty guests were seated there for dinner.

Some rental companies give caterers cash commissions or discounts at the end of each fiscal quarter based on the amount of business the caterer brings in. Sometimes they give a referral fee for directing the client to them and allowing the rental company to deal on its own with the client. (If you do this, though, get a copy of the rental list to make sure you get everything you need.)

Whether you rent or the client rents depends on what you are comfortable with. How much time do you have, and how much can you handle? The more you take on, the more careful you must be in budgeting your time and money, but the greater your opportunity for profit.

Another option is for you to invest in some catering gear yourself. Often home-based caterers end up catering small parties or weekly service clubs like Kiwanis or Elks consistently enough that they feel it's a worthwhile investment to buy dishes and flatware. You bill the client for the use of this equipment, which pays for itself after only a few parties. The money you generate this way soon becomes a fund for the purchase of more equipment.

For example: My partner and I bought beautiful burnished-brass chafers. They were better looking than any offered by the rental companies, yet I charged my clients half the going rental rate. After only twelve parties the chafers had paid for themselves. And then I found that if I needed to sweeten the pie in a competitive bid, I let clients have them at no charge. It was cheaper than giving food or my time away, yet it provided goodwill and stimulated referrals. And the chafers still looked great after 10,000 parties—they held up better than I did!

Setup Times

Estimated Time	Type of Function
½ hour	simple cocktail party, nearby delivery door
1 hour	simple party, distant delivery door
1½ hours	simple party, distant delivery door, heavy equipment
1½ hours	buffet, nearby delivery door, medium setup, moderate equipment
2 hours	buffet, distant delivery door, medium setup, moderate equipment
2½ hours	complex cocktail reception, nearby delivery door, heavy equipment
3 hours	sit-down dinner, nearby delivery door, heavy equipment
4 hours	very complex party with multiple food-serving stations and heavy equipment

At your first meeting and on-site inspection, decide the time your rentals must arrive and begin to estimate how long it will take to unload, set up, and break down the party. Study the party layout and place an X on each spot where you need personnel. Can you do it alone? If not, how long do you think each job will take?

Try to anticipate the amount of time for everything by walking through the party and the menu on paper from start to finish. Will you need an extra pair of hands to unload the van because there is no elevator? What about that grill ten minutes away from the kitchen in the backyard? Where can you put the bar so that it is easy for guests to get to it the moment they arrive without blocking anything or anyone? And do you have the rental representative's cell phone number or the driver's beeper number in case you've forgotten something?

I've gone as far as taking pictures of the location, props, and sample floral pieces to be sure that I know what I've discussed with a client. After the party the pictures go into my portfolio.

Moral of the story: Don't leave any pieces of your party to chance.

The Menu and Start-Up

If your client is having trouble deciding on the menu and the party is just two weeks away, stop suggesting items and tell the client that you'll choose. Usually this makes a client decide quickly. A common mistake of new caterers is allowing clients to make last-minute decisions and changes. They cost you money, time—and profit. Clients can be just like children about testing your limits. Some of them will run you ragged if they think they can get away with it.

Prepare kitchen "prep" sheets. These are lists describing the jobs that have to be done for your menu. Distribute the jobs over several days. Do anything you can several days early (but be sure to save chores like washing the lettuce till the very end). To come up with the most complete prep sheets, pretend that you are not going to be at the party and write the prep sheets as instructions for someone else. Give this someone else as much information as you can. Start your prep lists with the appetizers and move through the courses. List everything you have contracted for, down to coffee with cream and sugar or herbal tea. If peanuts are to be served at the bar, write it down. It is the only way I know to guarantee you won't forget to serve anything.

Underneath each menu item on your kitchen prep sheet, make a note of special equipment you will need to bring on the day of the event and how each dish will be served. Here is a sample prep sheet:

APPETIZERS FOR 25 GUESTS

Items: 3 types passed cold, 2 served warm (50 pieces each) = 10 pieces per guest = 250 total pieces

First item: 50 fluted ½-inch-tall cucumber rounds with 1 ounce piped salmon-cream mousse and lemon-fan garnish

Pack: pastry bag, star tip

Serve: silver tray with pink doilies, onion flower as tray centerpiece

Prepare at kitchen: Slice cucumbers, whip cream cheese, and make smoked salmon mousse. Slice lemons into fans. Pack all components, individually wrapped in plastic containers, in a foil pan. Cover with film wrap and label. Finish on-site.

Wrapped carefully in plastic containers, this appetizer can be prepared the day before the party. By placing all the components together, you save the trouble of trying to find something in the confusion of unpacking on the site. In general, pack ingredients for each course together. In this example you have designed an appetizer "kit." You could easily delegate the finishing work to someone else now. He or she has all the ingredients, equipment, and presentation instructions.

Break down every menu item this way so that your staff won't waste time looking for items that aren't there. With this method, if you have forgotten something, you'll discover it sooner—all you'll need to do is check your list.

From these prep lists you will be able to build your order sheet. Your order sheet is your shopping list. An organized order sheet should be easy to read and help keep your budget in line. I highlight products with colored pens when the orders are placed and confirmed.

At first, order sheets can be broken down into food groups; later on, as you become more experienced, you'll probably break them down by purveyors.

A blank piece of paper divided into four squares will get you started. Write "Meats/Seafoods" in the first square, "Produce" in the second, "Dry Goods/Paper Products" in the third, and "Dairy/Baked Goods" in the fourth. List the products you need directly from your prep sheets. If you have your pantry or kitchen set up as discussed in chapter 2, take inventory first and use as much stuff as you have on hand.

MEATS/SEAFOODS:

4 pounds salmon

_____

_____

_____

_____

_____

_____

_____

PRODUCE:

12 cucumbers

2 heads iceberg lettuce

10 lemons

_____

_____

_____

_____

DRY GOODS/PAPER PRODUCTS:

doilies

plastic containers

foil

napkins

_____

_____

_____

DAIRY/BAKED GOODS:

cream cheese

pastry shells

_____

_____

_____

_____

You'll make decisions about what food to make and what food to buy for every party you cater. You'll learn to balance the menu ingredients by cost, quality, time, preparation, and presentation. You'll learn to have every single menu item you can prepped or partially cooked the day before the party.

I have experimented with all kinds of food over the years, looking for dishes that can be made ahead. I find that a good many, in fact, taste better made ahead than cooked at the last minute. Lasagna is a prime example of something that tastes better the second day, so cook it the day before the party and just reheat it on-site. Bourbon cake also tastes better when it's been baked ahead and wrapped, resting for a week. Black bean soup with ham hocks is another dish that's best the second day, when the flavors have melded and are rich and smoky.

As your parties grow in size, you'll learn the necessity of what I call "food suspension." This is the art of storing perfectly prepped food in the refrigerator for a day or two, just waiting to be finished. Experiment and test items yourself. I bet you know some already, such as marinated flank steak or chicken teriyaki on skewers.

Sometimes it will be well worth your while to buy certain products already prepared. For example, when I first met my partner, she'd stay up all night baking rolls for the parties she catered. She thought that because she was a caterer, she had to make everything herself. After we got together, I convinced her to buy the best rosemary-garlic rolls from a local bakery instead. I suggested that she could put those baking hours she saved into something else she really needed—like sleep.

I spend a lot of time looking for new products, trying samples of ready-made items, and discovering wholesale caterers' products I can buy and highlight on my menus. I am careful to pick caterers, purveyors, and manufacturers who sell only high-quality products. It's important that the food products you purchase are fresh and uncontaminated and have been handled with the utmost care to ensure their safety. Whenever something is delivered that you are doubtful about—the wrong temperature or not as fresh as you like—don't accept it, and tell that purveyor why.

With each party you cater, you'll learn more about what products you want to buy and use regularly. This will ease your workload, help you manage your time, and gradually help you perfect your menu. Better to make three dishes perfectly than five that are just average.

Along the way you'll learn to save yourself storage space and refrigeration yet guarantee freshness by having products delivered right to the party site. Ice, wine, bread, pastries, appetizers, and whole fruit can come straight to the party. This means less for you to carry to the party site and one more job you don't have to do yourself.

The luxury of a carefully planned catering menu with a correct guest count means that you know exactly what you need to buy and nothing more. I work with both new and experienced caterers every day who haven't spent enough time in preparation. Because they don't really know the scope of the event they're catering, they are scared. To compensate they make extra food, buy extra cakes, or run to the store for an extra leg of lamb "just in case"—anything to avoid running out of food. You can imagine what happens to their bottom line.

Rules to live by: Deliver what you promised, stick to your menu, guide your client to what's best for both of you, and stay within your budget.

Ten Easy Food Presentation Tips

1. Always garnish with an ingredient from the dish. For example, if you're serving Chicken with Thyme, save three stalks of whole thyme to tuck under the breast. Run the stalks under warm water and dry before plating.

2. Experiment with fresh lemon or lime zest on top of soups, salads, or desserts.

3. Buy two plastic cheese shakers; fill one with powdered sugar and one with cocoa. Take them to every party. If your dessert needs an uplift, sprinkle powdered sugar on top; use the cocoa for the edge of the plate.

4. When serving pasta, don't be afraid to mix two different colors. Egg with spinach fettuccine looks more healthful.

5. Uplift any coffee service with a bowl full of chocolate chips for sweetening or cinnamon sticks for stirring.

6. Hollow out red cabbages or green bell peppers for "edible" dip bowls on your vegetable platters. Try mini-pumpkins for soup in the fall.

7. Paint your grapes or edible flowers with whipped powdered egg whites and roll in sugar. Fill a basket for a centerpiece.

8. Use whole, cleaned green onions as swizzle sticks in vegetable cocktails.

9. Serve your chili or clam chowder in a bread bowl. Hollow out a sourdough round, heat in the oven until warm, fill, and serve.

10. Learn to carve a watermelon basket. They never go out of style. Or buy a Styrofoam "tree" at a hobby store. Glue it to a base, cover entirely with lettuce or mint, and hang cooked shrimp or chocolate-dipped strawberries with toothpicks all over it. It's a show stopper.

Scheduling Staff and Assistants

As you break down party preparation into time slots, you'll discover the most efficient use of your time and waitstaff. In wholesale or "drop-off" catering, where you drop off food ready for the host or hostess to serve, you can work alone.

For most social affairs, civic functions, or corporate meetings, however, a caterer needs a helper or two. Remember the simple saying I tell my students: You can be

Making a Flow Sheet

Here's what I include in a party flow sheet for every staff member:

- Correct party date

- Location, address with map attached, and parking details

- Where I can be reached and what time I'll be at the location

- My phone numbers

- What staff members are to wear and where to put a change of clothes

- Their call time (the time they are to arrive) and their job from the moment they arrive throughout the evening

- Timing of the party: when guests arrive, when food is served, and when the wrap-up starts

- How many guests to expect, type of occasion, and what kind of service

- Menu description

- When they will get a break and dinner

- What time I think they will be finished

- Why this party is important to my company

- Why their attitude is important to the party

- When their check will be ready for pickup

- Why I appreciate their help

in only one place at a time. So if your client has twelve guests for dinner and the hostess wants appetizers passed throughout the cocktail hours, ask yourself: Who is going to be in the kitchen getting the salads and dinner ready if I'm out on the floor passing appetizers?

After the site inspection and menu breakdown, you'll be ready to decide how much staff you'll need. If you need only one pair of hands to help, hire a person who is a jack-of-all-trades, an assistant who is well rounded and dependable. This person should be able to tend bar, wash dishes, wait, and serve.

It helps to develop a party flow sheet. This is party timing on paper. A flow sheet simply says who does what when. It's the party script. Without it no one knows when to do what. Divide up the work on a party flow sheet and assign jobs to yourself and your assistant. Mark off jobs when completed. That way you won't forget anything. Whether I have one assistant or ten for a job, I send everyone a party flow sheet in the mail or e-mail. They get it about five days before the party. This saves time and fosters the behavior I want in the people I hire. If I don't take the time to tell my staff clearly and precisely what I want them to do, who will?

The more information you share with assistants or staff, the easier it is for them to live up to your expectations. If my clients have concerns about strangers coming to work in their home, I send them a copy of the party flow sheet. It puts their fears at rest knowing that my staff is directed by me and that I am responsible.

Most of the staff I work with today have worked with me for years. We like and respect one another. My goal is to make it as easy as possible for my staff to do what I need them to do. We make entertaining look easy.

Arranging Transportation and Packing Out Your Party

If you have catered even one party, you have already confronted the urge to lug everything you own to the party and then lug it all back. Try not to bring anything you aren't going to use. Buy the smaller size of such staples as film or foil wrap. Make it as easy as possible to pack and unpack. Twelve hours after your day began, you won't want problems repacking the van.

My partner and I established a standard equipment checklist. Then we customized it on the computer with the menu for every party. Not only did the checklist keep us from forgetting something, but it also stopped us from bringing anything unnecessary.

Stand next to the van and don't put anything in without checking it off on your list. Careful packing saves you tons of trouble at the site and potential problems with the food en route. (When carrying liquids, sauces, or soup, tape the lid of the container to the bottom with masking tape so that the contents can't spill.)

One way to organize is to clearly label or color-code food on the menu with small colored self-adhesive dots widely available at office-supply stores. Any food to be served before dinner might be marked with pink dots; food to be prepared and served with the entree might be marked with green dots; any products served for dessert might get orange dots. (This system really works well if you have two parties in one day.) If you've started your cooking several days in advance, use these dots in all three phases of production: ordering, prepping, and transportation.

On pages 170–171 is an example of a food and equipment pack-out list for a Mexican-theme wedding for one hundred guests, serving appetizers only.

The decision to rent a van or a refrigerated truck depends on the size of your party and what the location is like. Usually a van does nicely. (Add $2 to $3 per person to your menu price for parties of fifty people or more to pay for the van rental.) Rent from companies that promise roadside service in case of a breakdown.

Vans with double doors that slide make packing and unpacking easier. If you are working out of a small kitchen, the van can double as your pantry or refrigerator at the site. Bring in products as you need them. Cook from course to course, using your coolers or hot boxes stored in the van.

In an effort to make the day of the event less stressful, rent your van for two days. Get it the morning before the event and pack all the dry goods and equipment first. Be sure to leave room for the food. Then when you get to the site, reverse the process. Unpack the food first, ensuring proper food handling and temperature control. Then off-load dry goods, equipment, or linens in the order you'll use them.

Food handling is a big responsibility. I always ask my clients to empty their refrigerators before the party so that I can use every inch. I also order a hundred extra pounds of ice with the liquor order to replenish ice in any coolers I've brought.

If you don't know about correct food handling, it's imperative to learn. Cold food must stay below 45 degrees and hot food must stay at 145 degrees or above; otherwise the food enters a danger zone where bacteria multiply rapidly. In chapter 2 I recommended asking your local health department for written advice and guidelines. I also suggest contacting the Educational Foundation of the National Restaurant Association (www.nraef.org), 175 W. Jackson Blvd., Ste. 1500, Chicago, IL 60604, and requesting a copy of Applied Foodservice Sanitation, an excellent reference book for professionals.

Equipment List

- ☐ Aprons
- ☐ Bain Marie Set (for sauces)
- ☐ Broom & Dust Pan
- ☐ Bus Tubs
- ☐ Can Opener
- ☐ Carving Fork
- ☐ Charcoal
- ☐ Chinoise (cone shaped)
- ☐ Coffee Kit
- ☐ Cookie Sheets
- ☐ Corkscrew
- ☐ Cutting Boards (plastic)
- ☐ Cutting Boards (wood)
- ☐ Deep Fry Oil Setup Pot & Oil
- ☐ Display Kit
- ☐ Doilies
- ☐ First-Aid Kit
- ☐ Flat Beds (4 wheels)
- ☐ Foil Pans (½ gift or food)
- ☐ Foil Wrap
- ☐ Gloves (food service)
- ☐ Gloves (rubber-scullery)
- ☐ Grill Kit & Grill Brush
- ☐ Hats/Hair Nets
- ☐ Hotel Pans (400) for Chafer Frame
- ☐ Hotel Pans (200) Chafer Insert
- ☐ Kitchen Matches (box)
- ☐ Knives (cheese)
- ☐ Knives (chef)
- ☐ Knives (serrated slicer)
- ☐ Ladles (large 8 oz.)
- ☐ Ladles (medium 6 oz.)
- ☐ Ladles (small 2 oz.)
- ☐ Lighter Fluid
- ☐ Lucite Tubs
- ☐ Mesquite
- ☐ Oven Mitts
- ☐ Paper Plates
- ☐ Pastry Brush
- ☐ Pastry Piping Bag w/ Star Tip
- ☐ Pizza Wheel
- ☐ Plastic Wrap
- ☐ Sauté Pans (10 inch)
- ☐ Sauté Pans (12 inch)
- ☐ Sauté Pans (Teflon 10 inch)
- ☐ Sheet Pans (½)
- ☐ Sheet Pans (full)
- ☐ Soap Kit
- ☐ Spatula (offset)
- ☐ Spatula (rubber)
- ☐ Spatula (steel)
- ☐ Spatula (Teflon)
- ☐ Stainless Bowls
- ☐ Stainless Serving Spoons
- ☐ Standard Utensils
- ☐ Sterno (large _____ small _____)
- ☐ Strainer (wire mesh)
- ☐ Tongs (long)
- ☐ Tongs (short)
- ☐ Toothpicks
- ☐ Towels
- ☐ Towels (paper)
- ☐ Trash Can Liners
- ☐ Whisk
- ☐ Wire Chafer Frames
- ☐ Wire Strainer for Deep Fryer or Colander
- ☐ Wooden Skewers (6 inch)
- ☐ Wooden Skewers (9 inch)
- ☐ Ziploc Bags

Party Prop Checklist

Designer _____   Party coordinator _____

Please attach miniature party blueprint or photocopy

Event name _____   Event date _____

Theme _____

Decor costs billed _____

Budget, including labor _____

Estimated actual costs _____   (save copy of receipts for completed party file)

In-house props used _____   Or prop house _____

Address: _____   Contact name _____

Delivered _____   Or van pickup _____

Date props checked out _____   Special instructions _____

Date props checked in _____   _____

New props/purchased _____   Or borrowed _____

QUANTITY	ITEM/DESCRIPTION	WRAPPING NEEDED

Information on return _____

Responsible _____   Initials _____

Party coordinator approval upon completion _____

Profit $ _____

Date: _____   Party address _____

(Check off with initials)

MENU ITEMS	PREPPED	WRAPPED	ON THE TRUCK
jalapeño cheese palmiers	_____	_____	_____
mushroom olive empanaditas	_____	_____	_____
macho quesadillas	_____	_____	_____
flour tortillas, smoked chicken	_____	_____	_____
refried beans	_____	_____	_____
nachos	_____	_____	_____
tortilla chips, cheese	_____	_____	_____
salsa, green onion	_____	_____	_____
sour cream, jalapeños	_____	_____	_____
crudités basket	_____	_____	_____
black bean dip, guacamole	_____	_____	_____
seafood brochettes	_____	_____	_____
chicken brochettes	_____	_____	_____
tomatillo sauce	_____	_____	_____
seafood bar	_____	_____	_____
steamed clams, mussels	_____	_____	_____
scallop seviche	_____	_____	_____
salsa, sour cream	_____	_____	_____
round tortilla chips	_____	_____	_____
spice kit, cilantro	_____	_____	_____
oil for frying	_____	_____	_____
fresh fruit display	_____	_____	_____
wedding cake cookies	_____	_____	_____
lemon and lime wedges	_____	_____	_____
coffee, tea	_____	_____	_____
half and half, creamer	_____	_____	_____
sugar, artificial substitute	_____	_____	_____

GARNISH, DECOR, PROPS	PREPPED	WRAPPED	ON THE TRUCK
cactus leaves, pepper ropes	_____	_____	_____
whole onions, kale	_____	_____	_____
sombreros, clay pots	_____	_____	_____
risers, piñatas, terra-cotta trays	_____	_____	_____

EQUIPMENT			
spatulas	_____	_____	_____
wooden spoons	_____	_____	_____
tongs	_____	_____	_____
plastic wrap and foil	_____	_____	_____
first-aid kit	_____	_____	_____
fire extinguisher	_____	_____	_____
slotted spoons	_____	_____	_____
sheet pans	_____	_____	_____
oven mitts	_____	_____	_____
whisk and ladles	_____	_____	_____
oyster shucker	_____	_____	_____
paper towels	_____	_____	_____
trash bags	_____	_____	_____
sponge and detergent	_____	_____	_____
Sterno	_____	_____	_____
aprons and towels	_____	_____	_____
ashtrays	_____	_____	_____
assorted baskets	_____	_____	_____
knife roll	_____	_____	_____
serving bowls	_____	_____	_____
corkscrew	_____	_____	_____
cutting boards	_____	_____	_____
pitchers	_____	_____	_____
toothpicks	_____	_____	_____

Driver Instruction List

Name of party _____   Today's date _____

Date of party _____   Coordinator _____

Location _____   Map page number _____

Directions to location _____

_____

Where to park upon arrival _____

Transportation or packing instructions _____

_____

Beverages/Ice _____

Dry ice _____

Decor _____

_____

_____

Rentals _____

_____

_____

Special delivery instructions _____

_____

_____

Other _____

_____

Catering a Buffet

Buffets usually end up costing less than a very similar menu served as a plated meal, so it is a good idea to offer clients this money-saving alternative. Buffets that are colorful, interesting, well-planned, and well-maintained can stretch your food budget. Follow these tips for a successful buffet!

Create Height and Interest

Elevate your food by placing serving plates on risers or pedestals. If these are not decorative, they should be covered with table linens. Risers should be sturdy: bricks, small crates, sturdy empty boxes, overturned baking dishes, telephone books, or even stacks of paper plates. Glass bricks create both height and ambiance when illuminated from behind with votive candles. You can make your own risers by covering or painting clean aluminum cans or inexpensive terra-cotta flowerpots turned upside-down. Make sure whatever you use is stable and supports the entire serving dish.

Setting Up the Day Before

- Leave as little as possible to do at the last minute. This will save you valuable time, and will also relieve you of last-minute party stress.

- Set up all tables.

- If tables are inside, cover with tablecloths.

- Write the name of each food you are serving on a piece of note paper and put the note paper in the serving dish you are planning to use. Or just place on the table in the area about where you plan to place the food.

- Put risers in place and cover, if necessary.

- Put out glasses, utensils, napkins, salt and pepper, coffeepot, sugar bowl, and anything else that doesn't have to be refrigerated.

- Plate nuts, candy, crackers, or anything else that can stay at room temperature overnight. Cover with plastic wrap and put into place on buffet or side tables.

Create a Focal Point

A classic buffet may have a centerpiece of flowers or, in the olden days, an ice sculpture. This works if you have lots and lots of table space. It is much more likely that your table space will be tight, so consider using several smaller flower arrangements that are staggered along the table at different heights using risers. Or use a garland-style arrangement and snake it through the buffet. Begin with a garland of silk leaves and add fresh flowers to it.

A thrifty alternative to flowers are baskets of beautifully arranged bread, fruit, or vegetables. Save the produce after the party to use the next day. Pillar candles or candelabras at different levels will add a sense of drama to your table. Allow enough space for the guests to serve themselves safely without getting burned. Check local fire codes before using candles and use fire-retardant cloths. Invest in a small fire extinguisher and keep it under the table in case of emergencies.

How to Set Up a Buffet

- Place buffet table in a shaded, well-ventilated area.

- If using your client's tables, place a protective cloth between the tables and the rental linens.

- Set up a separate smaller table for appetizers to avoid congestion. This also allows you to fill the main buffet table without having to push through crowds. Or pass the appetizers or first course. If serving soup, spoon into coffee cups.

- Serve dessert and coffee at another location, room, or table so that it is easier to clear the main buffet table.

- Keep your party moving by placing food in different areas.

- Make a scullery station that is obvious to your guests to keep kitchen commotion to a minimum. A small card table or counter will do. It should be close enough to the buffet so guests will get the idea. Have well-marked recycling bins handy.

If your table is too bare, scatter with rose petals, loose flowers, candy, crackers, or bunches of fresh herbs or dried whole chili peppers. Or use an item that ties in with your theme, like chocolates, shells, fortune cookies, playing cards, etc.

Make the Most of Your Food

Use serving dishes that complement the color of your food. White will work with almost anything, so invest in a few basic platters, cake stands, plates, and bowls.

Buy one or two multi-tier servers with removable plates. These will add instant height to any table.

If you are serving a beautiful multicolored salad, display it at its best in a large glass or clear plastic salad bowl.

Pieces of marble, the kind used in countertops, are available at hardware and tile stores and can be used for a number of great food presentations. Look for damaged or broken pieces and ask the store to break them into different sizes for you. As the surface of marble stays reasonably cool, it is perfect for a cheese and fruit display. Use longer pieces, supported by risers, to create a series of dramatic shelves for the food.

Beveled mirrors or mirror tiles can also be used for cheese. Placing mirrors under bowls of food will give a suggestion of depth to the buffet.

Baskets are a must for caterers. Inexpensive and available in all different shapes and sizes, they can be easily recycled with a little spray paint. Or wrap the handles with fabric or ribbons. Line with linen napkins or aromatic herbs before adding food.

Avoiding the Slow-Moving Buffet Line

- Serve dishes that guests can easily place on their plates one-handed. If they have to put their dishes down to serve themselves, it slows down the line.

- Serve dishes that are easy to eat. No knives necessary.

- For larger crowds, have plated salads brought to the guests' tables. This will slow the rush to the buffet. Serve salad dressing separately, as most people like to dress their own salads.

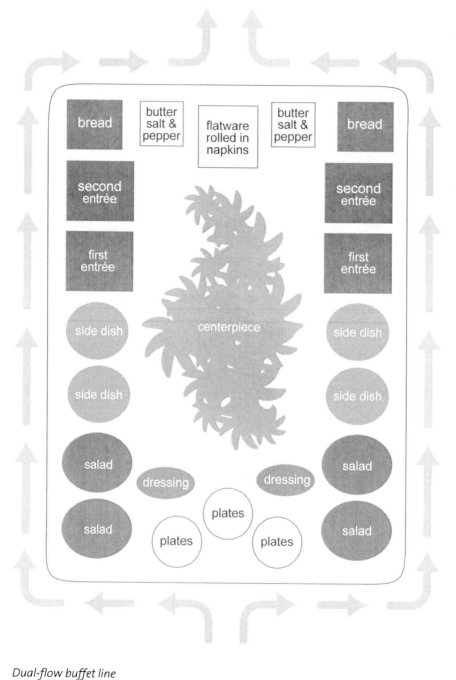

Dual-flow buffet line

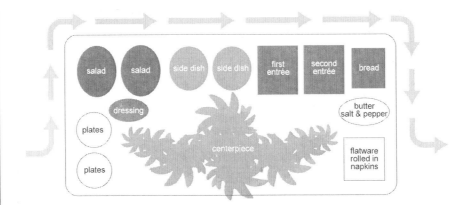

Single-flow buffet line

For crudités, line baskets with nontoxic leaves like lemon leaves, ornamental purple or green kale, baby bok choy, banana leaves, curly green lettuce, or Savoy cabbage.

A chafing dish is a must for hot food. To avoid the usual industrial look of multiple chafing dishes lined up in a row, use different shapes or mix copper with silver and place them at different angles. Make your own rustic-looking chafing dish by stacking red bricks to form a base and place a cast-iron griddle or skillet on top. For the heat source use Sterno or votive candles set on a terra-cotta plant saucer and place underneath. Another alternative to a chafing dish is a Crock-Pot or slow cooker. Set on low, it can be used to keep stews, soups, chowders, chili, or even beans warm. If the design of your Crock-Pot doesn't match your party decor, wrap a piece of fabric around it.

Maintaining Your Buffet

A properly maintained buffet will look more attractive and appetizing and will prevent food spills and waste. Provide your guests with the proper serving utensils. Tongs are the most guest-friendly utensils for a buffet, as they can be used one-handed.

Select utensils that are the correct length. Ladles should be long enough so that they don't sink beneath the surface of soups, and serving forks large enough to spear that slice of beef.

Provide a spoon rest or small saucer for utensils used in saucy dishes that can drip.

Precut casseroles like lasagna into serving sizes before placing on the buffet so that guests don't have to try to cut through the whole thing with the serving spatula. Make pieces on the small side to cut down on waste.

All buffet foods should be in manageable-size pieces that will fit easily on plates. For example, if you are using large chicken breasts, consider slicing them into two or three pieces. Cut whole corn in half and trim broccoli into florets before serving.

Avoid round food like peas and melon balls that may roll off plates. If soup is on the menu, use deep bowls or mugs and provide a ladle that gives the correct portion.

Check on the buffet occasionally to monitor the food. Are you going to run out of beef bourguignon? If you are expecting a rush of guests, keep an extra pan or two of the hot beef bourguignon in a cooler under the buffet. Having the hot food this close will ensure a quick change-out when one pan becomes low. Because coolers

Tablecloths for Buffets

Make sure the tablecloth is the correct size so that it drops all the way to the floor. If tables are not against a wall, the cloth will need to drop to the floor on all sides.

It's a good idea to invest in a couple of neutral, machine-washable tablecloths that can be used again and again. A standard black tablecloth can be used for evening and formal events or as a base on which to display different-color tablecloths.

Layer different colors and textures of cloth on top of your basic cloths. Look in the bargain bins at fabric stores for remnants or for bargain-priced twin-size sheets.

Use something other than a standard tablecloth to complement the theme of your party, like burlap, Hawaiian shirts or grass skirts, Mexican serapes, large Hawaiian ti leaves, beach towels, vintage board games, Astroturf, floor tiles, pebbles, placemats, pages from garage-sale picture books, etc.

If using paper or cloth tablecloths outside, remember to secure with tape on the underside or to weigh the ends down with weights. Make your own decorative weights by spray-painting wooden clothespins.

are insulated, they will keep food hot for limited periods of time. Put the pan of food into the cooler just before serving. This method of storing food should only be a fifteen- to twenty-minute temporary measure when you expect a quick turnaround. Do you need to replenish the pasta? If you do run out of something, simply remove the plate or tray. Fill the space with an extra breadbasket or another bowl of salad until the replacement food is brought in.

A great secret of catering buffets is to place the most expensive food, or the food that you have least of, at the end of the buffet line. That way your guests will have filled their plates and will have limited space left for the expensive item.

Building Crudité and Cheese Displays

Crudité and cheese displays can be used to fill spaces on the main buffet table or they can be placed on smaller tables in other areas of the party to take the pressure off the main table. Arrange cut vegetables in a large shallow bowl or on a decorative tray, with the dip in a small bowl or cup placed in the center or off to one side. Alternate colors so you don't have broccoli (green) next to celery (green). Instead, have red bell pepper strips or carrots between the broccoli and celery. Stand vegetables upright in tureens or wide vases instead of laying them flat. Add tiny yellow tomatoes or snow peas to your display—whatever is in season and available. Blanch green beans, broccoli, and asparagus for half a minute in boiling water; they will turn a bright, lovely green.

Cheese displays can be built on any clean surface. Use pieces of marble, wooden cutting boards, or large tiles. Group three, four, or five different cheeses together. Mix different textures and flavors. Try a soft goat cheese with a hard cheese like Parmesan and a semi-hard cheese like cheddar. Throw in a blue cheese or a soft-ripened cheese like a Brie for fun. Add fresh fruit like grapes, pears, apples, and figs or dried fruit like apricots and dates. If your cheese display surface is large enough, place the fruit and crackers around the cheese. If you don't have enough space on the cheese board, put the fruit in bowls and scatter the crackers directly on the tablecloth or on folded napkins. Warmed spiced nuts or herbed olives are a welcome addition to cheese boards.

Getting Down to the Wire

During the days before the party, it's important to keep in close contact with your client. You may be confident, organized, and prepared, but the client is probably a nervous wreck as the day approaches. Nothing calms a client down better than knowing that you are on top of details.

Look for ways to make the day of the event as simple as possible. If you're working in a private home or at a location that allows deliveries the day before the event, have your rentals or dry goods or even the flowers arrive then. You can meet the delivery people there, recheck your orders, and even put some pieces of the party in place.

I like to ask for a spot where I can leave a basketful of brochures, business cards, or matchbooks. I also like to squirrel away a party folder with extra copies of the menu, staff sign-in sheets (to verify the time the staff arrives and departs, for payroll purposes), and party instructions. I make sure to leave the client my phone number and an estimated schedule of the time the staff and subcontractors will arrive.

Another task I like to complete the day before is to set up a mini recycling station for bottles, cans, and plastic so that it will be easy for anyone working the party to help me recycle as soon as the party begins. The day before is also the perfect time to walk through the place with the client to find out where the light switches, the fuse box, the garden hose, or the smoke detectors are. Anything you might need to know while on the premises, find out now. I usually get a copy of the guest list or the boxes of the bride's party favors or guest book at this time. (I hate to bother clients with these details when they should be enjoying their party.)

If I plan to give my clients a present of a basketful of goodies or a special bottle of champagne, I do it the day before—I want to be sure the client knows it is from me.

Before the rooms are full of guests is a good time to talk with the host or hostess about where to put coats or baby bags or unexpected gifts or, for that matter, where to put a guest who is ill. This is the moment to talk about putting away any irreplaceable household items. If you are using the client's equipment, you'll want to jot down a list to make sure it gets put back where it belongs.

In chapter 10 you'll see how all your organizing techniques and checklists work. Whether or not you want to admit it, how well the party comes off is a direct reflection of your preplanning, communication skills, and attitude. I am not saying that you can control everything. There are four legitimate exceptions: monsoons, flu epidemics, union strikes, and war. But as a professional caterer, you'll be expected to handle just about everything else.

10

Pulling It Off with Ease

Doing as much work as you can on a job beforehand makes pulling it off, well, a piece of cake. If you can get more than half the work done before the event, you can't help but feel confident on the big day itself. By working ahead you give yourself the gift of self-assurance, a gift that clients and staff feel, too. Like the coach of a winning team, you need to provide inspiration as well as guidance and controls on party day.

The Day of the Party

Get a good night's sleep the night before. The better you take care of yourself, the more patience and strength you will have to cope with the unexpected. Put on comfortable clothes, support hose (men, too), and walking shoes. Plan on changing into party clothes, or at least a clean chef's jacket, before the guests arrive. One thing I hate to see is staff or kitchen help walking through a party in dirty uniforms or casual clothes. Do they believe they are invisible? Who could miss them? Imagine a stagehand walking through a classical ballet performance wearing a sweatshirt and baseball cap! Good catering is like good dancing: The audience must never see you sweat.

Attention to detail and the ability to see your parties as a performance, not a perfunctory job, are two things that set you apart from your competition. To achieve that professional smoothness, make day-of-the-party lists like the one on page 183. It covers every aspect of the party for which you are responsible.

Getting to the Party

Allow enough time to get to the party without racing. Have clear and concise directions and a map. A cell phone is a time-saving tool because it enables a caterer to be on tap every minute for questions, to handle surprises, or even just to call the client and say, "I'm on my way."

If you work from a copy of your master checklist and your party information file, it will be difficult for you to put the wrong foot forward. I can't emphasize too often that the success of the party depends on hours of preplanning and anticipating possible problems.

On the day of the party, caterers sometimes make the mistake of going back to the kitchen or to the store for one forgotten item. This leaves the staff at the party site without a leader and without instructions. If you've forgotten the toothpicks with color-coordinated frills, either do without them or send someone else to find them. The coach is too important to leave the game on an errand.

Even with careful scheduling, mishaps occur. If a purveyor is late with a delivery to your kitchen the morning of the party, don't hold up the entire parade. Call and find out if the delivery can be made right to the party site, or decide if you should leave a kitchen assistant behind to accept the delivery. Be flexible. Be able to manage your time. Perhaps the item is for dessert and you have some time before you need it. Know that there is no problem you can't solve. Just think through each dilemma.

I've managed to solve some very thorny problems, and I know that you can, too. Once I was the executive chef in charge of a celebrity wedding on the island of Catalina. All the food had to be coordinated, prepped, weighed, wrapped, then sent on a barge the day before the wedding. The 150 guests, all television stars, were crossing the seventeen miles of water between Los Angeles and Catalina in luxury yachts. At five o'clock on the morning of the wedding, just as I was leaving the house for the helicopter pad to fly to the island, the phone rang. It was the baker of the wedding cake, who said she had missed the barge. This was summer. The yachts and other passenger boats were booked full. The baker was sorry, but she didn't know how she could get the four-tiered wedding cake to Catalina.

I told her to meet me at the helicopter pad. The helicopter carried only four passengers and there was no storage space, but I figured I could manage. As the wind from the copter's blades blew the baker and me around, I passed the first two tiers of the cake to total strangers in the helicopter, screaming, "Would you mind holding this for a minute?" My assistant and I took the last two tiers and climbed aboard. The ride took thirty-seven minutes. I smiled the entire time, looking straight into the innocent faces of my fellow passengers, all holding tiers of wedding cake. They said not a word. Neither did I. When we landed, I climbed out, took the cake from their tired arms, said my thank-yous, and put the cake in a waiting taxi.

PARTY INFORMATION FOLDER/
YOUR PAPERWORK

☐ Copy of completed and signed contract

☐ Date and final guest count given by client

☐ Copy of deposit and balance checks, in case client has a question

☐ Subcontractors' contracts and phone numbers

☐ Staff phone numbers, addresses, and arrival times

☐ Staff payroll sheet for signing in and out

☐ Priority job list or special instructions for all staff

☐ Copies of special fire permits, if necessary, and a certificate of insurance

☐ Several copies of final menu—one for kitchen staff, one for waiters, one for bartenders—and all staff briefed to answer guests' questions

☐ Printed instructions on the sequence of food courses, timing, and type of service

☐ Diagram of how to set up temporary kitchen and organize existing space

☐ Copy of rental orders

☐ List of customer's equipment that will be used

☐ Entire location layout: placement of bar, food displays, kitchen area, scullery, guest tables and chairs, coatrack, place for gifts, security,

barbecue, trash, recycling, fire extinguishers

☐ Rental company's conditions of equipment return (what must or must not be washed)

☐ Instructions for repacking food for kitchen crew and waitstaff

☐ Blank party-closing reports (staff feedback sheet) to delegate to two staff members

TRANSPORTATION CHECKLIST

☐ Van gassed; map of location; food, supplies, and equipment checked off and packed

☐ Rental-van keys or car keys on huge colored key ring, impossible to misplace

MENU

☐ All menu items color-coded to menu courses, tightly wrapped for transport, and packed in coolers, hot boxes, or crates

☐ Special cooking instructions or finishing details attached to appropriate ingredients with tape

☐ Signs to hang up for each course or food station, telling which area waiters are

☐ to use to pick up appetizers, salads, or desserts

☐ Appointment of buffet monitors to replenish from backup food supply

EQUIPMENT PLACEMENT/
BREAKDOWN INSTRUCTIONS

❐ Scullery supplies, dishwasher, plastic bags for napkins, soap, rubber gloves, bus tubs for dirty dishes, flatware cleaner, sponges, garbage cans, table for repacking, running water (Note: Not all of these items will be needed if the job is at a private home.)

❐ Breakdown of rentals for storage, packing, and security until pickup

❐ Pack broom, mop, and garbage can on van in case they are not available at location

❐ Appointed hours for cleanup of premises and next-day inspection

SERVICE STAFF/EVALUATIONS/EMPLOYEE
INFORMATION

❐ Appoint one member of the waitstaff to be your assistant and help you pass information to other staff as well as fill out party-closing report.

❐ Pack emergency toilet articles appearance bag: one extra bow tie, hair spray, pantyhose, safety pins, hairbrush, lint brush, portable iron, black shoe polish, deodorant, extra chef's jacket, mouthwash, portable razor, belt, portable sewing kit, aspirin, and tampons.

❐ Designate place for staff's purses or jackets and decide chain of command for breaks and meals. Set aside fruit or sandwiches for snacking and water.

❐ Post job assignments and list of staff arrival times in designated area.

❐ Post copy of menu with all ingredients listed and instructions for staff to initial after reading.

❐ Post description of service buffet stations, sit-down or combination.

❐ Post special instructions such as cutting and passing the wedding cake, security of presents, where coats go, scullery duties.

❐ Allow ten minutes for pre-party meeting with staff to answer questions about party and potential problems and at least three minutes for inspirational message about what you envision from this team effort.

❐ Appoint two bathroom monitors to check bathrooms every thirty minutes for toilet paper and towels. Monitors must know where the plunger is, too. (Most toilets in private homes aren't used to being flushed one hundred times in four hours. Crowds create plumbing problems.)

Arriving at the Party Site

It's a good idea to get to the party before any of your staff. If they are standing there waiting for you, it's costing you money.

Make a job-priority list (see the example on page 189) that contains names of staff by each job, with written instructions for everything. Post the list in a prominent place so that all staff can refer to it. As each staff member completes a task, he or she checks it off and initials it before moving on to the next.

A job-priority list is a form of delegation. I need to know that my staff won't need me every second. I may need to be on the phone, finishing instructions about a party the next day or answering another set of nervous questions by the bride's mother, or trying to find a place for the family dogs away from the barbecue while the chef is grilling burgers.

A job-priority list is also a systematic way of making sure that your party is ready when the guests arrive, that you are using your staff effectively, and that you have left time for yourself to take pictures or to be available in case your client needs you.

It also keeps your party on schedule.

Winding Down: Why Your Party Has to End On Time

To stay within your budget, you need to stick to the time schedule you laid out in your contract. If the contract called for a four-hour party, give your client four hours, not four and a half. As the guests start through the sequence of events—cocktails, dining, dancing—you and your staff should be cleaning up behind them. Service the client, serve the food, and start to repack in an effort to organize the breakdown as the party winds down. For example, once the appetizers have been served, have someone repack any leftovers into the ice chests, clean the trays, and put all equipment you brought for the appetizers back on the truck. Clean up your party and repack as you go along.

Occasionally you'll encounter guests who don't want to leave even when the party is over. You'll have to enlist your host and explain that your job is done. If the client wants the bartender to stay another hour, you can, of course, agree, but only if the client is willing to pay extra for the bartender's time. Remember that you have to pay for every minute your staff works, whether or not you collected the correct amount of dollars from your client.

Manager Information Sheet

Client name _____ Contact _____

Function date _____

Salesperson _____ If not at party, try _____

Party manager _____ Kitchen manager _____

Guest count _____ Party hours _____

Breakdown hours _____

RENTALS

Rental company _____ Phone number _____

Contact _____ Delivery date _____

Address _____

Pickup date _____ Time _____

Where will rentals be located? _____

Where should rentals be left? _____

Special instructions _____

FLOWERS

Company _____ Phone number _____

Contact _____ Scheduled delivery time _____

Deliver to _____

What was ordered? _____

Return vases to _____ Leave at party _____

Instructions _____

BEVERAGE SERVICE

Company _____ Delivery date _____

Delivery time _____ Who provides _____

Ice by _____ Returns _____

Trash removal _____ Recycling instructions _____

What beverages should be left for client? _____

_____

Report Cards from Staff and Clients

The easiest way to get honest feedback and to document the results of your parties is to develop party-closing reports (see pages 190). I think of them as report cards. Ask two staff members—one from the floor, one from the kitchen—to each fill out a closing report the day of the party. I ask each client to fill out a report a couple of days later. These reports make it simple to see and correct mistakes in order to perfect your home-based catering business.

How a Staff Report Works

For example, if after two parties in a row your kitchen assistant says that he didn't have any pot holders, do the following: (1) Go back to your equipment pack-out list and verify whether or not you packed them, (2) determine whether your kitchen assistant is looking in the wrong box, and (3) determine whether the pot holders got left at another party.

If you learn that your staff felt rushed when the guests arrived, you know that you need to rethink timing. Either you are not allowing enough time for setting up, your staff needs clearer directions so that they don't waste time, or you are cutting it too close and need another pair of hands to help.

Staff reports are particularly valuable if you have two parties on the same day and can get to only one of them. You'll want to be informed about everything, good or bad, before you ask your client to fill out a report card and give you referrals.

Also, several months later, when the details of a party are fuzzy at best, staff reports may protect you from an employee or a guest who complains of an injury after the fact. You will be able to produce paperwork showing that no injury was reported at the time or that you took steps to gather information about any accidents with the intention of dealing with them.

I had a wonderful employee call me forty days after a party to say that he'd wrenched his back lifting a table and was filing a workers' compensation claim. When I checked my computer index for that date, I discovered that not only had he not worked for me then, but I didn't even have a party that day. It isn't unusual during the busy season for professional waiters to work for four different caterers in one week. In the time that had elapsed since his injury, he remembered the wrong caterer.

Client Reports

Asking for honest feedback from a client is harder than asking for it from staff. After the energy, effort, and anxiety you've put into an event, you want to believe your performance was flawless. You don't want to hear anything but praise. This attitude can work against you. To get over this I learned to take responsibility for my actions as a professional. At the end of a party, if I felt I had worked my butt off and not made enough profit, I had no one to blame but myself—I couldn't blame the client. I had not protected myself and educated the client about what was best for both of us, so I could not be angry with him or her.

I meet caterers all the time who are unable to turn a negative into a positive. Their inability to admit a mistake and learn from it contributes to burnout, dissatisfaction, and frustration in their jobs. They don't feel that clients appreciate what they do, yet they can't handle critiques that would improve their performances. I suggest that they refer to their contracts and ask themselves these questions: Did I do what the client expected and paid for, or did I do things I wanted and maybe not what the client paid for? Am I angry at the client or at myself? Is my perfectionism working against me? Without a good look at what they have done, I'll bet dollars to doughnuts they make the same mistakes over and over again.

You need perspective about each of your performances, and sometimes it's hard to look at a party honestly when your back still aches from all that cooking the night before. The client's party-closing report will help you clarify both your thinking and your client's about the final results of the event. When you are honest with yourself, trust me, the complaints are few and far between, and the ones you do get are useful.

On page 191 is a sample questionnaire to send to your client after the party.

The Day After

How you feel the day after may depend on how much natural energy you have and how well your party planning worked. Because you are your own boss, you can rest whenever it is best for you. In December it's common for small companies, big companies, or any other company to work nonstop for three or four days or weeks in a row. It becomes a habit, and your body gets on a roll. You are exhausted by Christmas. You expect to be, but you made enough money to support yourself in January, a slow month for caterers.

Job Assignments

Initial each line as you complete each task.

☐	Carol	Check rental delivery against the delivery sheet.
☐	Michael	Put every piece of equipment in place.
☐	Carol	Pass out linens, drape them, and roll silverware or fold napkins.
☐	Marie	Refrigerate food.
☐	Marie	Verify deliveries from outside suppliers.
☐	Gary	Make sure bar supplies are adequate and ready for first guests.
☐	Denise	Meet with waiters to discuss menu and party timing.
☐	Marie	Build salad and have appetizers ready.
☐	Michael	Be dressed in your waiter's uniform, ready to meet early arrivals.
☐	Gary	Make sure that all caterer's equipment is out of sight.
☐	Michael	Greet guests, handle guest book sign-in.
☐	Carol	Escort guests to their tables.
☐	Denise	Seat wedding party at bride's table.
☐	Marie	Finish beef in oven.
☐	Denise	Tell disc jockey to announce when the buffet will open.
☐	Marie	Take carving knife to buffet.
☐	Michael	Place bread baskets and butter curls on all tables.
☐	Gary	Fill water glasses and add lemon slice.
☐	Gary	Pour champagne into flutes for toast at 3:00 P.M.
☐	Michael and Gary	Bus dishes and glasses to scullery.
☐	Carol and Marie	Break down buffet at 4:15 P.M.
☐	Gary	Continue to pour champagne from bar.
☐	Michael and Carol	Cut and serve wedding cake.
☐	Gary	Set up coffee station.
☐	Marie	Wrap all leftover food.
☐	Marie	Feed staff and subcontractors.
☐	Marie	Separate rentals; store in safe place.
☐	Gary	Close bar at 5:00 P.M.
☐	Carol	Help family with gifts to car.
☐	Denise	Pass out bride's candy party favors for departing guests.
☐	Marie	Wrap extra wedding cake for bride's mother.
☐	Anybody not otherwise occupied	Reload van.
☐	Michael	Mop floors.
☐	Denise	Fill out staff time sheets.
☐	Carol	Fill out party-closing sheet.
☐	Marie	Fill out party-closing sheet for kitchen.
☐	Gary	Check location for any equipment.
☐	Anybody not otherwise occupied	Help repack van with equipment and recycling.

Party Closing Report/Staff Evaluation

Event _____   Date _____

Actual guest count _____   Filled out by _____

Staff on duty _____

1. Was client happy? _____

   Explain _____

2. Did problems arise that the client was aware of? _____

   If so, who handled the problems? _____

   How were the problems handled? _____

3. Were there problems with subcontractors? _____

   Explain _____

4. Would you hire these suppliers again? _____

5. Did the event start on time? _____

   If not, why? _____

6. Was the staff ready on time? _____

7. Did the event go overtime? _____

   Why? _____

8. Was there enough food for guests and staff? _____

   If not, what did we run out of? _____

9. Were there any complaints? _____

   Explain _____

10. Were there any injuries to staff or clients? _____

    Explain _____

11. Did you discuss these injuries with the host or hostess? _____

12. Evaluate the organization of this party and how I did as coordinator. _____

13. How would you rate your fellow service staff? _____

14. Were there any personality conflicts among staff members? _____

15. Were staff members clear about their responsibilities? _____

16. Could you suggest anything that might make it easier for all of us next time? ___

    _____

Client Complaint Form

Note: It is important to be tactful, thoughtful, and thorough when handling a client's complaints. If injury or accidents are involved, try to get the facts, take pictures, and record the names of any witnesses. Don't suggest or discuss who's responsible.

Completed by _____   Position _____

Date of incident _____   Time _____

Name of client _____

Address _____

Home phone number _____   Work phone number _____

Nature of complaint

_____

_____

_____

Employee comments

_____

_____

_____

Was there any accident or injury? _____   Was first aid offered? _____

Witness _____   Phone number _____

Witness _____   Phone number _____

Witness _____   Phone number _____

Were police called? _____   Officer's name _____

Badge number _____   Was a police report filled out? _____

Was an ambulance called? _____   To which hospital did it go? _____

Please return this completed form to the offices of FOOD FANATICS, or call (310) 836-3520. Thank you.

In my house the day after any party is a day of rest. I'm tired and exhilarated. I bask in the glory of my achievement. I reflect on how I would do the same party again, but better and more profitably. I make notes in red pen on my master check-list of items and circle things I wouldn't do again. I scribble notes to myself about the menu, staff, equipment, and suppliers while the facts are all fresh in my mind. This takes me thirty minutes, tops.

I review the closing reports carefully and try to make decisions that will eliminate problems in future parties. On the back of the reports, I list the pieces of the party that I loved and was proud of—for example, the decor was charming, the food was fresh and tasty, my staff worked hard and looked great. I take the time to savor what satisfied me as an owner, a businessperson, a chef, and an artist.

I've learned to hear and accept the compliments without adding "Yes, but . . ." or "Well, I'm glad you enjoyed the six-course dinner, but I wish the rolls had been a little bit warmer." Strive for excellence, not perfection.

If, in a tense moment, I wasn't the perfect manager, coach, player, or boss, I ask myself if I owe anyone an apology. If so, I call the person. I also ask myself whether I'm owed an apology. If so, does it really matter if I get one?

If during this reinspection of the event I determine that there was misconduct on the part of an employee, I make a note in that person's folder and decide if I should speak to him or her about it. Accidents are accidents and mistakes are mistakes, but neglect is grounds for dismissal.

Two Days Later

Send your client a Quality and Service Report questionnaire in the mail. If you haven't talked to him or her since the party, now's the time. Call and tell your client to look forward to the questionnaire, and explain why you're sending it. Enclose a stamped, self-addressed envelope and a handwritten thank-you note.

If there are loose ends, tie them up. Does the client owe you for two dinners? Send an invoice for them separately. Did you pick up the client's spatula by mistake? Tell the client what day you'll drop it off. Do you need to go to the location to verify a burn mark on the table from your chafer or a steam mark on a painting from your coffeepot?

If there is any damage, call your insurance agent, take a digital picture of the item, find out what your deductible is, negotiate the value of the damage, and be

Quality and Service Report

1. Are you glad that you were referred to my company? _____

2. Did you feel that I explained my policies promptly and courteously when we went over the menu package and party proposal? ___

   _____

3. From our meetings and discussions, do you feel as though you received the party you were promised? _____

   _____

4. Are you satisfied that we completed our contractual agreement?

   _____

   _____

5. Was the quality of the food as good as I promised? _____

   Did you enjoy it? _____

6. Which dish was your favorite? _____

7. Did the food presentation meet your expectations? _____

8. Did you receive compliments from your guests? _____

9. Was the temperature of each dish correct? _____

10. Do you feel that you got value for your dollars? _____

11. On a scale of 1 to 10, please rate the service staff. _____

12. Were there any problems I should know about that you are reluctant to bring up? _____

13. Was your home or the party site left in satisfactory condition? _____

14. Please tell me anything you feel would enable me to serve you better next time. _____

15. May I use your name as a reference? _____

16. Would you be comfortable writing me a letter of recommendation? _____

   Please mention what you liked best about working with me. _____

   _____

17. Please list below the names of two friends or colleagues who might need my services in the future.

   _____

   _____

Thanks again. I hope I have the opportunity to do another party for you in the future.

done with it. A hundred dollars to fix a problem when it involves a client who may send you thousands of dollars in business is an easy solution.

Write thank-you notes or e-mails to any purveyor or supplier who helped you—the butcher, the baker, the band. Many busy businesspeople forget how important a sincere thank-you can be.

Do your bookkeeping and accounting now. As discussed in chapter 8, bookkeeping is easy if you do a little every day, like exercise and flossing your teeth. Figure your final party profit sheet. Take a blank budget worksheet like the one used in chapter 5 and insert your actual costs. It's a great way to see how close you came to your estimates. Most new home-based caterers quickly get the hang of judging food quantities, but bidding correctly on labor costs takes experience. You have to be able to visualize parties, know what each staff position does, and how parties flow before you will be able to stop underbidding labor costs and stop working yourself to death.

Pay your purveyors, your staff, yourself. Organize all the information you have in your party folder: staff sheets, final accounting sheet, recipes to document the menu. A copy of the original proposal and your closing party reports belong here, too. Any information that applies to the party goes in the party folder: the rental order, the purveyors you used, the store where you bought the balloons, the bid from the designer who built the incredible archway. Why keep all this paper? Because if the party was as good as you think it was and it received glowing reviews, a guest from that party may call and order one just like it. By reselling a party you can make more money with less stress. Most of your planning has been done and you know your costs to the penny. Catering parties is like making crepes: The more you make, the better your pan gets.

For you to resell this party now, with all that you know, would be like taking candy from a baby.

Three Days Later

After you've done your bookkeeping, call your staff and tell them when their paychecks will be ready. Thank them again for their support and talent. It's a good time to ask each one what he or she thought of the party, the food, and the guests' reaction. Listen and look at your party through their eyes. Know that many of the waiters you hire also work with your competitors. They know a lot about the catering clientele in your area. Staff is a great source of information and insight.

Call the rental company and make sure that all its property was picked up properly and that your account is clear. If the company has complaints, now is the time to answer them.

One classic complaint of rental companies concerns napkins. The number of cloth napkins rented is never the same as the number returned. When the rental company sends you an invoice at the end of the month, it always charges you $5 a napkin, or whatever its replacement cost may be. Calculate how much money you will spend during two years in business if you lose between two and five napkins at each party.

Here's how it happens. One napkin went into the garbage can because the new prep cook grabbed it (he didn't know where the kitchen towels were) to clean the client's incredibly dirty grill. When he saw the mess he made of the napkin, he buried his mistake in the garbage can. Kiss that one good-bye. Another napkin was left in the hostess's bathroom by a guest, so the hostess keeps it next to her phone to remind her the next time she calls you. The third napkin is in one of your waiter's cars. His defroster wasn't working, so he took it when he left the party to wipe off his windshield.

You get my drift. It's important to stress to the staff the value of rental equipment. Count the rentals when you arrive. Count the rentals when you pack up to leave, and get the staff to help you account for them. Be sure to explain exactly how much replacements cost.

Two Weeks Later

Contact the three leads from your client's Quality and Service Report. Write each lead an email. If you have a recent promotional piece, a descriptive menu from a charity fund-raiser, a free recipe card, or a copy of your newsletter, enclose it along with your standard marketing package. Ask each of the three leads if he or she was at the party. If so, the person knows a lot about you already. Your goal is to make an appointment with all three of them to talk about future jobs. You'll make back the price of a cup of coffee and a brownie many times over.

Select the best ten photographs that you took during the party and e-mail them to your client. I call two days later to ask if the client got the pictures and if he or she liked them. Again I say how much I appreciate the business. I'm from the school that says you can't be too considerate or too thoughtful to clients.

Go to the stationery store and buy shiny gold stars just like the ones you were given in kindergarten. On every calendar in your life—in your organizer, on your desk calendar—stick those stars on the dates of every party you complete. Put them wherever you can to remind yourself that you are accomplishing your goals and living your dream.

Looking back on more than twenty years of catering, I know I wouldn't have missed a single party. Even the parties that made me cry, forced me to admit mistakes, and "built my character" were worth it.

I feel a real sense of accomplishment and joy when I see a near-perfect party come together because of my ideas and designs. To start with a vacant buffet or empty backyard and, in a few hours, create an entirely new fairy-tale setting and wonderful memories—and then get paid for it—still seems to me a miracle.

11 Solving Problems

I can anticipate the problems you'll be having after you've catered three or four parties. I know. I've been there. Apparently you aren't alone, because these are the questions I am asked repeatedly when teaching. The most important advice I can give you is try not to make the same mistakes twice. Learn from your experience, tuck the knowledge away, and use it when planning the next time.

Question One

I called my client the day before the party, and she gave me her final guest count. At the party twenty more guests arrived, and I ran out of rolls and salad. Fortunately I had lots of roast beef and shrimp to feed them. What should I do differently next time?

- In your sales presentation be even firmer when addressing your need for an accurate guest count. Make sure the client understands that she will pay for every guest you feed, even if the guests are a surprise to everyone. You are only trying to ensure her success as a hostess.
- When guests arrive, it's important to have someone at the door counting. The earlier you know about a soaring guest count, the sooner you can send someone to the store.
- Salad and bread are the cheapest items on your menu. You need to figure one and one-half rolls per person for a buffet, at least two for a sit-down dinner. Better to bring a few extra rolls than ten extra pounds of roast beef (two dozen rolls cost $4; ten pounds of roast beef cost about $60). Remember that if you buy too many rolls, you can use the leftovers to make great bread crumbs, bread pudding, or croutons for Caesar salad.

- Instead of running out of rolls, you could have cut the existing rolls in half when you refilled the bread basket.
- If you ever begin to run short of salad or any other self-service item, put a waiter on the buffet to serve it. He will control the portions and make it stretch.
- As a last resort, look in the refrigerator of the hostess to see if she has any lettuce. Or does she have a garden in the backyard? You can replace the items you use later.

Question Two

No matter how organized I try to be, I always forget one or two items. What can I do?

- Are you making lists? Or are you trying to remember details in your head instead? The latter is a no-no. Be sure to make foolproof prep lists and equipment lists from your menus. Mark off each item as you pack it in your car or van.
- Put together an on-site box for yourself. Keep it stocked and bring it to every party. Pack the following items: wooden matches, sugar cubes, toothpicks, dry coffee creamer, herbal tea bags, pot holders, plastic food-storage bags, doilies, bamboo skewers, a small fire extinguisher, and a box of birthday candles. Add the things you have been forgetting.
- Designate a backup driver or "gofer" for your party. It can be a neighbor or teenager you pay for a few hours to sit next to the phone and be available to bring you anything you've forgotten.
- Allow enough time to pack out your party. The less stress you are under, the easier it is to remember.
- Delegate: When you think of items you keep forgetting, ask someone else—a staff or family member—to help you remember next time.
- Schedule your waiter to call you at the party site before arrival. He or she can pick up the things you've forgotten.

Question Three

I've been afraid to do anything but the food for my caterings, but recently I've noticed I come up with more ideas than the wedding consultants or the party planners that hire me. How can I make more money?

You should definitely try your hand at the flowers and the decor to easily increase your profits. Let me give you an example from my own experience.

I was catering a beach wedding. The bride's florist wanted $35 per table for fifteen arrangements of tropical plants. Knowing that the budget was tight, I suggested to the bride that she consider using sand, shells, and two goldfish in a bowl on every table. She loved the idea. In the end each table cost me $6 to decorate—I charged $18. Everybody was happy: The bride spent half as much as she expected, and I made $180 for an hour's work and a good idea.

I used the same process I use in menu pricing to calculate my price. I estimated what my costs would be, analyzed the labor, was flexible, and budgeted my profit on a worksheet.

Selling centerpieces or getting involved in other aspects of the party planning can be a lifesaver if you discover that you've underpriced a menu. In my experience, even the best-prepared caterer sometimes makes a mistake or quotes a menu price that's too low. In that case, see whether you can interest your client in some wonderful centerpieces or a fabulous balloon sculpture or two singing waiters. The money you make in "upselling" the client this way may make the difference between a party that puts you in the black and one that puts you in the red.

Question Four

My food tastes great and I love to cook, but I'm not good at setting up my buffets. Are there any tricks I can learn for presentation that don't cost a lot of money?
Here are twelve tips for effective buffet presentation:

1. Use different sizes, colors, and textures of cloth as accent overlays with banquet rental cloths. Drape the tablecloths to the floor to cover the table legs. Buy the swatches of cloth at closeouts in fabric stores. I've even used twin-size sheets in various patterns that I bought at a white sale as overlays.

2. Create height. Elevate food with plastic risers or glass bricks (available at a builder's supply store). Votive candles behind the bricks create a wonderful light at night. Crates and boxes, even stacks of paper plates hidden under the cloth overlays, also add height.

3. For free risers, cover empty coffee cans with faux marble contact paper and put trays across the top for a dramatic high-tech look. I've also used

tall terra-cotta pots turned on their sides with a napkin liner to serve tortilla chips and Mexican bread.

4. Place cheese and fruit on mirrored squares or broken pieces of marble from a hardware store or marble quarry. Line different-shaped baskets with aromatic herbs to serve bread. Put salads in glass bowls to show off the colors.

5. Spray paint is the recycler of props. I own baskets that have been gold, black, red, or whatever other color I needed. I go over them with a wire brush for a burnished look and then spray them again.

6. Mix copper and silver chafing dishes, oblong with round. I've found antique-looking serving pieces at garage sales for less than $20 each.

7. Look around your garage or at garage sales for junk that can be used as props. An old fishbowl might be perfect on a Chinese stir-fry display, with one goldfish, or koi, as the center of attention.

8. Have your florist make two or three different-shaped arrangements instead of one standard buffet piece. Stagger the arrangements or group them on pillars behind the buffet. Or hang them from a beam behind the buffet. Or have a garland made and snake it through the chafing dishes. Ask your florist to give you any broken-stemmed flowers for free to scatter on the dessert table. Imagination is all it takes.

9. Tier candles in different-shaped holders. (Before you do this, be sure that props and cloths are fire retardant, and check local fire codes.) Use colored bulbs in ceiling lights or hang spotlights or Chinese lanterns. You can buy gel paper at photography stores to color lights, too.

10. Have your client rent battery-pack neon lights to highlight floral arrangements.

11. Dress your food servers in ethnic costumes to complement your theme or buffet. Coordinate your outfit to the color scheme. (I look great in peach, so I push that color theme.)

12. Rent sound effects from special-effect companies. Running water or a babbling brook under an Oriental display conjures up a Japanese garden.

Question Five

I get a lot of calls for jobs I have to turn away because I have only one pair of hands and I don't know how to handle volume. Do you have any suggestions?

Try not to turn away business. Try to solve the client's problems or work with another caterer or food source to pull the job off. At the very least you should be able to find another caterer and refer the job to him or her. Then ask for a finder's fee or barter a favor in return.

An example: A caterer I know had a problem. Her client wanted 500 box lunches at $5 each. The caterer figured that with overtime pay for helpers working all night and the small amount of refrigeration in her kitchen, it was an impossible feat for her.

I asked her what kind of box lunches her client wanted. "Oh, anything," she said. "Anything that tastes good. She doesn't really care."

In a shopping mall the week before, I saw a sign in a bakery window advertising box lunches for $3.99. I suggested to the caterer that she call the bakery. For an order that large, the bakery agreed to do boxes for $3.50 and to add an orange to the fresh croissant turkey sandwich, pasta salad, and cookie. The manager even agreed to deliver the boxes to the location in a refrigerated van. The caterer asked the bakery to leave its sticker off each box so that she could add hers and enclose a business card. She made $1.50 profit on each box lunch before taxes. The bakery was delighted with the order, the client got a wonderful lunch at the price she wanted to pay, and everyone lived happily ever after.

This was one smart business deal that worked in every way and took only one phone call.

Question Six

I was so careful ordering my rentals, but I still ran out of glasses, dinner plates, and cloth napkins at my party. Why?

This is a universal catering problem. You have to plan on guests' using about five glasses each for an average four-hour party. They do not hold on to the same glass. Every time they go to the bar, even if it's only for mineral water, guests get a clean glass.

Here are some solutions:

Glasses

- Rent five glasses per guest. Charge the client for them.
- If five glasses per guest cost too much, use glass only for the first two hours of the party, then switch to plastic.
- Be prepared to wash glasses. Have detergent, gloves, hot water, and someone to wash the dishes standing by, or plan on running the client's dishwasher.

Napkins

- Keep the cloth napkins under lock and key until you are ready to roll the silverware in them or fold them for placement. Chances are your staff grabbed them before the party and used them when they didn't have towels. Bartenders take them for opening wine. Chefs use them for pot holders, waiters for the bread baskets.
- Order twenty extra napkins (about 55 cents apiece) over your guest count and make the staff happy.

Plates

- If you're catering a buffet, plan on one and one-half dinner plates per guest. If your guest count is 100, put 150 plates out. This amount covers guests who come back for seconds, musicians, valets, waiters, and photographers. You want to make a great impression on everyone at the party, even subcontractors. They help build your reputation in the industry.
- Dessert for 100 guests probably means that you need only 110 plates. People often pass on dessert or even reuse their dessert plates, but not dinner plates.

Question Seven

When my rentals arrived, some cups were chipped, linens were faded, and the white chairs were scraped. We got through the party okay, but I was embarrassed. What can I do?

For next time:

- Always keep on hand the cell phone number of your rental representative. Call immediately to discuss the condition of the equipment and ask him or her to send replacement equipment on another truck.
- Demand a credit on the invoice. You feel cheated, and rightly so.
- Look for another rental company and go down to their warehouse to inspect the merchandise.
- Request the best equipment when you place your order, and tell them that your client is particular. Get the owner of the rental company's guarantee over the phone.

Question Eight

Sometimes clients ask me to leave the leftovers or their guests ask if they can take food home. How do I handle that?

Caterers differ on how they handle leftovers. Some leave them with the client. If you do that, I suggest that you leave written instructions on how the food is to be kept so that you don't run into complaints later.

I won't give leftovers to guests to take home, for a number of reasons. For one thing my product liability insurance doesn't protect me once the food is out of my sight. And what happens when the guest who took the leftovers lets the poached salmon salad with dill mayonnaise get warm, eats it, gets sick, misses several days' work, and wants to sue me? It takes my valuable time, attorneys' costs, and written documentation from my client to prove that he was the only guest who got sick.

My insurance policy extends only through the hours of the party. As far as I'm concerned, the client buys the food only for the time the party is held. Sometimes in my contract I put the specific times the buffet will be open and closed. Not only does this keep the food safe, but it also prevents clients from inviting a secret "second shift" to a party if they think you'll leave the buffet up for hours. They hope you won't notice twenty-five extra guests—latecomers—and that they'll eat for free.

Your best bet is to make the right amount of food so that you don't have left-overs after you've served the staff and subcontractors. I've found that leaving left-overs can work against me if the client sees a lot of food and thinks, "Gosh, if Denise hadn't made so much, maybe the party wouldn't have cost so much." Also, if they reheat a product and it doesn't taste good because it's dry and brown, they sometimes wonder if their guests really enjoyed it.

I had a client call me once to ask for a refund on a wedding cake a week after the reception. It seems she had tasted the last bite five days after the wedding and didn't think it tasted fresh-baked. "I was surprised by how dry it was," she told me. "Maybe that's why the guests didn't eat it all."

I told her that since her guests had gone back for seconds and thirds on the buffet (and, incidentally, raved about the entrees), they may have been too full for dessert. I had tasted the cake at the reception and knew it was delicious. When she admitted that she hadn't kept it tightly wrapped, it was easy for me to convince her that it wasn't right for me to give her a refund.

I admit that I'm stricter on this subject than many other caterers, but I work in California, which is a very lawsuit-happy state. I make sure my clients know at the outset that there may not be any leftovers, and that if there are, I won't leave them behind. I have found that they'll agree to anything as long as I tell them my policy at the outset.

Question Nine

My client supplied her own bar, and I hired a professional bartender from a personnel service; still one of the guests got drunk. When I asked the bartender how many drinks he served that guest, he said two, but apparently she drank the complimentary wine on the table during dinner. It was uncomfortable for everyone. Is there is a way to stop this in the future?

This is a serious problem in our industry. You want to be aware of the legal liabilities of your company and think about your moral obligation to the community. Call your local state Alcohol Beverage Control Board and ask about information and brochures they can share with you.

Remember that if a guest has a drinking problem, nothing will stop him or her from getting drunk. Serious drinkers carry small bottles in their purses or jackets. (You find the empties under the tables or in the bathrooms later.) But you can make sure that they don't drive away from the party.

In California that's why valet parking services have become so popular. The valet will not turn over car keys to an intoxicated driver. You can assist by suggesting a cab

Complementary California
Wine Selection List

White Wines

Sauvignon Blanc: A crisp, light, young wine with an herbal aroma and often fruity (apple) flavor. Served best with mild cheeses, appetizers, and seafood.

Chardonnay: Ranges from medium to full bodied. May taste of oak or have a smoky character. The lighter the Chardonnay, the more fruity the flavor; full-bodied varieties are often described as buttery. Will complement any chicken, fish, or light pasta dish.

Johannisberg Riesling: Delicate but complex with a spicy and fruity (peaches and apricots) character. Good with mild cheeses, light seafood appetizers, ham, and even desserts.

Red Wines

Zinfandel: Wide range of tastes, but a robust Zinfandel is spicy with black pepper and ripe berry flavors. Can hold its own with strong cheeses, beef, game, and a variety of hearty pasta dishes.

Cabernet Sauvignon: Cabs are distinguished by rich, full, fruit flavors (cherry and even raspberry) and aromas. Deep color with warm mouthfeel. Enjoy with strong cheeses, prime rib, steak, and chocolate.

Merlot: Merlot means "young blackbird" in French. Merlots are subtle and softer than a Cabernet and are dominated by fruit and herb flavors. Wonderful with beef, some poultry dishes, and even Chinese food.

or by calling the police. This is drastic, but sometimes necessary. At the very least ask the host or hostess, who might take the guest home safely.

Here are additional tips:

- Make some written notes that you alerted and discussed this problem with your client before the party. If you encounter a drunken guest, document what you did about it, too. You may have to take the lead because the host and hostess may have had a couple of drinks, too.
- Get information and brochures on the designated-driver program from your police or sheriff's department. When you are selling the party, ask the hostess if she would like to offer this to her guests. In each invitation make mention of the program or include a button. Tell designated drivers that they get chocolate-chip cookie bags from the caterer when they leave and free soft drinks during the party.
- I never purchase liquor for my guests or sell it to them. I am happy to supply a suggested bar list or to suggest a wine that goes well with the food (see page 205), but I don't profit from the sale of liquor; nor do I place the order or pay for it.
- Explain to clients that all wine and liquor should be poured and monitored by professional bartenders and waitstaff. If staff alerts you to a client who has had enough to drink, stand behind the staff in the decision to stop serving that person.
- Do you know other caterers who are selling liquor to their clients? They may own a liquor license or use one from a restaurant they own—or they may be breaking the law. Check the laws in your state and be sure to stay on the right side of them.

Question Ten

At my last party one of the waiters didn't show up. At the pre-party meeting I told all my staff to please work faster. We were shorthanded for the entire party. It made it stressful for everyone, and several of the staff complained. What else could I have done?

This will happen to you more than once in your career. Here are some alternatives to consider:

- The instant you know one waiter is a no-show, ask the other waiters if they know of anyone they can call to come help solve the problem. Even if he can't arrive for two hours, he'll get there in time to help clear the dinner dishes, lighten cleanup, and be a hero.
- Keep a list of waitstaff in your organized party folder. Assign one person to start calling until a replacement is found.
- When you schedule your party, ask a waiter to be on call. I've offered people $25 to be on call for the two hours preceding the start of my parties. It works. After two hours if I haven't called, they get the $25 and can do what they like.
- Make it understood when you are hiring staff that if they stand you up and aren't calling from a hospital to report why they are not there, they no longer work for you.
- If you can't reach anyone to help, tell the existing staff that you appreciate the extra effort and will disburse the pay of the missing waiter among them. A thank-you and up-front incentive work wonders.

Question Eleven

After doing four or five caterings, I am not making enough money. It seems as though I always forget to charge for something or something goes wrong and I have to pay for it. What can I do?

Promise to reread chapters 3, 5, and 8, and stop acting as though you don't understand math or that you are too creative to be bothered about money.

Catering is a business, and I bet you are not using a contract or writing proposal worksheets or calculating your costs. Because if you were, you would know to the penny what your parties are costing you. Instead I'd guess that clients call you and you are so glad to get the business that you say yes right away and start purchasing food, props, and equipment immediately. You never get deposit money or discuss the terms of who is paying for what. You just assume it will all be fine. Am I right?

Shortcuts can make you miss the most important parts of the deal. Start fresh today. Create a contract checklist and keep it next to the phone. The next time a client calls, start from the top. Don't promise or quote a price until you have worked the calculator. Don't undersell your talent or your product.

If you go through the process discussed in this book, you can't help but make money.

Question Twelve

I'm making good money in my business, but I only get calls from clients who never want to spend much. What can I do?

Change your attitude and expand your horizon. Look to target wealthier and more sophisticated clients. This is a marketing and image problem. I am a firm believer that you attract the clientele you deserve. That may be blunt and I'm sorry, but try to figure out whether your approach is at fault.

I look to competition I admire when I am trying to solve my problems. How are they getting clientele? What do their brochures or websites say? Maybe I can follow some of their steps without spending a lot of money.

Contact your chamber of commerce and find out if they have mailing lists available that target professional organizations. You know who is making the most money in your area. Who is providing services for them now?

Be sure not to make excuses for yourself. Get beyond the excuse stage and go after the clients you want. Error! Bookmark not defined.

12 Catering Menus and Quantity Recipes

I decided it would be helpful to include catering menus and foolproof quantity recipes for the new cook or caterer. The production notes, equipment suggestions, and step-by-step instructions provided with these recipes have proved to be successful.

The menus and recipes in this chapter are classic party foods that never go out of style. Actually, most trendy foods are just new twists on old classics. The menus have suggested titles, but many of them could be renamed to fit other occasions. Our Baby Shower Buffet Lunch could also serve as a wonderful Sweet Sixteen Luncheon or even a Grandmother's Birthday Brunch.

I know from teaching my catering courses that making too much product is often a problem for the new caterer. If you've had this problem, please go back and reread chapter 5.

If you calculate each portion of food per person, then multiply by the number of guests attending, you should come close to the right amount. There are resources listed in chapter 5 to help you in your quantity calculations.

Cooking Methods and Why It Is Important to Know Them
Unless you've worked in professional kitchens or have gone to culinary school, the chances are that you "know" a lot about cooking without knowing why or how you know. Unless you've had the opportunity to do something over and over and over again, you don't really know why something works and something doesn't. A little education goes a long way in this respect. Using the proper cooking method is the second step (after buying good quality ingredients) to a successful recipe. Below is a description of the basic cooking methods and their uses.

There are three basic ways to cook food: dry heat, moist heat, and a combination of the two. Dry heat methods result in highly flavored, crisp exteriors and moist interiors. Moist heat cooking methods are best for delicate, tender meats, fish, and poultry and produce a texture that is consistent throughout. Combination cooking methods are perfect for tougher cuts of meat, making them extremely flavorful and tender.

Dry Heat Cooking Methods

Food prepared this way should be naturally tender, as dry heat cooking does not have any tenderizing effects. You can add some moisture by marinating food before cooking.

Grilling and broiling (including grilling on a grill pan) foods is cooking foods through radiant heat from a source below or above the food. This results in a smoky, slightly charred flavor from the juices and fats that are cooked out. Steaks, ribs, chicken, whole or non-delicate fish and shellfish, and most vegetables are all good choices for grilling or broiling.

Roasted and baked foods are cooked through contact with dry, hot air, as in an oven. The food's juices turn to steam and deeply penetrate the food. Pan drippings make a very flavorful sauce. Meats from the rib and loin areas and top round are excellent roasted, as are whole poultry and fish. Many vegetables are excellent to roast, including potatoes, garlic, onions, squashes (both summer and winter), peppers, mushrooms, eggplants, carrots, tomatoes, and artichokes. (See Oven-Roasted Turkey recipe, page 228.)

Sautéing food produces excellent exterior color and flavor. Sautéing requires little fat and a medium to high heat. Once you've added your meat to the hot pan, don't move it or turn it over until it stops sticking or you will tear the surface of the meat. Sautéed food is sometimes lightly dusted with seasoned flour to enhance the crispness of the exterior. Fond (the browned bits stuck to the pan after cooking) make an excellent base for pan sauces. Chicken, lean cuts of meat, fish, and shellfish all respond well to sautéing, as do most vegetables. (See Chicken Breast in Wild Mushroom Sauce recipe, page 223, and Tenderloin of Beef recipe, page 241.)

Pan frying is similar to sautéing but with more fat or oil in the pan and over a less intense heat. Pan frying produces a crisp brown crust and a moist interior. Food is often breaded or dipped in a batter before cooking. The food is cooked through its contact with the hot oil rather than through its contact with the pan. Fruit and

Basic Pan Sauce

For the best flavor, use the appropriate liquid to complement your meat. When using canned broth, always choose the best-quality unsalted broth you can find. The salt content in most canned broth is overwhelming when cooked down.

Beef or lamb—use ½ cup veal or beef broth and ½ cup red wine, or use all broth.
Chicken—use ½ cup chicken broth and ½ cup white wine, or all broth.
Pork—use ½ cup chicken broth and ½ cup apple or regular brandy, or all broth.

1 cup liquid (see note above)
1 tablespoon fresh herbs, chopped (parsley, sage, thyme, or rosemary)
Juices from cooked meat (if any)
1 tablespoon butter
Salt and freshly ground black pepper

When your meat is finished cooking, place it on a dish and cover to keep warm. Remove all but a tablespoon of the excess fat from pan. Add ½ cup liquid to pan and place over medium heat. Cook about 3 minutes, stirring constantly to loosen any stuck-on browned bits. Turn heat to high and add the remaining liquid, herbs, and any juices that have collected from the meat you've set aside. Let boil until liquid is reduced by half, about 3 minutes. Taste and adjust seasoning. Remove from heat and add butter, swirling gently into the sauce. Spoon over meat before serving.

Makes about ½ cup.

vegetable fritters, chicken, fish, pork, and lamb chops are good candidates for pan frying, especially if they are floured or breaded.

Deep frying cooks foods by completely submerging them in hot oil. Food is almost always breaded, battered, or dusted with flour, potatoes being a notable exception. Foods should be cut into consistent sizes so that they will cook through quickly and evenly. Deep frying is excellent for battered or breaded chicken, all kinds of fish and shellfish, and vegetables. Deep-fried herbs make a beautiful garnish. Always completely dry any items before you put them into hot fat to avoid splattering.

Moist Heat Cooking Methods

Cooked by submerging foods in liquid that is kept at a consistent temperature, moist heat cooking tends to be more subtly flavored than foods cooked with dry heat. Naturally tender foods work best.

Poaching is cooking by placing foods in a flavorful liquid that is held at a temperature below the simmering point, about 160°F to 185°F. There is little loss of flavor with poaching. Tender foods like chicken, fish, fruit, and eggs work best. (See Chardonnay Poached Salmon recipe, page 216.)

Simmering foods requires slightly higher temperatures, 185°F to 200°F. There is a greater transfer of flavor from food to cooking liquid with simmering than with poaching. This is the method to use when making richly flavored stocks and broths.

Boiling (212°F) is used for beans, pasta, grains, and some vegetables. Boiling is not recommended for meats, as it makes them tough and stringy. Lobster is a notable exception. (See Just like Mom's Mashed Potatoes recipe, page 231, and Shrimp Cocktail recipe, page 235.)

Steaming surrounds foods in moist, hot air. Food can be either set into a small amount of liquid or placed above it, covered and cooked over low heat. Cutting food into consistent sizes ensures even cooking. Steaming is best with tender cuts of meat, since this method does not tenderize foods. Lean fish, vegetables, and chicken breasts can all be steamed.

Combination Cooking Methods

Stewing and braising are the two methods that use both dry and moist heat cooking. Usually this involves browning or searing meat before adding it to other ingredients and stewing or braising it. This imparts more complexity and flavor than you can get with a single cooking method. Meats prepared this way come out meltingly tender. This is the ideal way to cook tougher, cheaper cuts of meat. But even tender foods like seafood and vegetables can be successfully braised and stewed if you use less liquid and a lower heat.

Chuck, blade, whole skirt, and flank steak cuts of beef are ideal for braising and stewing. Shoulder, butt, and shank of pork are excellent when braised or stewed. Lamb shoulder and chops also work very well. Osso buco is a heavenly dish of seared and braised veal shanks. Legs and thighs of poultry work very well, as do breasts if you keep a closer eye on them. All vegetables can be braised and stewed successfully.

Board Room Breakfast for 25

Butter Croissants
with Assorted Preserves
Fresh Homemade Blueberry Muffins
Applewood-Smoked Bacon
Creamy Free-Range
Scrambled Eggs
Orange Juice, Coffee and Tea Service

Baby Shower Buffet Lunch for 25

Mixed Field Greens with
Raspberry Vinaigrette*
Chardonnay Poached Salmon
with Dill Remoulade*
Steamed Spring Asparagus Lemony Rice Pilaf*
Chocolate Walnut Biscotti*
Coffee Service*

Family Brunch for 25

Assorted Fresh Bagels, Lox, and Cream Cheese
French Toast with Maple Syrup and Sweet Butter
Spinach, Herb, and Swiss Cheese Frittata
Roasted Garlic and
Rosemary Red Potatoes
Strawberries with Chantilly Cream
Champagne Bellinis
Coffee and Tea Service

Business Lunch for 50

Classic Caesar Salad with Parmesan Curls*
Chicken Breast
in Wild Mushroom Sauce*
Three-Cheese Potatoes au Gratin*
Garden Fresh String Beans
with Toasted Almonds*
Rustic Rolls and Butter*
Fresh Seasonal Fruit Platter*

Traditional Holiday Dinner for 50

Oven-Roasted Turkey,* Turkey Gravy*
Cornbread Stuffing*
Just Like Mom's Mashed Potatoes*
Candied Yams*
Fresh Cranberry-Orange Relish
Pecan Pie* with Whipped Cream

* Recipe follows

The difference between braising and stewing is that stews contain food that is cut into bite-size pieces and generally contains more liquid than braises, which are most often whole cuts of meat. They can both be prepared either on top of the stove or in the oven.

Catering Menus

Deliciously Healthy Dinner for 12

Shaved Artichoke Salad*

Roasted Salmon* with

Lemon Almond Pesto*

Colorful Wild Rice Pilaf*

Roasted Root Vegetables with Coriander*

Warm Baguettes and Butter

Poached Pears with Brandy Whipped Cream

Family-Style Vegetarian Dinner for 25

Frisée, Escarole, and Beet Salad*

Moroccan Eggplant Stew*

with Noodles

Warm Whole Grain Bread

Sweet Oranges

in Red Wine*

Semolina Almond Cake*

Crowd-Pleasing Tasting Menu for 50

Melon Soup Demitasse*

Potato Onion Tarts

Spicy Shrimp Skewers

on Shredded Napa Cabbage*

Sausage and Spinach Stuffed Phyllo*

with Fresh Tomato Sauce*

Trio of Mini Chocolate Desserts

Southern Picnic for 50

Finger Food Fried Chicken*

with Peach Salsa*

Cheesy Corn Muffins*

Ambrosia*

Chilled Green Bean Salad

Dilly Macaroni Salad

Lemon Bars and Fudge Brownies

* Recipe follows

Mixed Field Greens with Raspberry Vinaigrette

PRODUCTION NOTE: Salad can be dressed just before service, or dressing can be served on the side.

Yield: 25 servings
Portion size: approximately 3 ounces
Equipment: tongs, stainless steel bowl, 36-inch-diameter salad bowl, whisk

Ingredient	Amount
Mesclun salad mix	32–40 ounces (16–20 cups)
Mayonnaise	2 ounces ($\frac{1}{4}$ cup)
Raspberry vinegar	2 ounces ($\frac{1}{4}$ cup)
Dijon mustard	1 ounce (2 tablespoons)
Raspberries, fresh or frozen and thawed tablespoon)	$4\frac{1}{2}$ ounces ($\frac{1}{2}$ cup + 1
Honey	3 ounces ($\frac{1}{3}$ cup)
Safflower or olive oil	24 ounces (3 cups)
Salt and pepper	to taste

Method

1. Combine mayonnaise, raspberry vinegar, Dijon mustard, raspberries, and honey in a stainless steel bowl. Using the back of a spoon or fork, mash raspberries into mixture.
2. Gradually whisk in oil until mixture is emulsified.
3. Season with salt and pepper.
4. Place a third of the dry lettuce in a 36-inch-diameter stainless steel or plastic bowl.
5. Add $\frac{1}{2}$ to $\frac{3}{4}$ cup of vinaigrette.
6. Using tongs or your hands in disposable plastic gloves, incorporate dressing with lettuce until well coated.
7. Taste salad and add more dressing as needed.
8. Place on buffet serving platter.
9. Repeat with remaining lettuce mixture and vinaigrette.

PRODUCTION NOTE: Serve the remoulade in individual ramekins or place in a pastry bag and pipe onto each filet. Remoulade can be made one day in advance.

Yield: 25 servings, 6$\frac{1}{2}$ cups of sauce

Portion size: 6 ounces

Equipment: two 8-quart (12$\frac{3}{4}$ x 20$\frac{3}{4}$ x 2-inch) steam table pans or four 4-quart (6x10x2-inch) steam table pans, heavy-duty aluminum foil, large stockpot, ladle, mixing bowl

Ingredient	Amount
Chardonnay or other dry white wine	6 bottles (750 mil each)
Fresh dill, chopped	4 bunches (about 1$\frac{1}{2}$ cups)
Lemons, cut into slices	6
Salmon fillets, center cut, skinless	25 pieces of fillet, 6 ounces each

Dill remoulade:

Mayonnaise	24 ounces (3 cups)
Fresh dill, chopped	1 bunch (about $\frac{1}{2}$ cup)
Fresh chives, chopped	1 ounce (2 tablespoons)
Dijon mustard	$\frac{1}{2}$ ounce (1 tablespoon)
Salt and pepper	to taste

Method

1. Preheat oven to 350 degrees.
2. Bring Chardonnay to a boil in a large stockpot.
3. Turn off heat and add dill and lemon slices.
4. Allow mixture to infuse for 10 minutes.
5. Divide the salmon fillets between the steamer pans in a single layer.
6. Ladle the hot wine over the salmon fillets.
7. Cover pans tightly with heavy-duty aluminum foil and place in oven.
8. Bake for about 20 minutes or until salmon is just cooked through. The salmon is cooked through when it turns a lighter color. Do not overcook.
9. Meanwhile, make the remoulade by mixing together mayonnaise, dill, chives, and mustard. Season with salt and pepper. Refrigerate until ready to serve.
10. Remove foil and allow fish to cool in liquid.
11. Carefully transfer salmon to serving platter and refrigerate, covered with plastic wrap until ready to serve.

Yield: 25 servings

Portion size: approximately ¹/₃ cup

Equipment: large sauté pan (14-inch), one 8-quart (12³/₄ x 20³/₄ x 2-inch) steam table pan or two 4-quart (6x10x2-inch) steam table pans, heavy-duty aluminum foil, fork

Ingredient	Amount
Butter	3 ounces (¹/₃ cup)
Onion, finely diced	5 ounces (²/₃ cup)
Long-grain white rice	2 pounds (5 cups)
Chicken or vegetable stock	72 ounces (9 cups)
Lemon juice	8 ounces (1 cup)
Bay leaves	5
Salt	3 teaspoons
Pepper	1 teaspoon

Method

1. Preheat oven to 350 degrees.
2. Melt butter in sauté pan over medium heat.
3. Add onions and cook for 2 minutes, or until softened.
4. Add rice and stir to coat with butter.
5. Transfer rice to steam table pan.
6. Add hot stock, lemon juice, bay leaves, salt, and pepper.
7. Stir to incorporate ingredients.
8. Cover pan tightly with aluminum foil.
9. Bake in oven for 25–30 minutes, or until liquid is absorbed and rice is tender.
10. Fluff rice with fork and transfer to buffet.

PRODUCTION NOTE: Can be made up to two days ahead.

Yield: 48 3-inch cookies
Portion size: 2 biscotti
Equipment: 18x26-inch or two 9x13-inch sheet pans, medium mixing bowl, large mixing bowl

Ingredient	Amount
Eggs, at room temperature	4
Vanilla extract	2 teaspoons
Granulated sugar	11 ounces (1$\frac{1}{3}$ cups)
Cake flour	10 ounces (2$\frac{1}{2}$ cups)
Unsweetened cocoa powder	5 ounces ($\frac{2}{3}$ cup)
Baking powder	2 teaspoons
Salt	$\frac{1}{2}$ teaspoon
Chocolate chips	4 ounces ($\frac{1}{2}$ cup)
Walnuts	5 ounces ($\frac{2}{3}$ cup)
Butter for greasing pans	

Method

1. Preheat oven to 350 degrees.
2. Beat eggs in medium mixing bowl until light and fluffy. Slowly beat in vanilla and sugar, scraping sides of bowl as needed.
3. In a large mixing bowl, sift together cake flour, unsweetened cocoa powder, baking powder, and salt.
4. Stir flour mixture into eggs. Stir in chocolate chips and walnuts.
5. Butter an 18x26-inch sheet pan.
6. With buttered hands, form mixture into four 3x10-inch logs and place on baking sheet.
7. Bake for 30 minutes. Remove from oven and let cool for 10–12 minutes.
8. Using a serrated knife, cut each log diagonally into 12 slices.
9. Place biscotti, flat side down, on a baking sheet.
10. Bake for 7 minutes. Carefully turn over and bake for an additional 5–7 minutes, or until crisp.
11. Remove to cooling racks. Let biscotti cool completely. Store in an airtight container until ready to serve.

PRODUCTION NOTE: For perfect coffee use freshly ground coffee, bottled water, and a clean coffeepot.

Yield: 40 cups
Portion size: 6–8 ounces
Equipment: 25–42 cup capacity coffeemaker

Ingredient	Amount
Ground coffee	16 ounces (1 pound)
Bottled water	$2\frac{1}{2}$ gallons
Cream, milk, or half & half	32 ounces (1 quart)

Classic Caesar Salad with Parmesan Curls

PRODUCTION NOTE: Look for five-pound bags of prewashed, ready-to-use romaine lettuce in large discount or club stores. This will save you time and labor cost. You can also serve this salad on individual salad plates. Use two anchovy fillets placed in an "X" on top of each individual salad for garnish. Because of food safety concerns about raw eggs in salad dressings, it's best to hard-boil your eggs instead of using raw ones. Chop the egg whites fine and use as an optional garnish for your salad.

Yield: 50 servings
Portion size: 3 ounces lettuce, 5–7 croutons, and $\frac{1}{2}$ ounce Parmesan curls
Equipment: large stainless steel bowl, tongs, disposable gloves, whisk

Ingredient	Amount
Caesar dressing:	
Anchovy fillets	30
Garlic cloves, minced	8 (about 2 tablespoons)
Egg yolks, hard-boiled	8
Lemon juice	12 ounces ($1\frac{1}{2}$ cups)
Olive oil	40 ounces (5 cups)
Salt and pepper	to taste
Romaine lettuce, trimmed, washed, and cut or torn into 1-inch pieces	20 pounds (about 12 heads)
or Romaine, prepacked, ready-to-use, chopped	160 ounces (10 pounds)
Croutons (recipe follows)	32 ounces (2 pounds)
Parmesan cheese curls	32 ounces (2 pounds)

Method

1. Place anchovy fillets, garlic, and egg yolks in bowl.
2. Mash together with a fork to form a paste.
3. Whisk in lemon juice until smooth.
4. Slowly drizzle in olive oil, whisking constantly until mixture thickens.
5. Season with salt and pepper.
6. Place romaine lettuce in a large stainless steel bowl.
7. Add dressing 1 cup at a time. Toss well with tongs or with gloved hands.
8. Continue to add dressing until romaine is well coated.
9. Taste and adjust seasoning with salt and pepper.
10. Add croutons and cheese just before service. Toss to coat.

PRODUCTION NOTE: It is easier to cut bread when it's a day old. An alternative method to sautéing the croutons is to place them on sheet pans and drizzle olive oil over them. Toss to coat and bake in a 350-degree oven until golden. Croutons can be made up to one week in advance. When completely cool, store at room temperature in an airtight container.

Yield: 2 pounds
Portion size: 5–7 croutons
Equipment: large sauté pans

Ingredient	Amount
Bread loaves, presliced	32 ounces (2 pounds)
Olive oil	8 ounces (1 cup)
Salt and pepper	to taste

Method
1. Trim crusts from bread.
2. Cut each slice of bread into $3/4$-inch cubes. Each slice of bread should yield about 12 croutons.
3. In batches, sauté croutons in oil until crisp.
4. Season with salt and pepper.

PRODUCTION NOTE: Instead of buying one large piece of parmesan, look for the precut wedges available in the cheese section of your grocery store. They are easier to store and handle.

Yield: 50 servings
Portion size: ¹/₂ ounce, about five 1-inch curls
Equipment: vegetable peeler

Ingredient	Amount
Parmesan cheese, cut into wedges	2 pounds

Method

1. Hold cheese in one hand with the long edge facing upward.
2. With the vegetable peeler in the other hand, form curls by peeling thin strips of cheese from the surface of wedge.
3. Store curls in an airtight container in the refrigerator for up to 1 week.

PRODUCTION NOTE: You can sauté the chicken, let it cool down, cover with plastic wrap, then refrigerate it the day before your event. If you are using a household-size oven, use four 9x13-inch sheet pans, also called half-sheet pans.

Yield: 50 servings
Portion size: 1 chicken breast and 2 ounces wild mushroom sauce (¹/₄ cup)
Equipment: two 18x26-inch sheet pans, large sauté pans, small saucepan, fine-mesh sieve, 8-quart stockpot, 2-ounce ladle

Ingredient	Amount
Wild Mushroom Sauce:	
Dried porcini mushrooms	2 ounces (²/₃ cup)
Chicken stock, low-sodium	16 ounces (2 cups)
Olive oil	4 ounces (¹/₂ cup)
Mushrooms (white, button, shiitake, crimini, oyster) cleaned and thinly sliced	96 ounces (6 pounds)
Garlic, chopped	1¹/₂ ounce (3 tablespoons)
Fresh sage leaves	¹/₄ cup (or 1 tablespoon dried)
Dry vermouth	16 ounces (2 cups)
All-purpose flour	2 ounces (¹/₂ cup)
Heavy cream	40 ounces (5 cups)
Salt and pepper	to taste
Chicken breasts, boneless, skinless, and trimmed	50 (6 ounces each, ~20 lbs)
Butter, cut into 1-ounce pieces	1 pound

Method

1. Make mushroom sauce by placing dried porcini mushrooms and chicken stock in a small saucepan. Bring to a boil.
2. Turn off heat and allow to stand for 1 hour. Drain mixture, reserving liquid.
3. Squeeze porcini mushrooms to extract liquid, rinse in cold water, then finely chop. Strain reserved liquid to remove any sediment. Set aside.
4. Heat oil in sauté pan over medium heat. Sauté fresh mushrooms in batches until lightly brown. Add porcini mushrooms and sauté for 2 minutes.

1. Add garlic and sage and sauté for 1 minute more, add vermouth and cook for 2–3 minutes until slightly reduced, then pour in stockpot.

2. Mix flour with reserved mushroom liquid to form a paste. Turn heat to low and add paste to stockpot, stirring constantly until smooth.

3. Bring to a boil, lower heat, and simmer for 5–10 minutes, or until flour mixture has cooked and sauce has no raw-flour taste.

4. Stir in heavy cream and simmer 5 minutes. Adjust seasoning. Serve immediately or cover surface with a layer of plastic wrap to prevent a skin from forming.

5. Preheat oven to 350 degrees. Season each chicken breast with salt and pepper.

6. Heat butter in sauté pans over medium heat. In batches, sauté chicken on each side until golden, then place chicken in single layer on sheet pans and put in oven to bake for 10–15 minutes, or until cooked through.

7. Ladle sauce over chicken before service.

PRODUCTION NOTE: It will take about one hour to reheat each 12x20x2-inch pan in a 350-degree oven. Cover with foil to prevent overbrowning. This can also be made in four 6x10x2-inch pans. This dish can be made one day ahead and reheated.

Yield: 50 servings

Portion size: 6 ounces

Equipment: two 8-quart (12x20x2-inch) steam table pans, large (6-quart) saucepan, large stainless steel mixing bowl.

Ingredient	Amount
Potatoes	15 pounds
Cheddar cheese, shredded	1 pound
Mozzarella, shredded	1 pound
Swiss cheese, shredded	1 pound
Salt and pepper	to taste
Heavy cream	1 gallon (8 cups)
Butter, melted	8 ounces (1 cup)
Seasoned bread crumbs	2 cups
Butter for greasing pans	

Method

1. Preheat oven to 350 degrees.
2. Butter pans.
3. Peel potatoes and cut into $1/4$-inch thick slices. Store covered with water to which a few drops of milk have been added. This will keep potatoes from turning brown.
4. Mix all cheeses together in a stainless steel bowl.
5. Divide potatoes into thirds and layer one third on bottom of both pans.
6. Season potatoes with salt and pepper.
7. Divide cheese mixture equally into thirds and sprinkle one third over potatoes.
8. Repeat layer with another third of the potatoes and another third of the cheese mixture, seasoning potatoes with salt and pepper.
9. Repeat with remaining potatoes and cheese.
10. Heat cream over low heat in saucepan.
11. Pour cream over potato-cheese mixture in pans.
12. Drizzle each pan with $1/2$ cup of melted butter.
13. Sprinkle top of each pan with 1 cup of bread crumbs.
14. Bake for 1 hour, or until top is golden-brown and potatoes are tender. (If top browns too quickly, cover with foil until potatoes are tender.)

PRODUCTION NOTE: Toasted almonds can be made one day in advance if stored in an airtight container at room temperature. If you are using a household-size oven, use two 9x13-inch sheet pans. Nuts can burn very quickly. Check the almonds frequently while in the oven.

Yield: 10 pounds string beans, 1 pound almonds
Portion size: approximately 3 ounces string beans, 2 teaspoons almonds
Equipment: two large (8-quart) stockpots, large stainless steel bowl, one 18x26-inch sheet pan

Ingredient	Amount
Sliced almonds	1 pound
String or green beans	12 pounds
Butter, melted	1 pound (4 cups)
Salt and pepper	to taste

Method

1. Preheat oven to 350 degrees.
2. Spread almonds evenly in one layer on sheet pan.
3. Bake for 6–8 minutes, stirring occasionally to prevent burning, until nuts turn golden-brown. Cool to room temperature.
4. Trim ends from string beans.
5. Fill stockpots with salted water and bring to a boil.
6. Add string beans to boiling water.
7. Reduce heat and simmer for 5–6 minutes, or until string beans turn bright green and are still slightly crunchy.
8. Place string beans in bowl.
9. Add butter and toasted almonds.
10. Toss to coat.
11. Season with salt and pepper.
12. Serve immediately, or hold for up to 10 minutes in a warm oven.

Rustic Rolls and Butter

1. Allow 1½ rolls for a buffet or 2 rolls for a sit-down, and 1 tablespoon butter per guest.
2. Avoid rolls that have a tough, chewy crust.
3. Avoid rolls that are too large.

Fresh Seasonal Fruit Platters

1. Allow 4–5 ounces of prepared fruit per guest.
2. Use only seasonal fruits. Fruits in season not only taste better but are also less expensive.
3. Prepare fruit so it is user-friendly: Slice melons into bite-size pieces; serve strawberries with stems still attached; cut grapes into small clusters containing 4–5 grapes.
4. Accent the platter with whole fruit cut in half (kiwi, papaya, pineapple).
5. Adding some lesser-known fruits will make the fruit platter more exciting. Try using starfruit, lychee, passionfruit, champagne grapes.
6. Avoid sliced fruits that will discolor (bananas, apples, pears).
7. If serving chunks of fruit (pineapple, melon), have tongs or toothpicks available for guests to serve themselves with.

Oven-Roasted Turkey

PRODUCTION NOTE: For more even cooking, separate legs and thighs from the breast. Place on separate pan from breast section. Cook as directed. Total cooking time will be less. Cook two turkeys for fifty servings.

Yield: 128 ounces (8 pounds) sliceable meat for 25 servings
Portion size: 4–5 ounces
Equipment: large roasting pan, carving knife

Ingredient	Amount
Whole turkey	22 pounds
Salt and pepper	to taste
Olive oil	4 ounces ($\frac{1}{2}$ cup)
Onions, chopped into small dice	8 ounces (1 cup)
Carrots, chopped into small dice	4 ounces ($\frac{1}{2}$ cup)
Celery, chopped into small dice	4 ounces ($\frac{1}{2}$ cup)

Method

1. Preheat oven to 325 degrees.
2. Remove giblets from turkey and reserve for the gravy.
3. Rinse cavity and dry well with paper towels.
4. Heavily season cavity with salt and pepper; rub outside of turkey with olive oil.
5. Lock the wings in place by twisting the wing tips behind and under the back of the turkey.
6. Place turkey on its side in the roasting pan.
7. Cook for $1\frac{1}{2}$ hours, basting every 30 minutes with drippings.
8. Turn the turkey over on its other side and roast for another $1\frac{1}{2}$ hours, basting every 30 minutes.
9. Turn turkey so it is breast side up.
10. Add onions, carrots, and celery to the bottom of the roasting pan.
11. Roast, basting occasionally for another 2–3 hours, or until an instant-read thermometer inserted into the thickest part of the thigh reads 180 degrees. If turkey browns too quickly, cover with foil until fully cooked.
12. Remove turkey from roasting pan. Reserve pan drippings and vegetables for gravy.
13. Allow to stand in a warm place for 20–30 minutes before carving.

PRODUCTION NOTE: Cook the giblets while the turkey is roasting.

Yield: 50 servings
Portion size: approximately 3 ounces
Equipment: medium-size saucepan, roasting pan, strainer, large spoon

Ingredient	Amount
Reserved giblets from turkey	
Chicken or turkey stock, hot	112 ounces (3 1/2 quarts)
Pan drippings from turkey	6 ounces (3/4 cup)
Reserved vegetables from turkey	
All-purpose flour	6 ounces (1 1/3 cups)
Salt and pepper	to taste

Method

1. Remove liver from giblets and discard or save for another use.
2. Place giblets in a saucepan and cover with cold water.
3. Bring to a boil, lower heat, and simmer until tender, about 2–3 hours. Set aside.
4. When turkey has cooked, remove from roasting pan. Pour off all but 3/4 cup of the drippings.
5. Place roasting pan on burner over medium heat.
6. Brown reserved vegetables in drippings.
7. Add 1 quart of stock to pan and deglaze pan by stirring and scraping up any cooked-on browned bits on the bottom of the pan.
8. Pour into a large saucepan. Skim off excess fat from surface using a large spoon.
9. Strain giblet broth and add to gravy.
10. Chop giblets very fine and add to gravy. Add remaining stock.
11. Mix reserved drippings and flour together to form a roux.
12. Whisk the roux into the gravy.
13. Bring to a boil, stirring constantly.
14. Reduce heat and simmer for at least 15 minutes, or until gravy is smooth and has no raw-flour taste.
15. Season with salt and pepper.

PRODUCTION NOTE: Can be made a day in advance. Reheat in a 300-degree oven. You can double this recipe to make fifty portions.

Yield: 25 servings

Portion size: 3–4 ounces

Equipment: one 8-quart (12³/₄ x 20³/₄ x 2-inch) steam pan or two 4-quart (6x10x2-inch) steam table pans, large sauté pan, large stainless steel bowl

Ingredient	Amount
Butter	1 pound
Onions, diced	1 pound
Celery, diced	¹/₂ pound
Prepared cornbread, cornbread muffins, or white bread	2 pounds
Parsley, dried	1 teaspoon
Sage, dried	1 teaspoon
Thyme, dried	1 teaspoon
Black pepper	¹/₂ teaspoon
Salt	2 teaspoons
Chicken or vegetable stock	2 pints
Pecans or walnuts, chopped	2 cups

Method

1. Preheat oven to 375 degrees.
2. In a large sauté pan, heat ¹/₂ pound of the butter.
3. Add onions and celery. Sauté until soft but not brown.
4. Cut cornbread into small cubes. Combine cornbread and cooked vegetables in a large stainless steel bowl.
5. Add parsley, sage, thyme, black pepper, and salt.
6. Slowly add stock and toss until dressing is moist.
7. Stir in nuts.
8. Spoon into a greased pan.
9. Chop remaining butter into ¹/₄-inch pieces and sprinkle over top of dressing. Cover with foil.
10. Bake for 45 minutes. Uncover and bake for 15 minutes longer until top starts to brown.

PRODUCTION NOTE: This is a generous recipe and portion size because whether it's a buffet or sit-down, everyone eats more homemade mashed potatoes than anything else.

Yield: 50 servings
Portion size: 8 ounces
Equipment: potato masher or food processor, electric hand mixer, large stockpot, large bowl

Ingredient	Amount
Russet potatoes	25 pounds
Butter, at room temperature	24 ounces (6 sticks)
Heavy cream, warm	2 cups
Salt and pepper	to taste

Method

1. Peel potatoes and cut into equal 1-inch-size pieces.
2. Place in a large stockpot and cover with cool water.
3. Bring to a boil, lower heat, and simmer until potatoes are fork-tender.
4. Drain well. Let potatoes air-dry for 5 minutes.
5. Mash potatoes by hand, or carefully pulse in a food processor in batches.
6. Add butter and cream.
7. Stir until butter has melted. Season with salt and pepper.
8. Whip with an electric hand mixer until potatoes are light and fluffy. Add more butter for a softer consistency.

Yield: 50 servings

Portion size: ¹/₂ cup

Equipment: one 8-quart (12³/₄ x 20³/₄ x 2-inch) steam pan or two 4-quart (6x10x2-inch) steam pans

Ingredient	Amount
Butter for greasing pan	
Canned yams	5 (28¹/₂ ounce) cans
Brown sugar, packed	3 cups
Unsalted butter, cut into ¹/₂-inch pieces	¹/₂ pound

Method

1. Preheat oven to 350 degrees.
2. Butter pan. Place yams in pan.
3. Cut into equal portion sizes to allow even cooking.
4. Sprinkle with brown sugar.
5. Distribute butter evenly over yams. Cover with foil.
6. Bake for 30 minutes.
7. Uncover and bake for an additional 15–20 minutes, or until yams are tender and slightly caramelized.

PRODUCTION NOTE: This comfortably serves twenty-five. Double recipe for fifty servings.

Yield: four 9-inch single-layer pie crusts
Equipment: four 9-inch pie pans, stand mixer

Ingredient	Amount
Unsalted butter for greasing pie pans	
Unsalted butter, chilled	20 ounces (5 sticks)
Sugar	6 ounces
Salt	2 teaspoons
Egg yolks	4
All-purpose flour	20 ounces (5 cups)

Method

1. Grease the pie pans.
2. Place butter, sugar, and salt in the mixing bowl of a stand mixer.
3. Mix on low speed until smooth and evenly blended.
4. Add egg yolks and mix until absorbed.
5. Gradually add flour until mixture forms a dough.
6. Cut dough into 4 equal pieces.
7. Flatten each into a disk shape.
8. Cover with plastic wrap.
9. Chill for at least 1 hour. You can prepare this up to 2 days in advance.
10. Roll out each disk into circles of about 14 inches.
11. Lay over pie plate and gently press into pan. Trim edges.
12. Cover with plastic wrap and chill for at least 30 minutes.

PRODUCTION NOTE: This makes twenty-five servings. Double recipe for fifty servings.

Yield: four 9-inch pies
Portion size: $1/_{12}$ pie
Equipment: electric mixer, mixing bowl, aluminum foil

Ingredient	Amount
Sugar	1 pound
Brown sugar	1 pound
Unsalted butter	8 ounces
Salt	1 teaspoon
Eggs	20
Corn syrup	$2^{1}/_{2}$ pints
Vanilla extract	2 teaspoons
Pecan halves	$1^{1}/_{2}$ pounds
Unbaked pie shells	4

Method

1. Preheat oven to 350 degrees.
2. Place sugar, brown sugar, butter, and salt in mixing bowl.
3. Mix until all ingredients are evenly blended.
4. With machine running, gradually add eggs until absorbed.
5. Add corn syrup and vanilla. Mix well.
6. Fill each pie shell with mixture.
7. Arrange pecans on top of filling in a circular pattern, beginning at the outer edge and working your way inward toward the center.
8. Bake for 40–50 minutes, or until edge of crust is lightly browned and filling is set. If crust begins to brown too quickly, cover with aluminum foil until cooked. Serve with whipped cream.

Shrimp Cocktail with Spicy Dipping Sauce

PRODUCTION NOTE: Shrimp is the most expensive single item on this menu. Have the shrimp cocktail passed to your guests rather than as a buffet item. This way you can control the amount consumed. To cut labor costs, consider buying the peeled and deveined precooked frozen shrimp.

Yield: approximately 50 servings
Portion size: 3–4 shrimp
Equipment: large 8-quart stockpot, large sauté pans

Ingredient	Amount
Colossal shrimp (21–30 count), peeled and deveined, with tail on	8 pounds
Spicy dipping sauce	4 cups
Lemons, cut into wedges for garnish	12
Butter (for Method Two)	2 pounds
Garlic, minced fine (for Method Two)	16 teaspoons
Salt	to taste

Method One for Shrimp Cocktail
1. Fill stockpot with water and add salt to taste.
2. Bring water to a rolling boil.
3. Add shrimp in batches and cook until just pink.
4. Remove shrimp, place in an ice bath, and allow to cool. Drain and refrigerate until service.
5. Arrange shrimp on platter. Serve with dipping sauce and garnish with lemon wedges.

Method Two for Shrimp Scampi
1. Heat sauté pan over medium heat.
2. Add 4 ounces butter and 2 teaspoons garlic per pound of shrimp to pan.
3. Add 1 pound of shrimp and sauté until just pink.
4. Repeat with remaining shrimp, butter, and garlic.
5. Cool and refrigerate until service.

PRODUCTION NOTE: Can be made up to three days ahead if stored in an airtight container and refrigerated.

Yield: 50 servings (4 cups)
Portion size: $1/2$ ounce
Equipment: large bowl, mixing spoon

Ingredient	Amount
Ketchup	2 cups
Chili sauce	$1^{1}/_{4}$ cups
Prepared horseradish, drained	$1/2$ cup
Lemon juice	$1/4$ cup
Worcestershire sauce	1 tablespoon
Hot red pepper sauce	1 teaspoon
Salt and pepper	to taste

Method

1. Combine all ingredients except salt and pepper. Mix well.
2. Taste and adjust seasoning with salt and pepper.
3. Refrigerate for at least 1 hour.

PRODUCTION NOTE: Can be made up to eight hours ahead of time and covered first with damp paper towels then with plastic wrap.

Yield: about 50 servings
Portion size: approximately 3 ounces

Ingredient	Amount
Any or all of the following assorted raw vegetables, peeled and cut: radishes, carrots, celery, broccoli, cauliflower, cherry tomatoes, jicama, asparagus, string beans, sugar snap peas	10 pounds
Yogurt	$1^2/_3$ cups
Mayonnaise	$1^2/_3$ cups
Buttermilk	$2^1/_2$ cups
Garlic, minced	1 tablespoon
Green onions, finely chopped	2 tablespoons
Salt and pepper	to taste

Method

1. Place yogurt, mayonnaise, buttermilk, garlic, and green onions in a large mixing bowl.
2. Whisk until combined.
3. Season with salt and pepper.
4. Refrigerate until ready to serve.

PRODUCTION NOTE: To cut costs, use whole chicken tenders. If you do not own a grill, these sates can be baked in a 400-degree oven for ten minutes, or until cooked through. If using a household oven, use the smaller steam table pans. To save time, purchase already roasted peanuts for the sauce.

Yield: 50 servings

Portion size: 1–2 skewers

Equipment: two 8-quart (12x20x2-inch) steam table pans, or four 4-quart (6x10x2-inch) steam table pans, 85 wooden skewers, 13x9-inch baking sheet, food processor or blender, medium saucepan, whisk, large stainless steel bowl

Ingredient	Amount
Marinade:	
Soy sauce	3 cups (24 ounces)
Red curry paste	⅔ cup
Garlic, chopped	1 cup
Lime juice	1 cup (8 ounces)
Coriander, ground	¼ cup
Peanut oil	2 cups (16 ounces)
Honey	2 cups
Chicken breasts, boneless and skinless	16 pounds
Peanut Sauce:	
Unsalted peanuts, skinless	1½ cups
Sugar	1 tablespoon
Peanut or canola oil	3 tablespoons (1½ ounces)
Red curry paste	2 tablespoons
Coconut milk	3 cups (24 ounces)
Soy sauce	2 tablespoons (1 ounce)
Lime juice	3 tablespoons (1½ ounces)

Method

1. Mix together soy sauce, curry paste, garlic, lime juice, coriander, peanut oil, and honey in a large bowl. Whisk until smooth.
2. Cut chicken into $1/4$-inch slices along the length of the breast.
3. Divide chicken between pans. Pour equal amounts of marinade over each pan of chicken. Mix well to coat.
4. Marinate for at least 2 hours or overnight, turning chicken occasionally.
5. Meanwhile, preheat oven to 350 degrees. Place peanuts on baking sheet in one layer.
6. Bake for 10–12 minutes, stirring occasionally, until peanuts turn golden-brown and are lightly toasted.
7. Cool to room temperature, then place peanuts and sugar in food processor or blender and grind peanuts until mixture is fine.
8. In a medium saucepan, heat oil over low heat. Add curry paste and coconut milk. Whisk together for 1 minute.
9. Add ground peanuts and bring mixture to a boil, stirring constantly.
10. Just before service, whisk in soy sauce and lime juice.
11. Soak skewers in water for 10 minutes to prevent them from burning during cooking.
12. Preheat grill (or oven).
13. Place 1 piece of chicken onto each skewer.
14. Grill chicken for 3–4 minutes on each side, or until cooked through.
15. Serve hot or at room temperature with Peanut Sauce.

Baby Spinach, Roquefort, and Toasted Walnut Salad with Champagne Vinaigrette

PRODUCTION NOTE: If you can't find champagne vinegar, substitute red-wine or balsamic vinegar. This salad should be dressed in batches as needed. You can also plate this salad and drizzle two tablespoons of vinaigrette over each salad. Nuts can burn very quickly when in the oven. Set a timer or check on the progress frequently.

Yield: 100 servings, 3 quarts vinaigrette, 2 pounds walnuts
Portion size: 3 ounces, 2 tablespoons vinaigrette
Equipment: large stainless steel bowls, tongs, disposable gloves, one 18x26-inch or two 9x13-inch sheet pans, whisk

Ingredient	Amount
Vinaigrette:	
Champagne vinegar	60 ounces
Lemon juice	³/₄ cup
Fresh thyme	¹/₂ cup, or 3 tablespoons dried
Salt	3 tablespoons
Pepper	3 tablespoons
Garlic, chopped	3 tablespoons
Honey	3 tablespoons
Olive oil	48 ounces
Salad oil or canola oil	24 ounces
Walnuts, chopped	2 pounds
Baby spinach, prewashed	16 pounds
Roquefort or other blue cheese, crumbled	2 pounds
Salt and pepper	to taste

Method

1. In a large stainless steel bowl, mix together champagne vinegar, lemon juice, thyme, salt, pepper, garlic, and honey. Whisk until smooth.
2. Gradually whisk in oils until mixture emulsifies. Set aside.
3. Preheat oven to 300 degrees.
4. Spread walnuts in a single layer over pan and place pan in center of oven.
5. Bake 15-20 minutes, stirring occasionally, until walnuts begin to darken slightly. Remove pan from oven and allow walnuts to cool completely before adding to salad.
6. Mix together spinach, Roquefort cheese, and walnuts. Add dressing gradually. Using tongs or gloved hands, toss spinach well. Season with salt and pepper.

PRODUCTION NOTE: Sauté the filet as close to service as possible. To avoid overcrowding and overcooking, use several sauté pans at once. Cook the tenderloins in two to three batches, depending on available equipment. The sauce can be made a day ahead if covered and refrigerated.

Yield: 100 servings, 8 cups sauce
Portion size: 5 ounces beef, 2 tablespoons sauce
Equipment: large sauté pans, tongs, large stainless steel bowl

Ingredient	Amount
Horseradish Sauce:	
Prepared horseradish	1 cup
Sour cream	2 cups
Mayonnaise	2 cups
Dijon mustard	3 tablespoons
Salt and pepper	to taste
Beef tenderloin (filet mignon), trimmed of fat	32 pounds
Vegetable or canola oil	4 cups
Salt and pepper	to taste

Method
1. Combine horseradish, sour cream, mayonnaise, and Dijon mustard in a mixing bowl. Whisk until smooth. Season with salt and pepper.
2. Slice the beef across the grain into 5-ounce filets.
3. Salt and pepper each filet.
4. Pour 1/4 inch of oil into sauté pan.
5. Heat oil over high heat.
6. Quickly sauté the meat until well browned. The filet should still be pink inside.
7. Serve immediately or hold for no longer than 15 minutes.

PRODUCTION NOTE: These can be made one day ahead. Bring to room temperature and place on sheet pans. Bake at 325 degrees until hot and crisp.

Yield: 100 servings
Portion size: 3 ounces
Equipment: large stainless steel bowl, large sauté pans, spatulas, paper towels, large colander, sheet pans for reheating

Ingredient	Amount
Potatoes, peeled and shredded	25 pounds
Onions, grated	4 pounds
Eggs	6
Salt	3 tablespoons
Pepper	2 teaspoons
All-purpose flour	About 2 cups
Oil for frying	

Method

1. Place potatoes in colander and squeeze out excess moisture. Place in mixing bowl.
2. Add onions to potatoes and mix together.
3. Add eggs, salt, and pepper. Mix well.
4. Stir in enough flour to bind mixture.
5. Fill sauté pans with $\frac{1}{4}$ inch oil. Place over medium heat.
6. Test-fry a small amount of potato mixture. If batter is too thin and pancake falls apart, add more flour. Adjust seasoning if necessary.
7. Using 3 ounces of potato mixture per pancake, cook until golden-brown.
8. Using a spatula, flip pancake and cook on the other side until golden-brown.
9. Drain on paper towels before serving.
10. Serve immediately or hold in a warm oven on sheet pans.
11. To reheat, place pancakes in a single layer on sheet pans. Place in a 350-degree oven until hot and crispy.

PRODUCTION NOTE: Use prepeeled and shaped, ready-to-use baby carrots, or fresh baby carrots with stems attached. Cut stems leaving $\frac{1}{2}$ inch of greenery.

Yield: 100 servings
Portion size: 2 ounces
Equipment: large stockpot, sauté pans, medium saucepan

Ingredient	Amount
Baby carrots	13 pounds
Butter, cut into 1-inch pieces	$1\frac{1}{2}$ pounds
Honey	3 cups
Orange juice	1 cup
Fresh parsley, chopped	$\frac{3}{4}$ cup

Method
1. Peel carrots if not using the prepeeled ones.
2. Fill stockpot $\frac{3}{4}$-full of salted water. Bring to a boil. Parboil carrots in boiling water until barely tender. Drain. (Carrots can be cooled and refrigerated for up to one day at this stage.)
3. Melt butter in sauté pans over medium heat. In batches, sauté carrots until almost tender.
4. Mix together honey and orange juice in a medium saucepan. Bring mixture to a boil. Add honey mixture to carrots. Toss to coat. Add parsley and season with salt and pepper.
5. Serve immediately or place in steam table pans and hold, covered with aluminum foil, for up to 30 minutes in a warm oven.

PRODUCTION NOTE: Fresh haricots verts require very little preparation. If fresh are not available, you can use frozen. Once defrosted, they need little cooking time.

Yield: 100 servings
Portion size: 2 ounces
Equipment: sauté pans, tongs

Ingredient	Amount
Haricots verts	13 pounds
Olive oil	1 cup
Salt and pepper	to taste

Method

1. Wash haricots verts and trim stalk end if necessary.
2. Heat oil in pans over medium heat.
3. Add haricots verts in batches and sauté for 30 seconds to 1 minute. Should be slightly crunchy. Season with salt and pepper.

Shaved Artichoke Salad

PRODUCTION NOTE: Dressing can be made a day in advance if refrigerated in an airtight container.

Yield: 12 servings
Portion size: about 3 ounces
Equipment: small stainless steel bowl, paring knife, spoon, food processor or blender, vegetable peeler

Ingredient	Amount
Lemon juice	1 cup, divided
Water, chilled	4 cups
Artichokes	2 large
Garlic	2 cloves
Extra-virgin olive oil	½ cup
Dijon mustard	2 tablespoons
Salt and freshly ground black pepper	to taste
Limestone lettuce, very roughly chopped	2 heads
Radishes, thinly sliced	1 bunch
Fresh tarragon, roughly chopped	¼ cup
Parmigiano-Reggiano cheese, shaved	1 cup

Method

1. In a small bowl, combine ½ cup of lemon juice and the water. Set aside.
2. Snap off outer leaves of artichoke; pare down to the heart. Scoop out and discard choke with a spoon. Place heart in lemon water.
3. Place remaining lemon juice, garlic, olive oil, and mustard in the work bowl of a food processor or blender and process until creamy. Season with salt and pepper and set aside.
4. Arrange lettuce, radishes, and tarragon on salad plates.
5. Remove hearts from water and, using a vegetable peeler, shave into very thin slices. Add to dressing, tossing to coat, and spoon over salads. Garnish with cheese and serve immediately.

PRODUCTION NOTES: If serving as a buffet, purchase two sides of salmon with the skin on, then slice into single-serving pieces through the flesh without cutting into the skin. This makes a very attractive way to serve the salmon, and helps you judge accurate portions. You can also purchase twelve five-ounce skin-on salmon fillets if a side of salmon is not available.

Yield: 12 servings
Portion size: 5 ounces
Equipment: two rimmed baking sheets, food processor, spreading spatula

Ingredient	Amount
Olive oil for greasing	
Lemons, cut into ¼-inch slices	4
Wild-caught or organically raised salmon	2 (2-pound) sides
Unsalted butter, at room temperature	12 tablespoons
Shallots, roughly chopped	4
Granulated sugar	2 teaspoons
Fresh rosemary leaves	2 tablespoons
Fresh chives, coarsely chopped	2 tablespoons
Salt and freshly ground black pepper	to taste

Method

1. Preheat oven to 450 degrees.
2. Grease 2 baking sheets with oil. Arrange lemon slices on prepared baking sheets. Place salmon on top of lemon slices, skin-side down.
3. Place butter, shallots, sugar, rosemary, and chives in the work bowl of a food processor and pulse until shallots are finely chopped and rosemary leaves are cut into small bits.
4. Spread butter mixture over top of salmon. Cook until salmon is just barely cooked through, about 15 minutes, depending upon thickness.
5. Remove from heat. Season with salt and pepper. Cover loosely with foil, and let stand for at least 5 minutes before serving. Serve hot or warm.

PRODUCTION NOTE: This pesto is milder than typical pesto, as the garlic is cooked to bring out the sweetness.

Yield: 2½ cups
Portion size: 2 ounces
Equipment: skillet, heatproof spatula, food processor, airtight container

Ingredient	Amount
Olive oil	1 tablespoon, plus ¾ cup
Garlic, peeled and coarsely chopped	1 head
Fresh flat-leaf parsley, coarsely chopped	¾ cup
Almonds, whole, roasted and unsalted	2 cups
Freshly squeezed lemon juice	½ cup
Lemon, zested	1
Salt and freshly ground black pepper	to taste

Method
1. Heat a tablespoon of olive oil in a skillet over medium-low heat.
2. Add garlic and cook, stirring frequently, until lightly golden but not browned, about 5 minutes. Transfer into the work bowl of a food processor.
3. Add parsley, almonds, lemon juice, and remaining olive oil and pulse until mixture is finely chopped, scraping down the sides of the bowl with a heatproof spatula.
4. Stir in lemon zest. Add salt and pepper.
5. Place in airtight container and refrigerate for up to 2 days.

PRODUCTION NOTE: Wild rice should be cooked covered, but you can lift the lid from time to time to stir and check on the cooking. Wild rice is done when about half of the kernels have burst open.

Yield: 12 servings

Portion size: ³/₄ cup

Equipment: large saucepan, large spoon, large skillet, heatproof spoon, large stainless steel bowl

Ingredient	Amount
Chicken broth, low sodium	9 cups
Wild rice	3¹/₂ cups
Unsalted butter	6 tablespoons, divided
Button mushrooms, diced	1 pound
Red onion, minced	1 large
Red bell peppers, finely chopped	2 medium
Fresh flat-leaf parsley, chopped	¹/₄ cup
Salt and freshly ground black pepper	to taste

Method

1. Bring chicken broth to a boil in a large saucepan over high heat. Stir in rice and bring to a boil. Reduce heat, cover, and simmer until kernels begin to burst open, about 45 minutes.
2. Meanwhile, heat 2 tablespoons of butter in a large skillet over medium-high heat. Add mushrooms and cook, stirring frequently, for 3–4 minutes or until lightly golden. Transfer to a large bowl.
3. Add 2 tablespoons butter to skillet along with onion and cook, stirring frequently, for 4–5 minutes or until lightly golden. Transfer to bowl with mushrooms.
4. Place remaining butter, bell pepper, and parsley in skillet and cook, stirring often, until bell pepper is soft, about 3 minutes. Transfer to bowl with mushrooms, stirring to combine.
5. Drain any excess liquid from rice. Add mushroom mixture to rice, fluffing to combine.
6. Season with salt and pepper and serve hot.

PRODUCTION NOTE: Substitute any of the vegetables below with yams or sweet potatoes, parsnips, turnips, or beets.

Yield: 12 servings
Portion size: 4 ounces
Equipment: two rimmed baking sheets, tongs

Ingredients	Amount
Carrots, peeled and cut into 2-inch pieces	6 large
Fennel bulbs, root end attached, cut into quarters	3 medium
Red potatoes, cut in half or quarters	8 medium or 12 small
Red onion, root end attached, cut into 8 wedges	1 large
Olive oil	1/4 cup
Lemon juice	2 tablespoons
Ground cumin	1/2 teaspoon
Fresh thyme leaves	3 tablespoons
Salt and freshly ground black pepper	to taste
Coriander or fennel seeds, crushed, for garnish	

Method

1. Preheat oven to 425 degrees.
2. Spread carrots, fennel, potato, and red onion over 2 baking sheets. Drizzle with olive oil and lemon juice. Sprinkle with cumin, thyme, salt, and pepper, tossing to combine.
3. Roast until browned, 35–45 minutes. Remove from heat and sprinkle with coriander seeds before serving.

Frisée, Escarole, and Apple Salad

PRODUCTION NOTE: Pears and pecans can be used instead of apples and walnuts.

Yield: 25 servings
Portion size: 4 ounces
Equipment: large stainless steel bowl, food processor or blender, paper towels

Ingredient	Amount
Gala or Fuji apples, cored and thinly sliced	5 medium
Lemon juice	1/4 cup, plus 2 tablespoons
Yogurt, plain (or a nondairy substitute)	1 1/4 cups
Rice vinegar	1/4 cup
Extra-virgin olive oil	1/4 cup
Fresh thyme leaves	1 tablespoon
Garlic, chopped	2 cloves
Salt	1 teaspoon
Freshly ground black pepper	1/2 teaspoon
Frisée, leaves separated	2 heads
Escarole, leaves separated	1 head
Walnuts, roughly chopped	1 cup
Thyme or chive flowers, optional for garnish	

Method

1. Place apple slices in a large bowl and add water to cover. Add 1/4 cup of lemon juice and set aside.
2. Place yogurt, vinegar, olive oil, remaining lemon juice, thyme, garlic, salt, and pepper in the work bowl of a food processor or blender and blend until smooth with just little flecks of green. Set aside.
3. Discard any tough or yellowing outer frisée and escarole leaves. Trim and discard any discolored root ends. Roughly chop larger leaves and divide among salad plates.
4. Drain apples and spread over paper towels. Pat to dry. Sprinkle apples over salads.
5. Drizzle dressing over greens, sprinkle with walnuts, and serve immediately.

PRODUCTION NOTES: Serve over hot noodles, rice, or couscous. For twenty-five servings, make four pounds noodles or three pounds rice or couscous. Israeli couscous is a great alternative. This stew can be made a day ahead and reheated before serving.

Yield: 25 servings
Portion size: about 1 cup of stew
Equipment: large stock pot or two large Dutch ovens, large ladle, large wooden spoon

Ingredients	Amount
Olive oil	3/4 cup
Red onions, roughly chopped	2 large
Japanese eggplants, sliced into 1-inch pieces	6 large
Whole tomatoes, coarsely chopped, reserving juice	4 (28-ounce) cans
Tomato sauce	4 (16-ounce) cans
Vegetable broth or water	6–8 cups, more or less as needed
Garbanzo beans, rinsed and drained	3 (14.5-ounce) cans
Carrots, peeled and cut into 1-inch pieces	5 large
Brown lentils, rinsed	1 cup
Garam masala	1 tablespoon
Salt	2 teaspoons
Freshly ground black pepper	1 teaspoon
Fresh cilantro, chopped	1 1/2 cups
Lemon juice	1/2 cup, more or less to taste

Method

1. Place oil in a large stock pot or 2 large Dutch ovens over medium heat. Add onion and eggplant and cook, stirring frequently, for 15 minutes.
2. Stir in tomatoes, tomato liquid, tomato sauce, broth, garbanzo beans, carrots, lentils, garam masala, salt, and pepper. Bring to a boil over high heat. Reduce heat and simmer for about 25 minutes or until lentils are tender. Add more broth if stew is too thick.
3. Remove from heat and stir in cilantro and lemon juice. Spoon over noodles, couscous, or rice and serve hot.

PRODUCTION NOTE: This recipe makes a generous amount. You can cut the recipe in half and use it as a lovely sauce for the Semolina Almond Cake.

Yield: 25 servings
Portion size: about 1 cup
Equipment: large stock pot, large wooden spoon, two large and one small stainless steel bowls, box grater

Ingredient	Amount
Spanish red wine, dry	4 (750 ml) bottles
Cinnamon sticks, broken in half	4
Granulated sugar	4 cups, plus ⅓ cup
Oranges	25 large
Sliced almonds, toasted	1 cup

Method

1. Pour wine into a large stockpot. Add cinnamon sticks and 4 cups of sugar and bring to a boil over medium-high heat, stirring until sugar dissolves. Let boil, stirring occasionally, for about 30 minutes or until liquid has reduced by about two-thirds. Discard cinnamon sticks and let cool completely. Transfer to a large bowl, cover and refrigerate for at least 1 hour or up to overnight.

2. Grate zest from 6 of the oranges on the small side of a box grater. In a small bowl, combine orange zest and remaining sugar.

3. Slice the peel and white pith from oranges. Cut into segments and place in a large bowl. Drizzle with wine syrup and sprinkle with sugared orange zest and almonds before serving.

PRODUCTION NOTES: This cake tastes best when made one or two days ahead. Rewarm in a 275-degree oven for fifteen minutes before serving. Serve with slightly sweetened whipped cream, vanilla ice cream, or Sweet Oranges in Red Wine.

Yield: 25–30 servings

Portion size: 2¹/₂ x 3-inch piece

Equipment: two 9 x 13-inch cake pans, parchment paper, three large mixing bowls, electric mixer, large wooden spoon, rubber spatula

Ingredient	Amount
Unsalted butter, at room temperature	3 cups, plus more for greasing
All-purpose flour	6³/₄ cups
Fine semolina	2¹/₄ cups
Baking powder	2 tablespoons
Salt	³/₄ teaspoon
Orange juice	1¹/₂ cups
Eggs, separated	9
Granulated sugar	2¹/₂ cups, divided
Orange zest	3 tablespoons
Almonds, chopped	2 cups
Almond extract	1 tablespoon

Method

1. Preheat oven to 350 degrees.
2. Grease two 9x13-inch cake pans with butter. Cover bottom of pans with parchment paper and grease with a little more butter. Set aside.
3. In a large bowl, whisk together flour, semolina, baking powder, and salt. Stir in orange juice until mixture is smooth. Set aside.
4. Place egg whites in a large clean bowl and beat with an electric mixer, gradually beating in 1¹/₄ cups of the sugar, until stiff peaks form. Set aside.
5. Place egg yolks in another bowl and, using an electric mixer, beat until creamy. Add butter, orange zest, and 1¹/₄ cups sugar, and beat until pale in color and very creamy.
6. Stir yolk mixture into flour mixture. Fold in egg whites. Pour batter into prepared pans and sprinkle with almonds.
7. Bake until deep golden brown and a tester inserted in the center comes out clean, about 40 minutes.
8. Remove from heat and let cool.

Melon Soup Demitasse

PRODUCTION NOTE: Cantaloupe or watermelon can be used in place of the honeydew.

Yield: 50 servings
Portion size: 3 ounces
Equipment: blender

Ingredient	Amount
Honeydew melons, peeled and seeded	3
Pineapples, peeled and cored	3
Hothouse cucumbers, peeled	6
Jalapeños, seeds removed and chopped	2
Fresh mint leaves	½ cup
Salt to taste	

Method

1. Coarsely chop honeydew, pineapple, and cucumber.
2. Working in batches, place honeydew, pineapple, cucumber, and jalapeño in a blender and blend until nearly smooth. Add mint and pulse just until chopped.
3. Add salt and chill until ready to serve.

PRODUCTION NOTE: If Napa cabbage isn't available or is too expensive, it can be replaced by green or red cabbage; one head of red or green cabbage will replace three to four heads of Napa.

Yield: 50 servings
Portion size: 2 shrimp
Equipment: two baking sheets, medium skillet, fifty 5-inch skewers

Ingredient	Amount
Olive oil	1 cup, divided, plus more for greasing
Jumbo shrimp, peeled and deveined	9 pounds
Garlic, peeled and minced	1 head
Salt	2 teaspoons
Red pepper flakes	1 teaspoon
Ground cumin	1 teaspoon
Freshly ground black pepper	1 teaspoon
Dry white wine	2 cups
Napa cabbage	7 heads
Lemons, cut into wedges	13

Method

1. Preheat oven to 425 degrees.
2. Grease 2 baking sheets with oil and set aside.
3. Thread 2 shrimp onto each skewer and place on prepared baking sheet.
4. Place 2 tablespoons olive oil in a medium skillet over medium-low heat. Add garlic, salt, red pepper flakes, cumin, and black pepper. Cook, stirring constantly to prevent burning, until garlic is light golden, or about 3 minutes. Increase heat to high, add wine, and bring to a boil. Boil for about 7 minutes or until liquid has reduced by half.
5. Brush sauce over shrimp and bake until cooked through, about 5 minutes.
6. Serve hot or at room temperature on a bed of cabbage and garnished with lemon wedges.

255

PRODUCTION NOTES: These can be assembled and frozen for up to one month if wrapped securely with plastic wrap. Let thaw in the refrigerator overnight before baking. Make this recipe in single batches to keep filling consistent. Serve slices on a plate with a little Fresh Tomato Sauce underneath.

Yield: 50–54 servings

Portion size: 2x3-inch slice

Equipment: three 9x13-inch baking dishes, large stainless steel bowl, damp kitchen towel

Ingredient	Amount
Unsalted butter, chilled and cut into small pieces	1½ pounds, plus more for greasing
Eggs, beaten	36
Sweet Italian sausage, cooked and crumbled	3 pounds
Feta cheese, crumbled	2 pounds
Spinach, coarsely chopped	9 cups
Pine nuts	2 cups
Phyllo dough, thawed	3 (1 pound) packages

Method

1. Preheat oven to 350 degrees.
2. Grease three 9x13-inch baking dishes with butter and set aside.
3. Place a third of the butter, eggs, sausage, feta, spinach, and pine nuts in a large bowl, stirring to combine. Set aside.
4. Unroll a package of phyllo dough and cover immediately with a clean, damp kitchen towel (to keep it from drying out when not using).
5. Cover baking dish with 10 sheets of phyllo dough, letting ends hang over edges of dish.
6. Scoop 3 cups of egg mixture into bottom of baking dish.
7. Loosely gather together a sheet of phyllo (like wadding up a piece of paper before tossing away) and place in bottom of baking dish, swirling in the liquid to moisten. Repeat with 9 more sheets of phyllo.
8. Pour remaining egg mixture over top. Fold ends of phyllo up and over filling.
9. Lay remaining phyllo over the top, tucking ends between phyllo and side of baking dish.
10. Bake until golden brown on top and puffed in the center, about 50 minutes. Remove from heat and let stand for 5 minutes.
11. Cut into 3x2-inch pieces. Serve hot or at room temperature.

PRODUCTION NOTES: This sauce can be made up to two days in advance if refrigerated in an airtight container.

Yield: about 13 cups
Portion size: about $1/4$ cup
Equipment: food processor, stockpot, large wooden spoon

Ingredient	Amount
Tomatoes, cut into wedges	30 large
Garlic, peeled and minced	1 head
Tomato paste	$3/4$ cup
Olive oil	1 cup, divided
Red pepper flakes, optional	1 teaspoon
Salt1 tablespoon, more or less to taste	
Low-sodium chicken broth	6 cups, more or less to taste
Fresh parsley, chopped	1 cup
Red wine vinegar	1 tablespoon

Method

1. Working in batches, place tomatoes, garlic, and tomato paste in the work bowl of a food processor and pulse until tomatoes are very finely chopped.
2. Place olive oil, red pepper flakes, and salt in a stockpot, stirring to combine. Stir in broth.
3. Place stockpot over high heat and bring to a boil. Reduce heat and let simmer for 15 minutes. Remove from heat and stir in parsley and vinegar.
4. Serve hot or cool.

Finger-Food Fried Chicken

PRODUCTION NOTES: Chicken can be made through step 5, then covered and refrigerated up to overnight. Serve with Peach Salsa spooned on top.

Yield: 50 servings
Portion size: 3 pieces
Equipment: four baking sheets, three large bowls, large deep saucepan or medium stockpot, tongs, paper towels

Ingredient	Amount
All-purpose flour	5 cups
Ground paprika	3 tablespoons
Salt	2 tablespoons
Freshly ground black pepper	1½ tablespoons
Dried oregano	3 teaspoons
Onion powder	3 teaspoons
Eggs, lightly beaten	24
Whole milk	1½ cups
Panko bread crumbs	12 cups (2 12-ounce bags)
Chicken breasts, boneless and skinless	50
Canola or other vegetable oil for deep frying	

Method

1. Line 4 baking sheets with several layers of paper towels and set aside.
2. Place flour in a large bowl. Add paprika, salt, pepper, oregano, and onion powder, whisking to completely combine.
3. Place eggs and milk in a large bowl, whisking to combine.
4. Place half of the bread crumbs in a third bowl (refilling with more bread crumbs as necessary).
5. Slice each chicken breast into 3 long pieces. Dredge chicken in flour mixture, shaking off excess. Dip chicken in egg mixture, then press into bread crumb mixture, shaking off excess.
6. Place 2 inches of oil a large, deep saucepan (or medium stockpot) over medium heat. Bring oil to 350 degrees. Fry 6–8 pieces of chicken at a time (depending upon size of saucepan; don't crowd pieces) until just golden and cooked through, about 5 minutes. Using tongs, transfer chicken to prepared baking sheets.
7. Serve chicken hot, warm, or cold.

Peach Salsa

PRODUCTION NOTE: This recipe can be made up to the night before if covered and refrigerated in a glass or plastic container.

Yield: 50 servings
Portion size: about ¼ cup
Equipment: food processor

Ingredient	Amount
Peaches, peeled, pitted, and roughly chopped	15 large
Plum tomatoes, roughly chopped	10 medium
Pineapple, peeled, cored, and roughly chopped	1
Lime juice	⅔ cup
Salt and freshly ground black pepper	to taste

Method

1. Working in batches, place peaches, tomatoes, pineapple, and lime juice in the work bowl of a food processor. Pulse until finely chopped but still a bit chunky. Season with salt and pepper.
2. Serve immediately or cover and refrigerate for up to overnight.

PRODUCTION NOTES: If you don't have enough muffin tins or oven space to cook all of these at the same time, refrigerate the excess batter then bake off as soon as you can. Muffins can be baked up to two weeks ahead of time if wrapped well and frozen.

Yield: 60 muffins
Portion size: 1 muffin
Equipment: five muffin tins, muffin tin liners, food processor, large bowl, whisk, fork

Ingredient	Amount
Cornmeal	9 cups
All-purpose flour	5 cups
Granulated sugar	1⅔ cups
Baking powder	3 tablespoons
Baking soda	2½ teaspoons
Salt	2½ teaspoons
Cayenne pepper	½ teaspoon
Freshly ground black pepper	¼ teaspoon
Unsalted butter, softened	2½ cups
Buttermilk	1½ cups
Eggs	20
Cheddar Jack cheese, shredded	4 cups

Method

1. Preheat oven to 375 degrees. Line 5 muffin pans with paper liners.
2. Working in batches, place cornmeal, flour, sugar, baking powder, baking soda, salt, cayenne, and black pepper in the work bowl of a food processor and pulse to blend.
3. Add butter and pulse until mixture resembles coarse meal.
4. Working in batches, place buttermilk and eggs in a large bowl and whisk to combine. Add cornmeal mixture and stir with a fork until just moistened. Add cheese and stir just to combine. Scoop into prepared muffin pans.
5. Bake until golden on top or until a tester inserted in the center comes out clean, about 17 minutes. Let cool at least 10 minutes before serving.

PRODUCTION NOTE: This is a fresh, undressed version of ambrosia. If you want something more traditional recipe, do the following: Stir in 1 (1-pound) bag mini marshmallows; replace the grapes with 6 cups maraschino cherries, cut in half; and stir everything together with 5 cups sour cream.

Yield: 50 servings
Portion size: about 1 cup
Equipment: large bowl, large mixing spoon

Ingredient	Amount
Mandarin orange segments, drained	6 (15-ounce) cans
Pineapples, peeled, cored, and chopped	4
Red grapes, halved	16 cups
Shredded coconut, sweetened	2 (14-ounce) bags
Pecans, chopped	1 (8-ounce) bag

Method

1. Combine all ingredients except pecans in a large bowl. Cover and refrigerate for at least 45 minutes or up to overnight.
2. Stir in pecans before serving.

Appendix

Culinary Schooling/Education

The Culinary Institute of America (CIA)
1946 Campus Dr.
Hyde Park, NY 12538
(845) 452-9600
www.ciachef.edu
The Culinary Institute of America offers a five-day catering course through its continuing-education department.

The CIA at Greystone
2555 Main St.
St. Helena, CA 94574
(707) 967-1100
www.ciachef.edu/california
The Culinary Institute of America has a second campus in the Napa Valley, offering a variety of short courses.

Institute of Culinary Education
50 West 23rd St.
New York, NY 10010
(212) 847-0700
www.ice.edu
Different catering courses are offered at various times each year on the school's schedule. Call for details and upcoming classes.

The International Culinary Center, New York Campus
462 Broadway
New York, NY 10013
(888) 324-2433

The International Culinary Center, California Campus
700 West Hamilton Ave.
Campbell, CA 95008
(866) 318-2433
www.frenchculinary.com
For serious French cuisine aficionados, the International Culinary Center (formally known as the French Culinary Institute) offers a 600-hour professional training course. The institute has total-immersion classes in the culinary arts, pastry, and bread baking. Shorter classes are available in wine fundamentals and restaurant management. Amateur classes in many subjects are also available.

Johnson & Wales University
Culinary Arts Division
8 Abbott Park Place
Providence, RI 02903
(800) 598-1000
www.jwu.edu/culinary
Johnson & Wales University is a prestigious cooking school, highly recommended for the professional chef. Special courses include catering/garde-manager (presentation of cold foods) and catering management. They also offer classes in Denver, Colorado; Charlotte, North Carolina; and North Miami, Florida.

New England Culinary Institute
56 College St.
Montpelier, VT 05602
(877) 223-6324
www.neci.edu
The New England Culinary Institute offers catering instruction in a two-year program.

New School of Cooking
8690 Washington Blvd.
Culver City, CA 90232
(310) 842-9702
www.newschoolofcooking.com
The New School of Cooking offers part-time professional cooking and baking pro-grams designed to fit within the schedules of working people. They also have a wide variety of recreational, single subject, evening, and weekend classes.

Sullivan University
National Center for Hospitality Studies
3101 Bardstown Rd.
Louisville, KY 40205
(800) 844-1354
www.sullivan.edu
Sullivan offers a unique degree in professional catering in conjunction with their eighteen-month Associate of Science Degree Program.

Westlake Culinary Institute
4643 Lakeview Canyon Rd.
Westlake Village, CA 91361
(818) 991-3940
www.letsgetcookin.com
The Westlake Culinary Institute offers short and long professional cooking, pastry, and catering courses.

Online Culinary Resources

Online industry magazine: www.catersource.com
Exotic and hard-to-find produce: www.melissas.com
Info on farmers' markets and locally grown produce: www.seasonalchef.com
Excellent info on wine: www.learnaboutwine.com
For recipe inspiration: www.epicurious.com
Industry website: www.chef2chef.net
Food writers' website: wwww.food52.com

Tons of culinary information: www.egullet.com
Used cookbooks: www.campusi.com, www.abebooks.com, www.alibris.com
Live butterflies: www.amazingbutterflies.com

Recommended Reading

An excellent reference book for cooking schools around the world is *The Guide to Cooking Schools 2005*, by ShawGuides. Contact ShawGuides at PO Box 1295, New York, NY 10023; (212) 799-6464; www.shawguides.com.

A must-have book for anyone who writes recipes is *Will Write for Food* by Dianne Jacob (Da Capo Press, 2010).

Along with the collection of cookbooks I know you already own, consider the following when you've got money to invest in your education:

Books from the heart that will inspire you to cook

Appetite for Life—The Biography of Julia Child, Noel Riley Fitch (Doubleday, 1997)
The Art of Eating, Special Edition, M. F. K. Fisher (Macmillan, 2004)
A Chef's Tale, Pierre Franey (Knopf, 1994)
An Omelette and a Glass of Wine, Elizabeth David (Lyons Press, 1997)
The Rituals of Dinner, Margaret Visser (Penguin Books, 1992)
A Woman's Place Is in the Kitchen, Ann Cooper (VNR, 1998)

Books that will impress your clients

Emily Post's Entertaining, Peggy Post (Harper Perennial, 1998)
Larousse Gastronomique, Jennifer Harvey Lang (Clarkson Potter, 2001)
The New Food Lover's Companion, Sharon Tyler Herbst (Barron's, 2007)

Books that will teach you how to cook

The All New All Purpose Joy of Cooking, Irma Rombauer, Marion Rombauer Becker, and Ethan Becker (Simon & Schuster, 1997)
Anne Willan's *Look and Cook* series, twenty-four volumes (Dorling Kindersley, 1997)
Classic Home Cooking, Mary Berry and Marlena Spieler (Dorling Kindersly, 2003)
Cookwise, Shirley O. Corriher (Morrow, 1997)
The Country Cooking of France, Anne Willan (Chronicle Books, 2007)
Essentials of Cooking, James Peterson (Artisan, 1999)

Lorenza's Pasta, Lorenza De Medici (Clarkson Potter, 1996)

Mastering the Art of French Cooking, Julia Child (Knopf, 2001)

The New Making of a Cook, Madeline Kamman (Morrow, 1997)

The Way to Cook, Julia Child (Knopf, 1995)

Books with quantity recipes

Cooking for Crowds for Dummies, Dawn and Curt Simmons (For Dummies, 2005)

Do It For Less! Parties, Denise Vivaldo and Cindie Flannigan (Terrace Publishing, 2005)

Do It For Less! Weddings, Denise Vivaldo (Sellers Publishing, 2008)

Food for Fifty, Mary K. Molt (Prentice Hall, 2005)

Books with beautiful pictures and presentations

Bouchon, Thomas Keller (Artisan, 2004)

Charlie Trotter's, Charlie Trotter (Ten Speed Press, 1994)

Charlie Trotter's Desserts, Charlie Trotter (Ten Speed Press, 1998)

Charlie Trotter's Vegetables, Charlie Trotter (Ten Speed Press, 1997)

Ducasse Flavors of France, Alain Ducasse (Artisan, 1998)

Entertaining, Martha Stewart (Potter, 1998)

The French Vineyard Table, Georges Blanc (Clarkson Potter, 1997)

The New InterCourses: An Aphrodisiac Cookbook, Martha Hopkins and Randall Lockridge (Terrace Publishing, 2007)

Pacific Flavors, Hugh Carpenter (Stewart, Tabori & Chang, 1988, 1993)

Books that you should buy when you are a student

Fish and Shellfish, James Peterson (William Morrow and Company, 1996)

How to Cook, Delia Smith (DK Publishing, 2001)

The New Kitchen Science, Howard Hillman (Houghton Mifflin, 2003)

The New Professional Chef, Culinary Institute of America (John Wiley and Sons, 2001)

On Cooking, Sarah R. Labensky and Alan M. Hause (Prentice Hall, 1999)

On Food and Cooking, Harold McGee (Scribner, 2004)

The Professional Caterer Series, vols. 1–4, Denis Ruffel (VNR, 1997)

Professional Cooking, Wayne Gisslen (Wiley, 2002)

Vegetables, James Peterson (William Morrow and Company, 1998)

Vegetarian Cooking for Everyone, Deborah Madison (Broadway Books, 1997)

The Whole Soy Cookbook, Patricia Greenberg (Three Rivers Press, 1998)

Books to buy if the bakery is closed

Baking with Julia, Dorie Greenspan (William Morrow and Company, 1996)

Bernard Clayton's New Complete Book of Breads, Bernard Clayton Jr. (Fireside, 1995)

The Cake Bible, Rose Levy Beranbaum (Morrow, 1988)

Chocolate, Nick Malgieri (Harper Collins, 1998)

How to Bake, Nick Malgieri (Harper Collins, 1995)

The Italian Baker, Carol Field (Harper Collins, 1985)

The Pie and Pastry Bible, Rose Levy Beranbaum (Scribner, 1998)

The Professional Pastry Chef, Bo Friberg (Wiley, 2002)

The Simple Art of Perfect Baking, Flo Braker (Chronicle Books, 2003)

Out-of-print books to look for at the flea market

The Art of Serving Food Attractively, Mary Albert Wenker (Doubleday, 1951)

Betty Crocker's Cookbook for Boys and Girls, General Mills (Simon & Schuster, 1957)

Jacques Pépin's La Methode (Random House, 1979)

Jacques Pépin's La Technique (Random House, 1976)

The Joy of Cooking, vols. 1 and 2, Irma S. Rombauer and Marion Rombauer Becker (NAL-Dutton, 1974)

Industry magazines

Catersource

Magazine, Conference, and Tradeshow

2909 Hennepin Ave. South

Minneapolis, MN 55408

(612) 870-7727, (877) 932-3632

www.catersource.com

Dedicated to the education and growth of the professional caterer through their educational and informative website, magazine, and trade shows. The largest catering resource network in the United States.

Fancy Foods and Culinary Products
Talcott Communications
20 West Kinzie St., Ste. 1200
Chicago, IL 60654
(312) 849-2220
www.fancyfoodmagazine.com
A good magazine to consult if you want to learn about new products on the market.

Food Arts: The Magazine for Professionals
Food Arts Publishing, Inc.
M. Shanken Communications
387 Park Ave. South
New York, NY 10016
(212) 684-4224
www.foodarts.com
Food Arts is an up-to-date voice of the food industry today, addressing restaurants and caterers.

Special Events Magazine
Primedia Business Magazines and Media
17383 Sunset Blvd., Ste. A220
Pacific Palisades, CA 90272
(800) 543-4116
www.specialevents.com
Special Events Magazine covers current party trends and offers informative articles about how industry professionals create their spectacular parties.

Bookstores catering to cooks

Jessica's Biscuit
Box 301
Newtonville, MA 02460
(800) 878-4264
www.ecookbooks.com

Kitchen Art and Letters
1435 Lexington Ave.
New York, NY 10128
(212) 876-5550
www.kitchenartsandletters.com
These bookstores take a serious interest in providing the most current and recommended reading on cooking. If these bookstores don't have the book you want, chances are you don't need it!

Trade Shows

Throughout the year, trade shows at which vendors in our industry introduce their products are held in cities all over the country. As a professional, attending these trade shows gives you an opportunity to research, sample, and update your knowledge of equipment and services. Along with miles of purveyors' booths, many of the shows also present keynote speakers in a relaxed and informal setting.

Check with your local convention center about upcoming trade shows affiliated with the hospitality industry. To purchase a general admission ticket requires only a business name and a business card. The following is a list of the most prestigious trade shows held every year. Registration fees usually run from $10 to $30.

Fancy Food Show
National Association for the Specialty Food Trade, Inc.
136 Madison Ave., 12th Fl.
New York, NY 10016
Convention information number: (212) 482-6440
www.specialtyfood.com
This trade show is held every six months in either San Francisco, San Diego, New York, or Chicago. Exhibitors from all over the world are on hand to introduce their products. This show used to be geared to chocolates, cookies, biscuits, and nuts but has expanded over the years to include a growing organic and specialty foods presence.

The National Restaurant Association Show
Convention information number: (312) 853-2525
www.show.restaurant.org
About 100,000 people from all over the United States and Europe attend this trade show, held at McCormick Place in Chicago every May. The kitchens built here are specifically designed to house the final tryouts for the US Culinary Team in the "Food Olympics." It is imperative to reserve a hotel room early. Complimentary shuttle buses from most of the major hotels are provided to and from McCormick Place throughout the show.

The Special Event
Stamford, CT 06907
Convention information number: (800) 927-5007
www.thespecialeventshow.com
Each January *Special Events* magazine creates the industry's first and foremost convention. This successful conference has been held in San Diego; New Orleans; and Orlando, Florida. Seminars are available on catering, decor, and successful business ideas.

Professional Organizations

Join as many professional organizations in your area as possible. They're a wonderful way for you to meet other caterers, food writers, and a host of other professionals involved in the food-service industry. Many of them also offer classes and other benefits.

American Culinary Federation
180 Center Place Way
St. Augustine, FL 32095
(904) 824-4468
www.acfchefs.org
Industry experience can earn you accreditation in this organization.

American Institute of Wine and Food

26364 Carmel Rancho Ln., Ste. 201

Carmel, CA 93923

(800) 274-2493

www.aiwf.org

This national nonprofit group was founded by Julia Child, Robert Mondavi, and other professionals. Monthly meetings are dedicated to the appreciation of exquisite food and excellent wine. Check to see whether your city has a chapter. Participate in the group's fund-raisers and you'll have a chance to rub shoulders with seasoned professionals who may recommend you for jobs.

International Association of Culinary Professionals

1221 Avenue of the Americas, 42nd Fl.

New York, NY 10020

(866) 358-4951

www.iacp.com

IACP is a not-for-profit professional association that provides continuing education and the opportunity for culinary development. It has become a worldwide networking organization. The membership is composed of food writers, cooking teachers, chefs, home economists, editors, caterers, food stylists, and just about anyone else connected with food.

Each year IACP hosts a six-day conference where experienced food pros mentor and share information through workshops and lectures. It's a wonderful opportunity to meet the very best of our profession.

The National Restaurant Association

2055 L St. NW, Ste. 700

Washington, DC 20036

(800) 424-5156

www.restaurant.org

By joining this organization, you can be assured that you will be up-to-date on state and federal legislation pertaining to the hospitality industry. The national association maintains a resource library for members and can refer them to state restaurant associations, many of which offer classes on food safety and other subjects at state restaurant shows in conjunction with the Educational Foundation of the NRA.

Women Chefs and Restaurateurs

115 South Patrick St., Ste. 101

Alexandria, VA 22314

(877) 927-7787

www.womenchefs.org

WCR is a wonderful resource for women business owners. Founded by America's foremost women chefs, this networking group reaches out to its members and tries to share as much business information and tips as it can dig up. Their quarterly newsletter alone is worth the annual membership fee.

Suggested Training

The single most informative food-service class I've ever attended is the ServSafe course offered by the Educational Foundation of the National Restaurant Association. Find your state's branch of the association at www.nra.org or contact ServSave directly at www.servesafe.com. Or just read the book.

ServSafe—Serving Safe Food

www.servsafe.com

Texts: *ServSafe CourseBook*

ServSafe Manager

ServSafe Food Handler Guide

ServSafe Alcohol: Fundamentals of Responsible Alcohol Service

ServSafe Allergens Online Course and Assessment

This nationally accredited program will bring you up to date on the issues of food safety. You'll learn to identify potentially hazardous foods that can cause food-borne illness; the guidelines, regulations, and codes related to food safety; and how to prevent contamination and cross-contamination of foods. This is our industry's most respected food safety training program. This course is offered in several different formats, and a certification exam can be taken online as well as in person (check with your state restaurant association, local health department, or culinary school to find out if there is a proctored exam site available in your area).

National Registry of Food Safety Professionals (NRFSP)

www.nrfsp.com

Texts: *Food Safety Management Principles*

A Beginner's Guide to Health and Safety

Food Safety Fundamentals

HealthGuard: Professional Food Manager Certification Training

NSF HACCP Manager Training

This organization is also nationally accredited and will train you in the critically important area of food safety. The tests are offered in print as well as online.

Index

About the Author

A seasoned food professional with over thirty years of experience, **Denise Vivaldo** has catered more than ten thousand parties and has cooked for such guests as George H. W. Bush, Ronald Reagan, Prince Charles, Bette Midler, Suzanne Somers, Merv Griffin, Cher, Aaron Spelling, Sly Stallone, Arnold Schwarzenegger, and Maria Shriver. She began her culinary training at the Ritz Escoffier and La Varenne in Paris, and then graduated Chef de Cuisine from the California Culinary Academy in San Francisco. Denise spent numerous years as a professor at UCLA's Culinary Program and at her alma mater, the California Culinary Academy.

In 1988 Denise founded Food Fanatics, a catering, recipe-development, and food-styling firm based in Los Angeles, California. Since that time she has catered for such events as the Academy Awards Governor's Ball, *Sunset Magazine*'s Taste of Sunset, and Hollywood wrap parties. She has also styled food for countless local and nationally syndicated television shows such as *The Ellen DeGeneres Show*, *The Tonight Show with Jay Leno*, *NapaStyle with Michael Chiarello*, and *Access Hollywood Live with Billy Bush*. In 2012 Denise sold the trademark name Food Fanatics. Offering the same services and more, the Denise Vivaldo Group, Inc., was launched.

Denise is also the author of *How to Start a Home-based Personal Chef Business* (Globe Pequot Press), *The Food Styling Handbook*, *Perfect Table Settings*, *Do It For Less! Parties*, *Do It For Less! Weddings*, *The Entertaining Encyclopedia*, and *Top 100 Step-By-Step Napkin Folds*. In addition to books, Denise is a contributing blogger for the Huffington Post as well as her own blog, Denise Vivaldo Blogs.

Denise is passionate about passing on what she has learned. She founded the Culinary Entrepreneurship Program, and she teaches catering and food styling seminars and workshops across the country and internationally.

Denise is a resident of Los Angeles, California. Contact her through her website, denisevivaldo.com.